THE WORLD TO COME

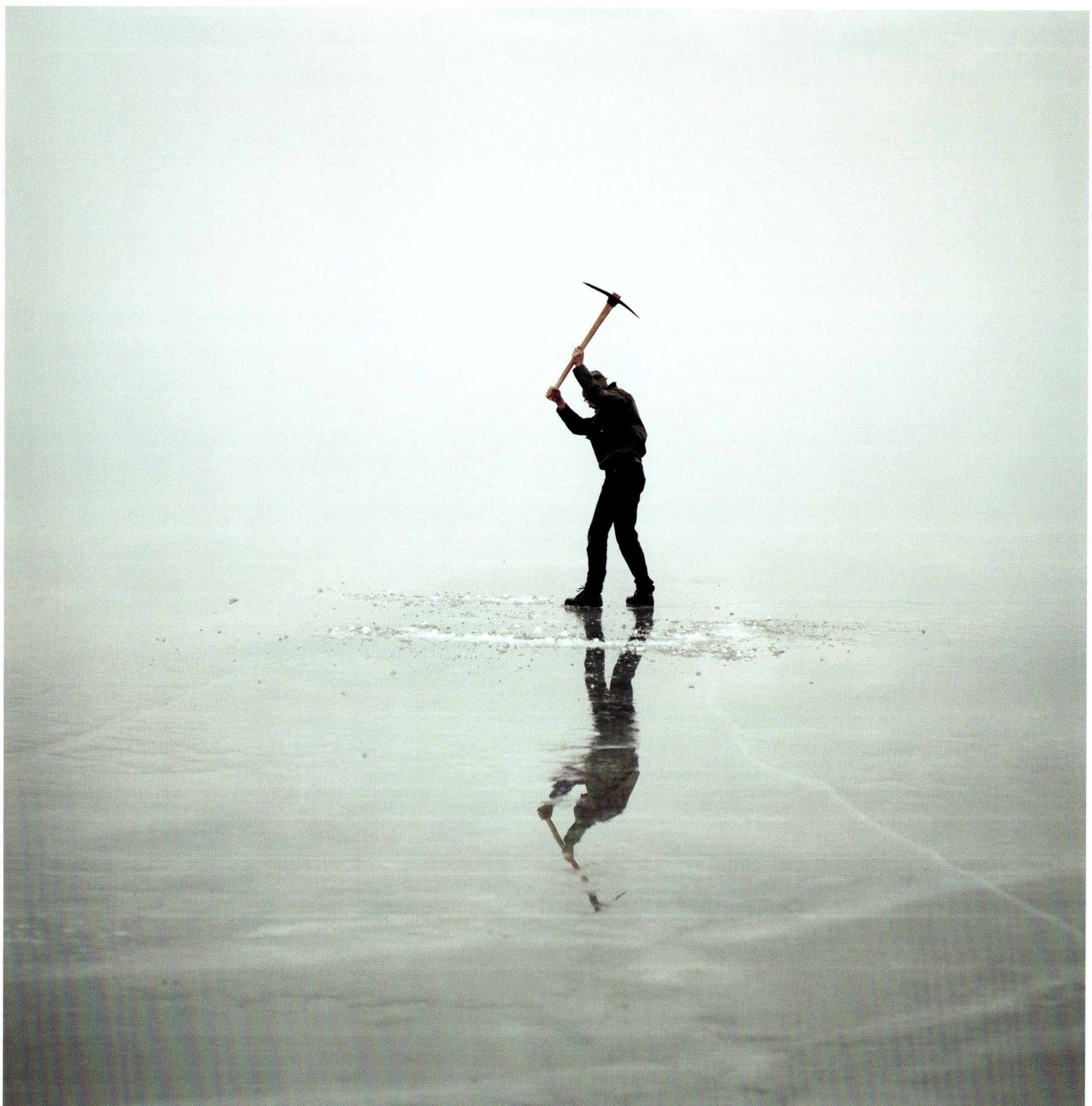

THE WORLD TO COME

ART IN THE AGE OF THE ANTHROPOCENE

Edited by Kerry Oliver-Smith

Samuel P. Harn Museum of Art • University of Florida • Gainesville

Cover, front: Gideon Mendel, *Adlene Pierre, Savanne Desolée, Gonaïves, Haiti, September 2008*, 2008 (page 72)

Frontispiece: Nicole Six & Paul Petritsch, *Spatial Intervention (1)*, 2002 (page 69)

Page vi: Subhankar Banerjee, *Caribou Migration* (detail), 2002 (page 68)

Page xii: Dana Levy, *Emerging from the Swamp* (detail), 2014 (page 113)

This publication is made possible by the Andy Warhol Foundation for the Visual Arts, University of Florida Office of Research and Office of the Provost, John Early Publication Endowment, and the Robert C. and Nancy Magoon Contemporary Exhibition and Publication Endowment.

Printed in Canada on acid-free paper

23 22 21 20 19 18 6 5 4 3 2 1

Library of Congress Cataloging-in-Publication Data
Names: Oliver-Smith, Kerry, editor.
Title: The world to come : art in the age of the anthropocene / edited by Kerry Oliver-Smith.
Description: Gainesville : Samuel P. Harn Museum of Art, University of Florida, 2018.
Identifiers: LCCN 2018003426 | ISBN 9780983308584 (pbk. : alk. paper)
Subjects: LCSH: Human ecology in art—Exhibitions. | Art, Modern—21st century—Exhibitions. | Future in art—Exhibitions. | History in art—Exhibitions. | Photography, Artistic—Exhibitions.
Classification: LCC N8217.E28 W67 2018 | DDC 709.05—dc23
LC record available at https://lccn.loc.gov/2018003426

Production by the University Press of Florida

Design and composition by Louise OFarrell

Published by the Samuel P. Harn Museum of Art
University of Florida
3259 Hull Road
Gainesville, Florida 32611-2700

www.harn.ufl.edu

UF | UNIVERSITY *of* FLORIDA

HARN MUSEUM OF ART
UNIVERSITY OF FLORIDA

This catalogue was published in conjunction with the exhibition *The World to Come: Art in the Age of the Anthropocene*, organized by the Samuel P. Harn Museum of Art, University of Florida.

Samuel P. Harn Museum of Art
University of Florida, Gainesville, FL
September 18, 2018–March 3, 2019

University of Michigan Museum of Art
University of Michigan, Ann Arbor, MI
April 27, 2019–July 28, 2019

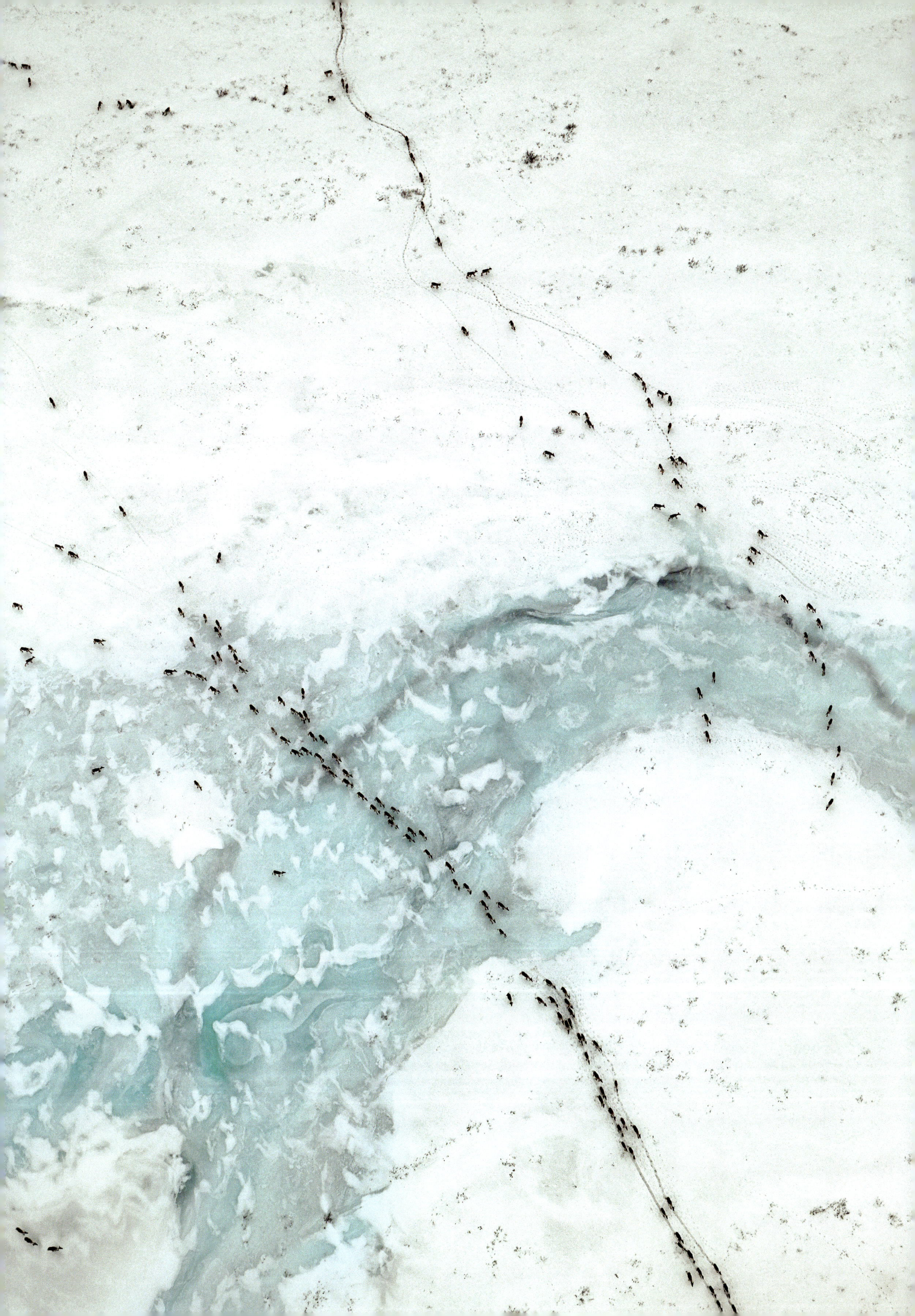

CONTENTS

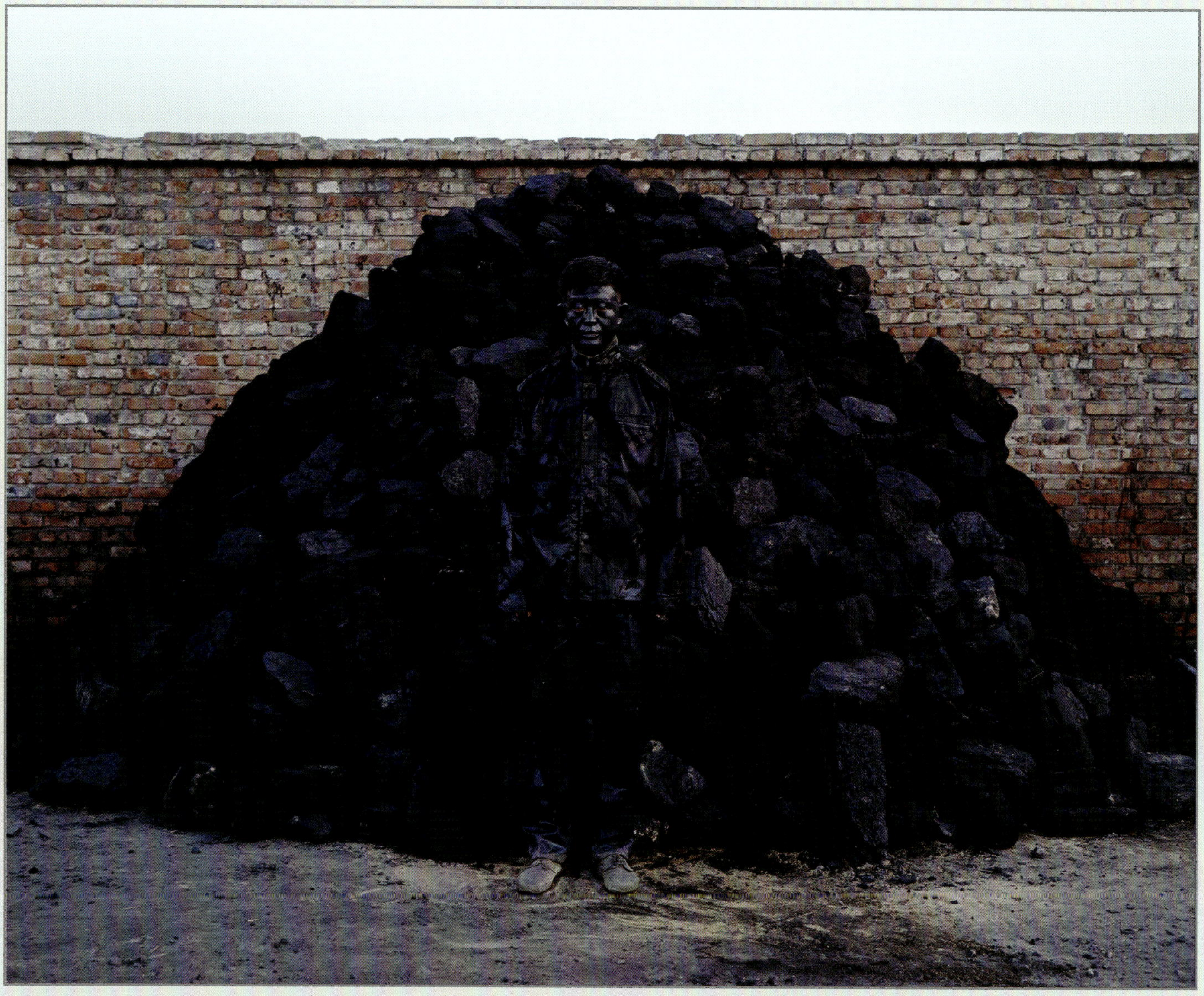

Liu Bolin

Hiding in the City, No. 95, Coal Pile

FOREWORD

Rebecca M. Nagy

Director, Harn Museum of Art

This exhibition is the fruit of several years of intensive research and an even longer period of reflection by Curator of Contemporary Art Kerry Oliver-Smith on artists' varied and powerful responses to climate change and other environmental threats to the well-being of life on Earth and the health of our planet.

The theme could not be timelier as the intensity and frequency of extreme environmental threats appear to be on the rise. I write these words at the end of a year during which our country has been ravaged by monster hurricanes and raging wildfires and other regions of the world have been beset with similarly disastrous events.

Here in Florida we feel ourselves to be targets every hurricane season, while our coastal cities routinely experience flooding caused by high tides. The beautiful natural springs in which north Florida takes great pride are no longer the pristine pools of crystalline water that we remember from just a few years ago, and some have dried up completely. The splendid Florida panther, threatened with extinction due to habitat loss, is a poster child for many other endangered animals and plants. Florida is a microcosm for the macrocosm of life on Earth.

At the University of Florida, scores of scientists and researchers devote their careers to the study of environmental issues such as these and to seeking solutions where those are still possible. We are fortunate to have partners in numerous university centers, institutes, and departments who are working with Kerry Oliver-Smith and museum educators to ensure that the impact of this exhibition is felt on campus, in the local community, and across the state. Artists speak powerfully about the very issues to which scientists and other scholars devote their energies, helping to communicate to wider audiences the beauty and fragility of nature, threats to a healthy planet, irreparable losses, and also opportunities to intervene and make a difference.

I am grateful to Kerry Oliver-Smith for bringing to the Harn and our audiences this beautiful, thought-provoking, disturbing but profoundly meaningful exhibition. She acknowledges elsewhere in this publication the generous donors who have supported the exhibition and publication; artists, collectors, and institutions that have kindly made works available for the show; members of the exhibition advisory committee who shared their insights and ideas to improve the presentation and interpretation of the art; and the many colleagues at the Harn who have worked tirelessly and with tremendous talent and creativity to make the exhibition, accompanying book, and a rich array of educational programs successful. I add to Kerry's acknowledgments my own heartfelt thanks to these friends and colleagues, without whom this important project would not have been possible.

ACKNOWLEDGMENTS

Kerry Oliver-Smith

Curator of Contemporary Art, Harn Museum of Art

The World to Come: Art in the Age of the Anthropocene project has come to fruition through the generous and creative support of many remarkable people. To begin, I am grateful to the forty-five international artists in the exhibition who have recognized and revealed the critical and precarious state of our planet. They challenge the assumed sovereignty of humans over nature and reenvision the bonds of humans to each other and to nonhumans. These artists defy inertia and denial; they insist on optimism as they strive to imagine and create a better and more beautiful world.

I extend my sincere thanks to the excellent galleries, museums, and collectors who have been instrumental in the realization of *The World to Come* project. Working with artists from as far away as Brazil, Ireland, South Africa, and Japan, these lenders have made the art available to the Harn Museum of Art. I am also indebted to the institutions and individuals whose generous financial contributions made this project possible. They include the Andy Warhol Foundation for the Visual Arts; National Endowment for the Arts; C. Frederick and Aase B. Thompson Foundation; John Early Publication Endowment; Robert C. and Nancy Magoon Contemporary Exhibition and Publication Endowment; Harn Program Endowment; and the University of Florida through the Office of the Provost, Office of Research, Center for the Humanities and the Public Sphere, Harn Eminent Scholar Chair in Art History (HESCAH) Endowment, Biodiversity Institute, Water Institute, Climate Institute, English Department "Imagining Climate Change" program, and Center for Latin American Studies. I am thankful for all of the many individual contributions, including those from Kenneth and Laura Berns; David, Edie, Gladys, Mary Ann P., and Paige Cofrin; Jack E. Davis; Paul Doughty; Daniel and Kathleen Hayman; Lynne and Robert Holt; Aida Hozić and Richard Scher; Ken and Linda McGurn; Susan Milbrath; Drs. Peter Stacpoole and Sara Nixon; Drs. Pamela and Douglas Soltis; and Robert and Carolyn Thoburn.

I am very thankful to the authors who have made important and key contributions to the exhibition catalogue: Marisol de la Cadena, T. J. Demos, Natasha Myers, Trevor Paglen, and Joanna Zylinska. The catalogue will extend information and insights to a broad and interdisciplinary field that includes art, science, law, literature, social sciences, and media. Many thanks go to Michele Fiyak-Burkley for her excellent production of the catalogue, Louise OFarrell for her elegant design, and Susan Murray for her excellent copyediting. The museum is also organizing a symposium to stimulate discourse and exchange ideas across the disciplines. I am grateful to my organizing partners, Terry Harpold and Maya Stanfield-Mazzi, as well as to contributors Marisol de la Cadena, T. J. Demos, Ellen Martin, Natasha Myers, Pedro Neves Marques, Brett Scheffers, Susan Paulson, and Les Thiel.

Early in our project, we formed an advisory group with University of Florida faculty and Gainesville community members. Their invigorating conversation and thoughtful advice helped guide the formation of the exhibition. I thank Thomas Ankersen, Cynthia Barnett, Ian Fletcher, Lesley Gamble, Terry Alan Harpold, Susan Nugent, and Kim Tanzer. It was a joy to have the contributions of interns to the *The World to Come*. They brought fresh ideas, great skills, and enthusiasm to the table. Interns included Kéla Jackson, Lindsey Jones, Paula Kroll, Ashley Peterson, Marissa Secades, Brett Taylor, Anna Toptchi, and Yixuan Zhu (Mia). In addition, art historians Karen Web and Eleanor Laughlin provided important research.

I am especially grateful to the remarkable members of the Harn Museum staff. Their expertise, dedication, talent, and humor made this project not only possible but a pleasure as well. Special thanks go to our very skillful registration and preparation team, Jessica Uelsmann, Liz Rodgers, Tim Joiner, and Erin Gordon, who deftly manage multiple projects at any one time, including loan agreements, contracts, shipping, installation, and more. The Education Department, headed by Eric Segal with Brandi Breslin, Elizabeth King, and Paige Willis, has excelled in creating innovative programs for the exhibition. They also connected and collaborated extensively with the University of Florida and Gainesville community. I greatly appreciate Tami Wroath, who has expertly coordinated the catalogue process while also guiding promotion for the exhibition. Thanks are deserved for our talented designer, Jessica Berube, for assistance with exhibition promotion and design.

A special note of appreciation goes to my smart, encouraging, and witty curatorial colleagues Dulce Román, Susan Cooksey, Carol McCusker, Allysa Peyton, and Jason Steuber. A heartfelt thanks goes to Amara McMann and Jane Hamel, both extraordinary exhibition coordinators whose contributions have been essential to the success of each curatorial endeavor. Appreciation goes to Mary Yawn, Director of Finance and Operations, for help with grant applications and budgetary aspects and to her talented administrative and technology team, particularly Matt Herring, who is working on several video projects in the exhibition. I am thankful for Director of Development Kelly Harvey for her skill in fundraising. Special thanks go to Harn Director Rebecca Nagy for her commitment and support that helped drive the project.

I am beholden to faculty members, friends, and family for invaluable conversations, suggestions, and exchanges that furthered the ideas for this exhibition. Warm thanks to Kaira Cabanas, Jill Ciment, Jesus Fuenmajor, Terry Harpold, Barbara Mennel, Susan Milbrath, Maya Stanfield-Mazzi, Kim Tanzer, and Sergio Vega. Longest conversations were saved for Tony Oliver-Smith, an anthropologist and expert in environmental disaster, displacement, resettlement, and forensic research. Being that Tony is my husband, it has been a special joy to sit over the kitchen table, questioning and exchanging exciting ideas. Thanks also to our sons, John and Daniel, who were interested and encouraging, ready to offer astute opinions, most often with a dash of wry humor.

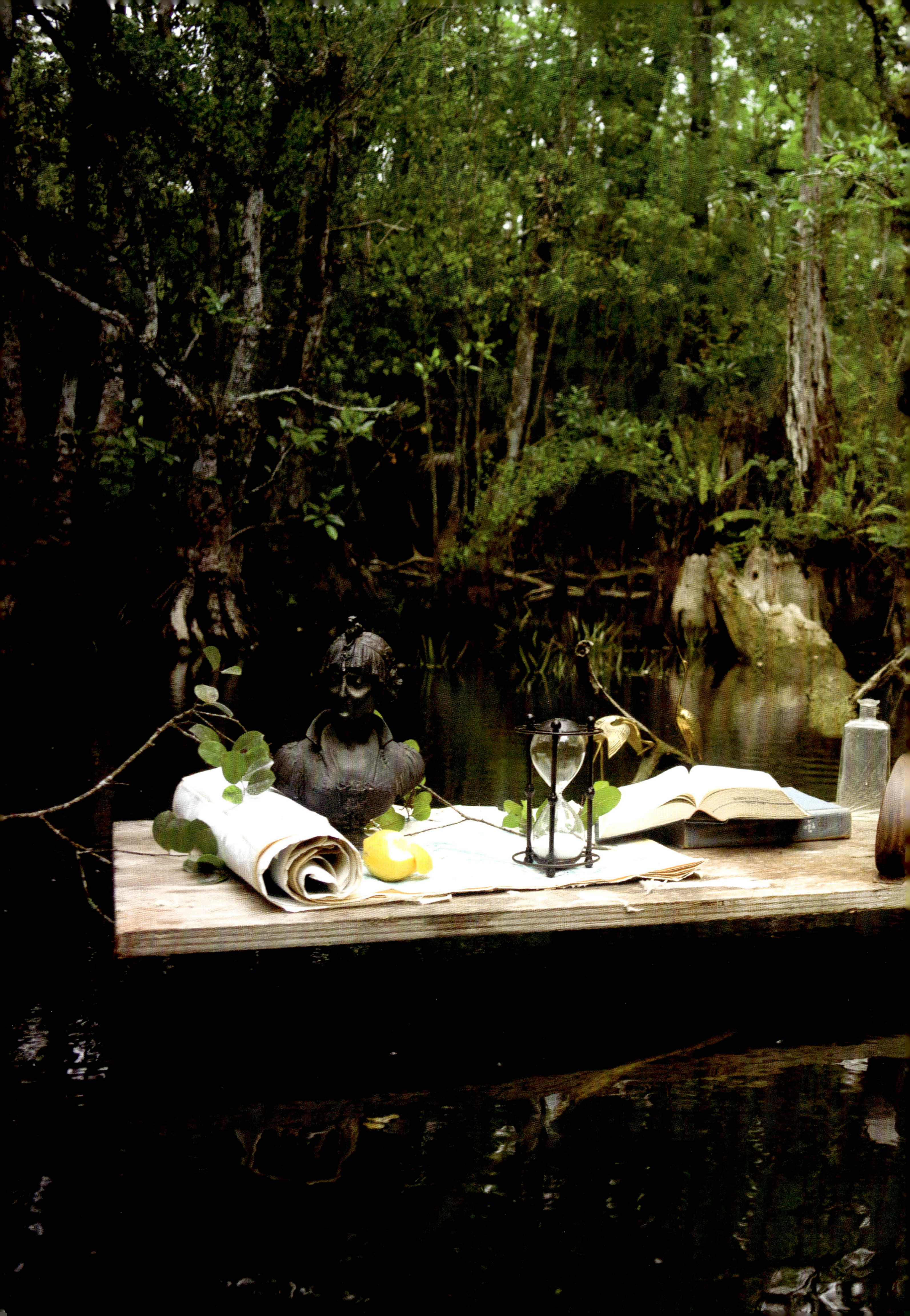

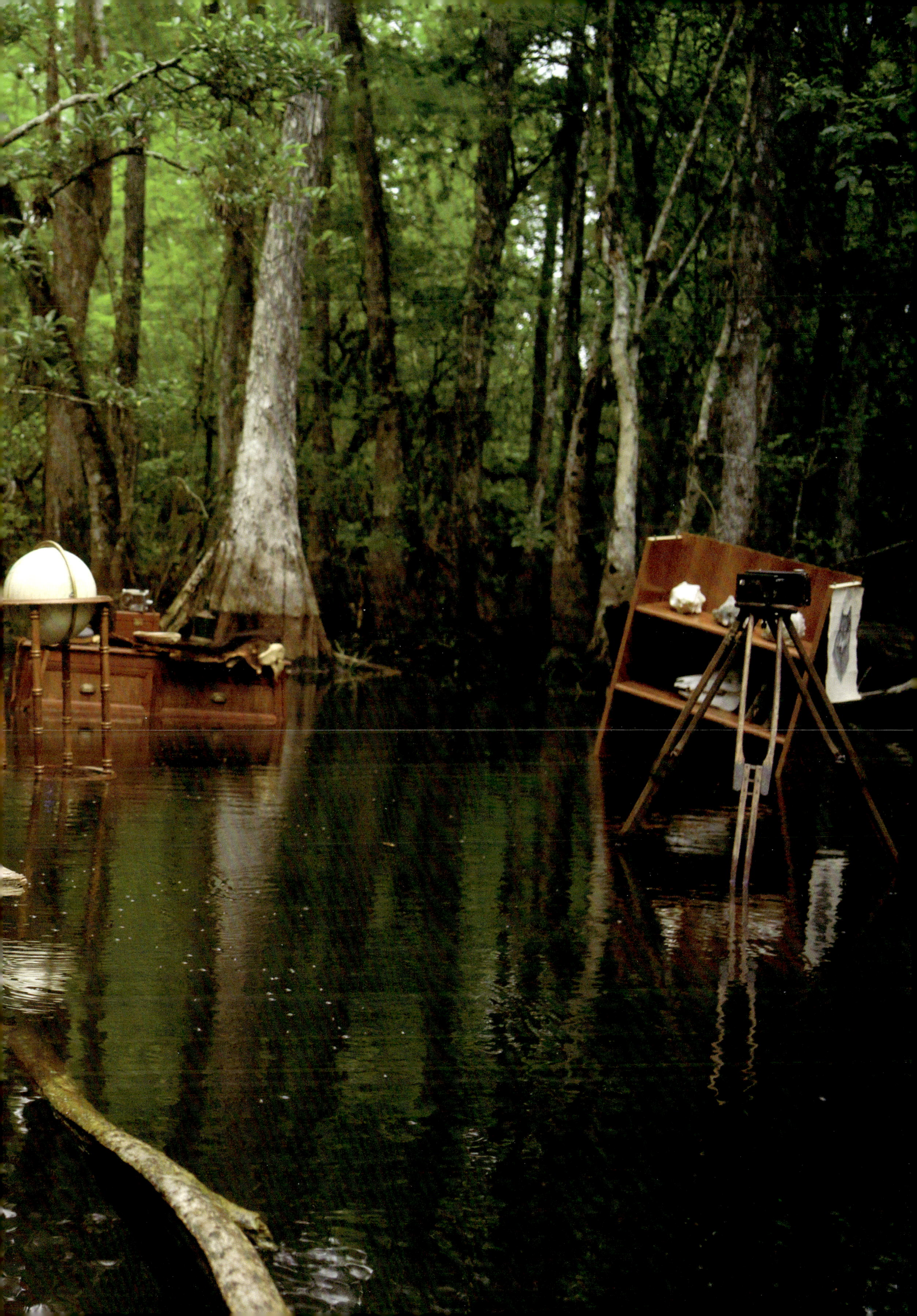

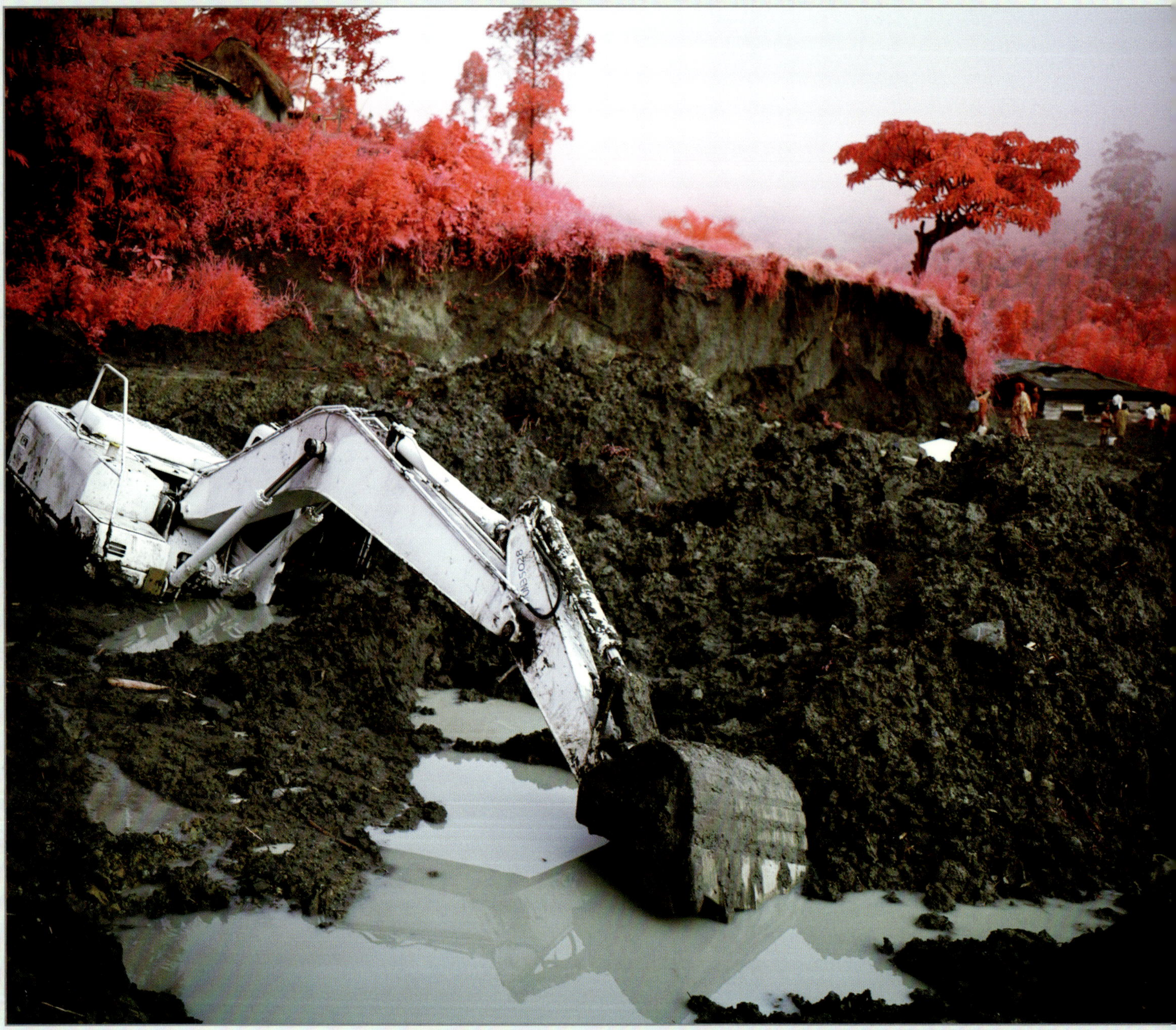

Richard Mosse

Stalemate

INTRODUCTION

Kerry Oliver-Smith

The World to Come: Art in the Age of the Anthropocene is a response to an era of rapid, radical, and irrevocable ecological change. We live in a world of imminent extinctions, runaway climate change, and the depletion of biodiversity and resources. Our age has been identified by Nobel Laureate Paul Crutzen as the Anthropocene, a controversial term used to name a new geological epoch defined by human impact. Whereas geological epochs are generally understood as products of slow change, the Anthropocene has been characterized by speed. Rising water, surging population, and new technologies compress our breathless sense of space and time. Philosopher Santiago Zabala, echoing Heidegger, warns, "The greatest emergency is the absence of emergency." He proposes that contemporary art has the capacity to meet this challenge by disrupting the status quo, energizing radical democratic action, making visible the invisible, and activating intervention.[1]

Scientists have searched for the "golden spike" that marks the beginning of the Anthropocene epoch. The 1600s, the Industrial Revolution, and the Great Acceleration of the 1950s have been suggested—all times characterized by a decoupling of nature from culture. Recently, the Anthropocene Working Group agreed on the mid-twentieth century as the beginning of the Anthropocene. They recommended a formal declaration of their findings to their parent organization: the International Commission on Stratigraphy, the official keeper of geological time.[2] The Working Group selected this marker in response to an accelerated and suddenly intensified human impact, including the worldwide spreading of radioactive elements generated by nuclear bomb tests. Confronted with evidence of the Earth being so profoundly changed, International Commission scientists have come even closer to announcing that we have stepped into the Anthropocene.

Over the last decade, the concept of the Anthropocene epoch has attracted enormous interest from scholars, artists, and activists worldwide. Critical philosophy has engaged with the fields of speculative realism, indigenous cosmologies, and new materialism inspired by theorists such as Bruno Latour, Timothy Morton, Jean-Luc Nancy, Isabelle Stengers, Donna Haraway, and Eduardo Kohn. Other outstanding scholars have also contributed to this exhibition catalogue, including T. J. Demos, Marisol de la Cadena, Natasha Myers, Trevor Paglen, and Joanna Zylinska.

Some theorists object to the term "Anthropocene," arguing that it reinforces the human-centric view of the world that has led us to the brink of global catastrophe. Others say the Anthropocene concept places the blame on all of humanity when in fact the damage has been inflicted by a privileged minority.[3]

Many have faith that climate change mitigation is fundamentally a technical challenge, a matter of innovation rather than a question of political will. For instance, the Breakthrough Institute hosted a conference on the theme of "The Good Anthropocene" in 2015. Organizer Erle Ellis advised that we should stop trying to save the planet and that we should be proud of an "artificial earth." He assured his audience that humans can "totally trash the planet and still survive." Another participant, Mark Lynas, said: "For the essential truth of the Anthropocene is this: neither God nor Gaia is in charge. We are. We now get to decide everything from the pH [acidity] of the oceans to the temperature of the biosphere to the very composition and future evolutionary path of life on Earth. . . . By virtue of our global influence, we have landed ourselves with this awesome task of planetary management!"[4]

Isabelle Stengers, a philosopher of science, suspects that people who claim that they can save the planet with techno-scientific resources are feasting on fear. They may promote the necessity of sacrifice for the good of all, presenting the situation as, "It's us as your saviors or it's the end of the world." Stengers warns of a potential turn toward global apartheid and a police state.[5]

Not everyone accepts the notions of the Anthropocene and climate change. Some politicians and media outlets declare that climate change is a hoax, the fabrication of mad scientists, or a conspiracy of the political Left. Others may deny climate change to further their own political or financial interests. Frustrated environmentalists recognize that despite the evidence, some people believe or want to believe "untruth" or "lies."[6] Political philosopher Jodi Dean remarks, "Climate change tethers us to a perspective that oscillates between the impossible and the inevitable, already and not yet, everywhere but not here, not quite."[7]

Contemporary art plays a crucial role in discourse on the Anthropocene, upending traditional ways of thinking about nature and culture. Crossing genres, disciplines, and species, artists investigate the interconnections and interactions of the material world. They attune us to new realities, helping us to see through the eyes of others and dismantle the binaries of life/matter, human/animal, organic/inorganic. Their work is inspired and informed by diverse cultures and indigenous cosmologies. Artists defy human mastery over nature, expose environmental devastation, seek justice, and ignite action. They witness social division, greater inequality, and civilization collapse. They also understand the experience of trauma and loss and expand the concepts of empathy and compassion.

The concept of the Anthropocene persists as a nexus for exchange of ideas, explorations, strategies, and experiences across the globe. It is in this context that *The World to Come: Art in the Age of the Anthropocene* unfolds. The exhibition is organized around overlapping trajectories, constituting a network of ecologies and stories within stories. The narrative traces states of being and becoming, from rupture, disaster, and loss to the emergence of nonhierarchical alliances in human/nonhuman relations. It also explores the realms of justice, aesthetics, ethics, and the role of technology while also considering the possibilities for a vibrant future. The stories in the next essay are structured by seven intersecting themes of the exhibition: Deluge, Raw Material, Consumption, Extinction, Symbiosis and Multispecies, Justice, and Imaginary Futures.

NOTES

1 Santiago Zabala, introduction to *Why Only Art Can Save Us: Aesthetics and the Absence of Emergency* (New York: Columbia University Press, 2017), 2.

2 Damian Carrington, "The Anthropocene Epoch: Scientists Declare Dawn of Human-influenced Age," 2016, www.theguardian.com/environment/2016/aug/29/declare-anthropocene-epoch-experts-urge-geological-congress-human-impact-earth.

3 Alex Blasdel, "'A Reckoning for Our Species': The Philosopher Prophet of the Anthropocene," 2017, www.theguardian.com/world/2017/jun/15/timothy-morton-anthropocene-philosopher.

4 Rory Rowan, "Extinction as Usual? Geo-Social Futures and Left Optimism," *e-flux journal 56th Venice Biennale,* 2015, http://supercommunity.e-flux.com/authors/rory-rowan/.

5 Isabelle Stengers, *In Catastrophic Times: Resisting the Coming Barbarism* (London: Open Humanities Press, 2015), 9, 22.

6 J. Hillis Miller, "Reading Paul de Man While Falling into Cyberspace," in *Twilight of the Anthropocene Idols,* ed. Thomas Cohen, Claire Colebrook, and Miller (London: Open Humanities Press, 2016), 130.

7 Jodi Dean, "The Anamorphic Politics of Climate Change," *e-flux,* 2016, www.e-flux.com/journal/69/60586/the-anamorphic-politics-of-climate-change/.

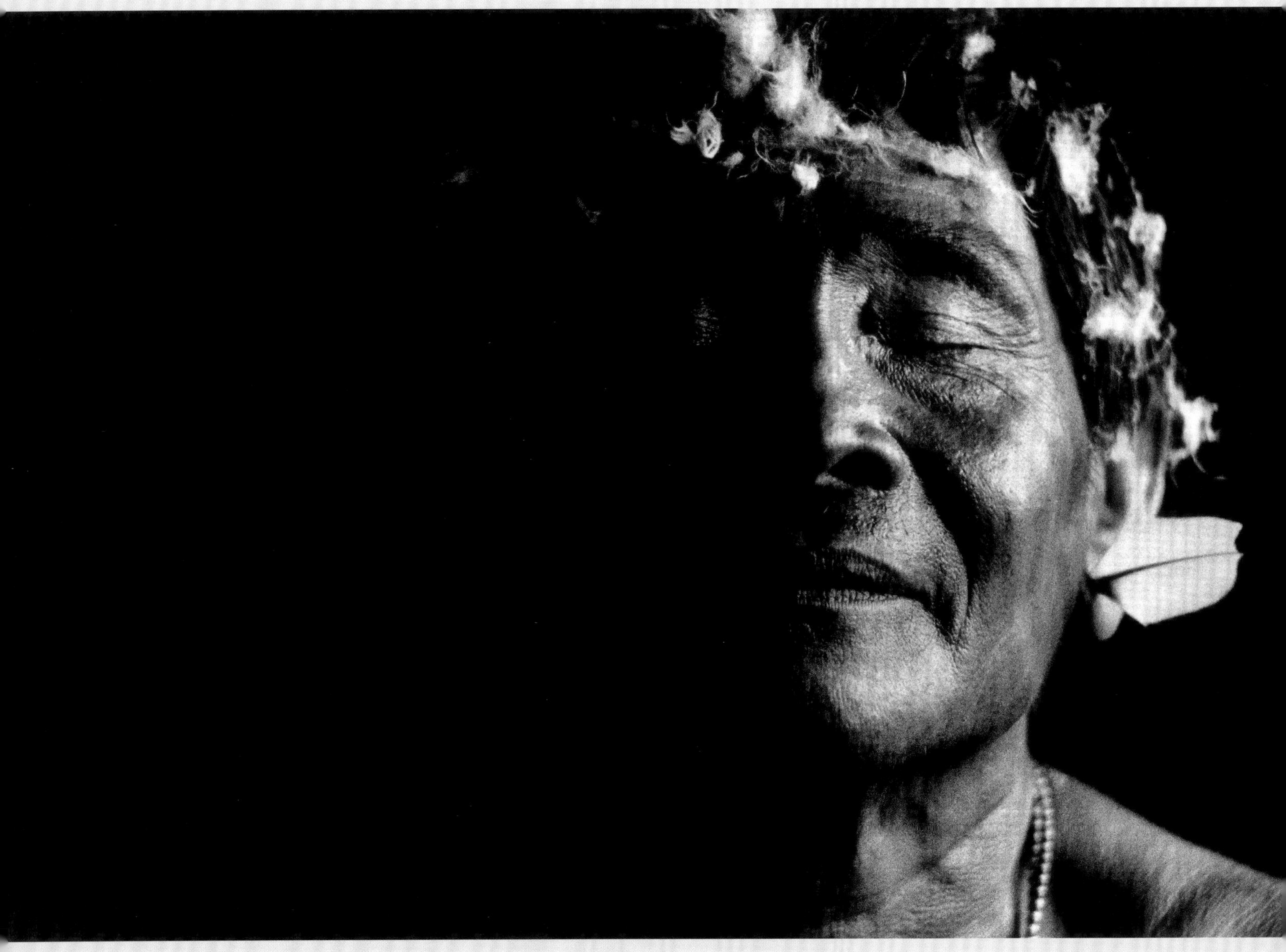

Claudia Andujar

Yanomami

THE WORLD TO COME

Art and Ethics in the Age of the Anthropocene

Kerry Oliver-Smith

The interplay of ethics and aesthetics moves throughout *The World to Come: Art in the Age of the Anthropocene*. In the realm of ethics, anthropologist Laura Ogden proposes that multinational corporations, development initiatives, and global economic institutions present a new form of socioecological governance. Constituting a "global assemblage," these entities are key drivers of environmental change, injustice, and inequality.[1] Nonetheless, Ogden rejects the inevitability of nature's commodification and the dominance of neoliberalism. In tandem with Ogden, artists in the exhibition resist the mastery and power of humans over nature. They engage, contest, and reveal the makings of challenges including colonialism, capitalism, technology, population growth, inequality, displacement, and issues of law, violence, and social justice. Taking an affirmative and ethical turn, these artists seek new ways of seeing and thinking about the world to come.

According to art historian Carol Armstrong, "the ethical purpose of art is to make you see, think, and feel anew . . . 'anew' in a generative sense."[2] The Anthropocene becomes a call to reimagine humans in the context of biology and geology, thinking through interconnections, interactions, and the senses. Artists are further guided by a speculative philosophy that embraces a rethinking and re-visioning of humanity's relationship to nonhuman life, revealing the mutual integration that binds the human and natural worlds. It also serves as a mode of perception that not only unveils the evident but also makes visible what is hidden and unknown. Parallel with the work of Isabelle Stengers, artists seek a life that explores connections through the powers of "acting, feeling, imagining and thinking."[3] Through this process, the artists sustain an openness to wonder and curiosity while keeping optimism in check and nihilism at bay.

DELUGE

"Deluge" comes from the Latin word *diluvium,* meaning flood. The verb "deluge" similarly means to overwhelm or inundate with something, particularly water. In the next century, sea levels may rise up to seven feet. If that happens, coastlines and entire cities will be indelibly altered and, in extreme instances, entirely lost. Sea-level rise comes from the ice melt in Antarctica and Greenland, an expanding ocean, and a slowing Gulf Stream. Excess heat whips the waves of ocean water into storms and hurricanes that rip away rocks, earth, and the homes in which we live.

The notion of deluge is relevant to Timothy Morton's concept of the hyperobject. Morton defines a "hyperobject" as an entity of such massive temporal and spatial dimension that it defies our sensory perceptions and, necessarily, our comprehension. An example of a hyperobject is climate change. Climate change is everywhere but rarely visible. We only recognize it by symptoms such as extreme weather, global warming, rising sea levels, and floods.[4]

Sandra Cinto's mesmerizing images conjure the massive scope of hyperobjects. She draws raging storms and tempestuous seas whirling through the deep night sky. Her fantastic seascapes recall human odysseys and dramas of ancient myth and biblical narratives. Now, episodes of extreme weather are being experienced globally more often and more forcefully. Cinto's work summons memories of the recent violent hurricanes in the Americas (pages 70 and 71).

Subhankar Banerjee took his photograph in the Arctic National Wildlife Refuge, the largest area of untouched wilderness in the United States. Banerjee records the migration of caribou to the core caribou calving area of the Porcupine River (page 68). Recently the caribou have experienced a trophic mismatch due to seasonal climate change brought on by global warming and melting ice. The change causes them to fall out of step with critical food sources—particularly dangerous during breeding time. The herd's calving ground is the most sacred space to the Gwich'in indigenous community. It lies within the area that was opened to drilling by the U.S. Congress on December 2, 2017.

In another odyssey, Gideon Mendel strives to document the magnitude of climate change for his photographic series *Drowning Worlds* (pages 72 and 73). Traveling to many countries, he captured portraits of flood survivors set in deep floodwaters in the remains of their homes or in other submerged landscapes. Most of Mendel's subjects are from the "Global South," where climate change and disaster have a disproportionate impact on poor nations and communities already devastated by inequality, neocolonialism, authoritarianism, and poverty.

Curator Hamza Walker states, "We flirt with extinction, an irrational provocation turned to desire."[5] The practices of denial and self-extinction are linked to the Anthropocene and to Derrida's law of autoimmunity.[6] The law maintains that human cultures have an unconquerable penchant for self-destruction, driven by our need to feel secure and safe. An autoimmune disease turns the body's defensive antibodies against its own tissues and organs. This impulse is played out in the film *Spatial Intervention (1)*, by artists Nicole Six and Paul Petritsch (page 69). Their work is an allegory of the Anthropocene, a poetic parable of human self-annihilation. Performing in the film, Petritsch stands in the center of a frozen landscape; no horizon is in sight. The artist lifts a heavy axe and relentlessly strikes the ice beneath his feet. At a mesmerizing pace, he carves a circle around his body, reaching deeper and deeper until the ice breaks around him. Regardless of his impending disaster, he denies his potential fate.

In her video *Shifting Zero: Don't Ask Don't Tell,* Laurencia Strauss carves her message on the beach in Miami, Florida (pages 74 and 75). *Shifting Zero* regards Florida as a ground-zero site for climate change, ocean warming, rising sea levels, and flooding. The message creates a link with climate change and the former military motto regarding recognition of gay men and women soldiers. Both situations suffered denial and hypocrisy. Strauss' message is continually washed away by the sea, but she persists in sending her message.

RAW MATERIAL

Clear evidence of detrimental human impact abounds in the Anthropocene. The Earth suffers large-scale mining, multinational land grabs, mountaintop removal, hydraulic fracking, and the extraction of Alberta tar sands. For the global assemblage of development initiatives, corporations, and financial institutions, matter exists only to be exploited and commercialized. In the spirit of defiance shared by artists, Isabelle Stengers challenges the unalienable rights claimed by multinational oil companies and speculators who "transform every form, every situation whatever it may be, into a source of profit."[7]

Jane Bennett advocates a shift in our relationship to matter from exploitation to respect. In her book *Vibrant Matter,* Bennett claims that agency is not exclusively the domain of humans and that "things" have a vital force. She dismisses the binaries between life/matter, human/animal, and organic/inorganic, arguing that a "vital materiality" runs through and across bodies, both human and nonhuman.[8]

Frank Thiel's photograph *Piedras Blancas* (White stones) reveals the orders of magnitude between human history and the scale of geologic time (page 79). The vast glaciers of the Patagonian Andes in Argentina are remnants of the last ice age and now a part of the third-largest ice cap in the world. In the photograph, receding glaciers expose the barren and raw fissures of the mountains left behind.

To see and/or experience the landscape is to connect with a world and universe possessed of a vitality infinitely greater than our own. Elena Damiani looks through a veil of fiction and fantasy, reworking material found in geologic and cartographic archives for her work *Fading Field N.9.* Drawing from multiple times and topographies, Damiani produces installations of uncanny and ghostly landscapes that hover between past and present, fading recollections and collective memory (page 78).

The Anthropocene, which some also call the "Capitalocene," is linked to the imperial and predatory practices of both colonialism and capitalism. Sammy Baloji brings both systems together in his photomontage series *Mémoire* (pages 80 and 81). Using archival and contemporary images, he explores and records the harsh mining history of his homeland in the Democratic Republic of the Congo. Art historian T. J. Demos remarks that we are living in a regime of resource colonization "rooted in paradigms of imperialism that go back centuries."[9]

Sociologist Liam Downey proposes that the relationship between humans and the natural world cannot be understood without considering a strong link between natural resource extraction, armed violence, and environmental degradation.[10] Resource extraction in the eastern part of the Democratic Republic of the Congo is inextricably tied to an ongoing civil war that has claimed up to 6 million lives since 1998. The country is rich in resources including diamonds, gold, cobalt, copper, and Coltan used in electronic devices, all much-desired for manufacturing high technology in the West. Profit goes to corporations, "illegal" mining operations, smugglers, warlords, government, and private militias—not to the people.

In response to the dire situation, artist Richard Mosse uses his camera to bring much-needed attention to the Democratic Republic of the Congo. Taking advantage of the unusual coloring created by a World War II infrared reconnaissance camera, Mosse denaturalizes the daily cycle of mining, smuggling, warfare, and family life, hoping to break the shield of indifference to human and environmental devastation. Mosse's photograph *Stalemate* depicts an abandoned United Nations digger stuck in mud. The machine conveys the frustrated efforts for peace and for healing the Earth and its inhabitants (page 82).

It is widely known that current energy sources cannot sustain the world population at the level of American consumption. For many who are poor, coal is the most accessible source of energy. However, coal mining has a severe impact on humans and the environment, including shortened human life; mountain-removal mining; air pollution from toxins and methane and carbon dioxide (CO_2) production; and destruction of ecosystems and wildlife habitats. Although China claims to be a leader in reducing fossil fuel dependency, Chinese corporations are building or planning to build more than seven hundred new coal plants at home and around the world. Himself covered in coal, Chinese performance artist Liu Bolin takes his stand in front of a pile of coal (page 83). In defiance of Chinese practices in coal production, he makes himself nearly invisible as a way to highlight government disregard for human life and environmental safety.

CONSUMPTION

In a startling and fantastic declaration, scholar J. Hillis Miller tells us we are "collectively living on a planet that is becoming one gigantic garbage dump." Miller's concerns are vast: carbon dioxide, methane, landfills, nuclear waste, plastic, and toxins. The list could go on. With a sense of dismay, Miller conjures Paul Klee's evocative image *Angel of History,* now looking backward on the ever-growing debris of history as he is propelled into a future he cannot see.[11]

The Anthropocene epoch is characterized by the push for endless growth and consumption. Those who were born to endless expansion cannot conceive of contraction. Artists in this section expose the toxic danger that threatens the planet due to consumption and waste. They address wanton waste on land and sea, as well as issues of accumulation, growing populations, and manufactured food.

Trash is the driving force for works by Allan Sekula, Yao Lu, and Kimiyo Mishima. Allan Sekula focuses on the world's oceans, a site of global exchange, extraction, and exploitation of labor. His work *Shipwreck and Worker, Istanbul* reveals not only the wreckage of a ship but also the risk of a capitalist system that prioritizes profit at the cost of human suffering and environmental devastation (page 87). Yao Lu's photomontage portrays massive trash heaps under the guise of a traditional Chinese landscape (page 92). Kimiyo Mishima focuses on the discarded objects of contemporary life including cans, newspapers, posters, and everyday objects of consumer culture, transforming them into highly realistic ceramic sculptures (pages 88 and 89).

Geologists from the University of Leicester inform us that humanity has accumulated an estimated 30 trillion tons of "Stuff" —5 million times the mass of the Great Pyramid of Giza and enough to fit more than one hundred pounds' worth over every square meter of the planet's surface.[12] Artist Mary Mattingly's work emphasizes the magnitude of our dependence on material things. In her photograph *Life of Objects,* she shows a bundled ball containing all of her belongings (page 93). The globelike ball rests on the back of a young man's body. Metaphorically bearing the world of human possessions, he recalls the myth of Atlas, who was condemned by Zeus to hold the heavens on his back.

Nine billion people are expected to live on Earth in 2050. Edward Burtynsky's photograph *Cape Coral, Florida #1, 2012,* is an aerial view of a preplanned city that may prove to be a model for housing the thousand people who move to Florida every day (page 91). Cape Coral has the largest canal system in the world, with four hundred miles of canals pinning together a seemingly endless number of houses in tight grids. The canal system is so extensive that the local ecology and tides have been affected. With rising sea levels and swiftly increasing populations on a global level, the future of such coastal cities looks dire indeed.

More than ever, nature is monetized as a human resource. Animal agriculture harms the Earth and transforms the human/animal connection to a consumer/commodity relationship. Industrial animal consumption and the use of fossil fuel for energy are the two leading causes of global warming, deforestation, pollution, and water consumption. Fifty-one percent of all greenhouse gas comes from the animal industry, in which confined cows are forced to eat an unnatural diet saturated with growth hormones and antibiotics. Most ranchers forbid the public to view their feedlots. Exposing the practice, artist Mishka Henner created an aerial view of a feedlot in Texas by cobbling together screen shots from Google Earth (page 90).

EXTINCTION

Ghosts remind us that we live in an impossible present—a time of rupture, a world haunted with the threat of extinction. Deep histories tumble in unruly graves that are bulldozed into gardens of Progress.

—Anna Lowenhaupt Tsing, ed., *Arts of Living on a Damaged Planet*

The ravages of poverty, pollution, and resource depletion have pushed humans and nonhumans alike toward the edge of extinction. It is estimated that the rate of biological extinction is now several hundred times beyond its historical levels. Some scientists predict that half of all plants, animals, and birds on the planet will die off before 2100, a problem for both individual species and ecosystems worldwide.

Some people attempt to move beyond mourning and melancholia, countering it with resistance, research, vigilance, and reaching into the past to understand the present. Still, philosopher Jean-Luc Nancy encourages us to remain alert and to allow ourselves to be "exposed" to the crisis. After reflecting on nuclear catastrophe, he writes: "Let us not hurry to hide this exposure. Let us remain exposed, and let us think about what is happening [*ce qui nous arrive*] to us: Let us think that it is we who are arriving, or are leaving."[13] With hope and determination, artists in this section consider impending extinctions. Foremost, they consider the potential causes of annihilation, including pollution, poaching, climate change, habitat destruction, displacement, and war. The stories behind their images are woven with elements of fantasy, fiction, the ghostly, and the uncanny.

Memory, histories, and allegories about extinction have important meanings for artists Bethany Taylor and Chris Jordan. Ghosts and the uncanny seem to inhabit Taylor's jacquard woven tapestries. Loosely based on emblematic tapestries of moral codes from the sixteenth to eighteenth centuries, her dreamlike and didactic textiles feature a menagerie of animals and ghostly figures (pages 96 and 97). In his *Midway: Message from the Gyre* series, Chris Jordan taps into the myth treated in Coleridge's poem "The Rime of the Ancient Mariner," that to kill an albatross brings bad luck (pages 100 and 101). Jordan followed albatrosses to Midway Atoll and found carcasses of nesting chicks and parents. They had choked to death mostly from the plastic trash in the ocean.

Plastic plays a vital role in the packing and distribution of global commodities. Synthetic polymers derived from oil are a kind of living dead among us, as these molecules refuse to interact with other carbon-dependent life forms. They do not biodegrade. It is projected that the amount of plastic created annually will reach 33 billion tons by 2020.

Big animals, or megafauna, are extremely vulnerable and face loss of habitat and "harvesting," and/or deliberate killing. Giant and big animals have existed across the globe from 40 million years ago until recently, when they began to lose a disproportional number of species. Artists Maroesjka Lavigne and Taryn Simon target the fate of large animals living in critical danger. Lavigne's eerie and ghostly image depicts a wild white rhinoceros crossing a white salt pan in the Namib Desert, a coastal desert in southern Africa (page 99). Rhinos have long been prized and killed for their horns, believed to be a source of healing and power. Due to poaching, rhinos are on the brink of total extinction. Taryn Simon's haunting photograph portrays Kenny, a white tiger caged in Arkansas (page 98). Kenny is the result of selective inbreeding that artificially creates the genetic conditions leading to white fur and ice-blue eyes. He has genetic defects and has difficulty breathing and closing his jaw. His teeth are malformed, and he limps because of abnormal bone structure in his forelegs. Humans are the driving force behind the extinction of the majestic tiger.

Many species of trees and plants are also endangered by humans. Trees absorb one-fifth of the Earth's carbon emissions. They provide cultural and ecological values, food, medicine, and timber. Of sixty thousand known tree species, ten thousand are threatened by deforestation, development, climate change, and invasive species. Beth Moon's photographs fight against extinction. The baobab trees she photographs are some of the oldest living beings on Earth (pages 104 and 105). These otherworldly and rare trees live past six thousand years and are usually found in remote, secluded, and unexpected places. The mythical dragon's blood tree, or bottle tree, grows on Socotra, a Yemeni island in the Arabian Sea (page 105).

Charles Gaines is also engaged with trees. Inspired by Tantric Buddhist art, he views the gridlike drawings and mandalas as maps of impulses and energies in the cosmos and a manifestation of a Zen-like practice. His number-based works highlight the relationship between the analog and the digital, the organic and unnatural, being and nonbeing (page 102).

The threat of extinction has extended to humans and groups of humans. Pollution dominates the stretch of land between New Orleans and Baton Rouge. Richard Misrach's *Swamp and Pipeline, Cancer Alley, Louisiana* has a backstory of 150 heavy industrial facilities that line the banks of the Mississippi River (page 103). They release toxins into the air, land, and water at staggering rates. Poverty-stricken African Americans, segregated by race and socioeconomic status, live nearby in clusters. Struggling with environmental racism, they suffer from pollution and high rates of cancer.

The Anthropocene also entails the mass movement of peoples. Within a decade, there will be millions of environmental migrants, with climate change as one of the major drivers. The effects of global warming are most felt in the developing world, with the poor suffering disproportionately in Asia, the Middle East, Africa, and Latin America. North-South conflicts will increase because of perceived injustice regarding who causes and who bears the effects of global warming. Eva Leitolf's *Postcards from Europe* project assembles photographs and texts that touch on conflict in the context of global migration. Her photography brings attention to scenes where incidents of exclusion, xenophobia, and violence have occurred—but that are empty of people (pages 106 and 107). The absence of the perpetrators and victims is eerie, but it makes the evocation of loss all the more poignant.

SYMBIOSIS & MULTISPECIES

The Greek word *symbiōsis* means a "state of living together." It relates closely to what Donna Haraway calls sym-poesis, meaning "making with," which brings the relationship much closer. Theorist and physicist Karen Barad has introduced the concept of "intra-action" regarding relationships. Different from the "inter" of interaction, "intra" means "within," and "intra-action" is a deep and transforming exchange, an experience that ignites the ability to act and create. In the context of these concepts, artists explore the ideas of immersion, entanglement, and being part of everything and everyone else.

Artists consider the many relationships and interactions between humans and nonhuman beings. On one hand, artists consider the negative effects of anthropocentric control and supremacy over nature, a perspective guided by dualisms—nature/society, individual/collective, body/mind, subject/object. On the other hand, artists share nonhierarchical alliances and symbiotic attachments, understanding that objects, beings, and ideas are always becoming a part of interconnected assemblages. Their relations extend to animals, plants, artifacts, images, and other forms of being.

The latter relations are reflected in Ana Mendieta's work. Mendieta endows things and nature with life, agency, and subjecthood. In her film *Creek,* Mendieta herself is immersed in the gentle waves of a creek, the water rippling over her body (page 111). She writes: "My art is grounded in the belief of one universal energy which runs through everything: from insect to man, from man to specter, from specter to plant, from plant to galaxy. My works are the irrigation veins of this universal fluid. Through them ascend the ancestral sap, the original beliefs, the primordial accumulations, the unconscious thoughts that animate the world."[14] Influenced by the aesthetic strategies of Marcel Duchamp, Gabriel Orozco focuses on the overlooked detail, the chance encounter, and the potential for play. In his two photographs, he highlights the symbiotic relationships between a whale and birds and in the encounter of spiders with a leaf (pages 114 and 115).

The Florida Everglades is the only wetland of its kind in the continent, but farming, dredging, engineering, developments, roads, and loss of clean water threaten its very existence. Invasive plants and animals combined with endangered species make the environment all the more vulnerable. For her film, Dana Levy chose the Big Cypress Swamp at the heart of the Everglades to stage a fictitious encounter between a colonial explorer and nature. Using vintage artifacts, she creates a floating study in the dense swamp (page 113). Colonial furniture and antiquities glide through the dark waters. Birds cry as a snake slithers over a desk, through documents and artifacts. This uncanny scene suggests that colonialism is not compatible with nature.

Thomas Struth's photograph *Paradise 14, Yakushima, Japan 1999* captures the dense, verdant, and haunting beauty of the island's forests, some thousands of years old. In this photograph, a clearing in the moss-covered rocks leads the viewer's eye into a labyrinth of vines and vegetation, creating an effect of total immersion (page 110). Today many have abandoned the Romantic idea of nature as a pristine and eternal entity, untouched by humans, a nature that never was.

Multispecies studies have attracted scholars interested in the interconnectedness and inseparability of humans and other life forms, ranging from animals, plants, and fungi to microbes. These entanglements also morph into fictitious and hybrid creatures such as those depicted by artists William Kentridge, Huma Bhabha, Wifredo Lam, Sergio Vega, Pedro Neves Marques, and Jackie Nickerson.

Against the background of apartheid, South African artist William Kentridge created *Promenade II,* a series of bronze figures. Each figure is part human, animal, plant, or machine, with elements that recall the dinosaur age, colonialism, industrialism, everyday objects, and even a figure of himself (page 119). These indeterminate figures suggest labor, displacement, and a seemingly endless migration. Huma Bhabha's colorful drawing takes the shape of an uncanny human-canine hybrid. Upon closer inspection, layered features of a woman and wolf or dog can be seen (page 121). Bhabha's work has been described as "having been improvised by some lone survivor of an unspecified catastrophe, reflecting on what has happened and on what may yet be."[15]

Less haunting is a terracotta black glazed relief with a figure, half woman and half fish, by Wifredo Lam (page 118). Inspired by the surrealists and the legacies of European, African, and Cuban culture, Lam began making fantastic, polymorphic, and hybrid figures that testified to human/animal connections and the multiple dimensions of any one being. Sergio Vega explores the link between humans and long-tailed monkeys through biblical and evolutionary perspectives. Vega makes the humorous proposal that the long-tailed monkey, not the gorilla, could have been tapped as our closest human predecessor were it not for the monkey's tail (page 120). With the catastrophic destruction of the Amazon habitat, the relationship is ever more distant but not forgotten.

Philosopher, environmental activist, and ecofeminist Vandana Shiva states, "Monocultures based on chemical inputs do not merely destroy plant biodiversity, they have destroyed soil biodiversity, which leads to the emergence of pathogens, new diseases, and more chemical use." She also condemns GMOs for the depletion of water sources and the increasing of greenhouse gases.

Industrial agriculture has often created a serious rupture in human/nonhuman relationships.[16] In his film *YWY, The Android*, Pedro Neves Marques explores the limits of technology and human life (page 117). He considers GMOs and their effects on humans and non-humans. Two Brazilian entities have a conversation—one is an indigenous female android and the other is a GMO cornfield itself. Despite the absence of human identity, they still talk about bodily rights, infertility, labor, and monocrops. In a companion film, he highlights the nebulous boundaries of biogenetics. In *The Pudic Relation between Machine and Plant,* the human element is omitted. The film portrays "romantic skirmishes" between a robot and a plant that is highly sensitive to touch (page 116). Tim Morton suggests that human beings are all cyborgs of a kind as they already carry all sorts of nonhuman components in their bodies.[17]

Jackie Nickerson is a longtime researcher of farmlands and farmworkers. In the series *Terrain,* she focuses on the positive synergy and entangled relationship between workers and the land they work. At the suggestion of a farmworker, she collaborated with farmworkers to stage a series of portraits exploring the connections between humans and nonhuman beings (pages 122 and 123).

JUSTICE

This section in the exhibition is devoted to justice for the indigenous peoples and lands of the Amazon Basin. It attunes us to new realities and relationships that guide us to see through the eyes of others across cultures and cosmologies. The Amazon Basin is rich in culture and nature and is the most biodiverse place on Earth. It has the planet's largest rain forest and the greatest number of plant and animal species in the world. It is also home to roughly 1 million indigenous people within the rain forest and in the highlands of the Andes. Amazon rainfall and rivers also nourish regions well beyond the Amazon Basin, and more than a quarter of all carbon is stored by tropical forests. Currently, indigenous lives, cultures, knowledge, lands, and resources are being threatened by rampant development and the extraction of raw materials.

Anthropologist Marisol de la Cadena is a defender of the lands and people of the indigenous world in South America. She resists and fights against the extraction of profitable resources and what she calls the "silent war" that takes place in even the most remote and unknown territories. She notes the remarkable and unparalleled speed and scope of environmental devastation and displacement caused by mining for minerals and fossil fuels, damming and polluting rivers, leveling trees, and the "destruction of networks that make local life possible."[18] De la Cadena also foregrounds the strong resistance of local people hoping to protect their territory and lives.

Indigenous knowledge of plants has been critical to medicinal scientists. Artist Abel Rodríguez was asked to help classify and identify different species. Rodríguez is known as a *sabedor* (man of knowledge), a savant, and namer of plants. Drawing from memory, he illustrated the botanical life of the forest in exquisite works of ink and watercolor (pages 126 and 127). Curator José Roca described his work as "visions of someone that speaks to the plants." Rodríguez fled the forest due to armed conflict triggered by illegal land grabs and gold mining.

Eduardo Kohn is an anthropologist and the author of *How Forests Think.* He states that any entity that communicates by signs can be considered as a "self." Kohn proposes that all beings are constitutively semiotic—using signs to convey meaning: "All life is semiotic and all semiosis is alive. In important ways, life and thought are one and the same: life thinks; thoughts are alive. Wherever there are 'living thoughts,' there is also a 'self.'"[19] Kohn's research has led him to the diverse cultures and cosmologies of indigenous people, most of whom recognize a kinship with rivers, plants, and animals emerging in an organic whole. In the 1970s, artist Claudia Andujar photographed the ways of life of the Yanomami

Indians of the Amazon Basin of northern Brazil. Though the Yanomami are one of the larger groups, they are still in danger of cultural dissolution. One blurred image by Andujar hints at the fading away of indigenous people and traditional life (pages 132–135).

Indigenous lands are facing massive threats from oil and gas companies, hydroelectric dams, illegal loggers, and drug traffickers. Brazil is planning a growth program to turn the Amazon Basin into an industrial heartland to fuel Brazil's fast-growing urban economy. In the summer of 2017, Brazil opened up 860,000 acres of protected Amazon rain forest to logging, mining, and farming. Today, many of the forests and savannas have been razed, burned, and converted to fields for agriculture and cattle ranching. When forests burn, tree carbon matter is released in the form of carbon dioxide. The rain forest is now emitting more carbon than it is taking in. Sergio Vega's photographs show the Amazon rain forest devastated by fire (pages 130 and 131). *Paradise on Fire* is part of an ongoing project, "Paradise in the New World." Vega plays on the discrepancy between utopian dreams of the Amazon and its severely damaged present condition. The original fantasy was inspired by seventeenth-century scholar Antonino de León Pinelo, who located the Garden of Eden in the Mato Grosso region of Brazil.

In 2008, President Rafael Correa of Ecuador was highly praised when he signed the "Rights of Nature" into the country's constitution, granting to nature rights equivalent to human rights: "The new constitution redefines people's relationship with nature by asserting that nature is not just an object to be appropriated and exploited by people, but is rather a rights-bearing entity that should be treated with parity under the law."[20] Unfortunately, the president did not keep his promises and bent to mining interests.

Indigenous peoples have strongly opposed the invasive practices of multinational extractive industries that threaten their lands and resources. Resistance has proved essential for justice in the Amazon. On October 12, 2013, nearly three hundred women from seven different indigenous tribes of the Ecuadorian Amazon went on a long march to the capital. They were fighting to save their ancestral land from impending oil drilling and mining. Artist Felipe Jácome collaborated with the women to create and document their portraits. On the frames of the photographs, the women wrote about their battles, fears, determination, and wishes (pages 128 and 129). Jácome considers the images not just as photographs but also as testimonies. Colombia's president declined to meet with the protesting women and later imprisoned some as terrorists.

Grassroots resistance may prove to be the most effective and courageous way to practice stewardship of our planet. T. J. Demos writes about the significance of civil action and the possibility of joyful rebellion. With the closing of conventional political routes to counter environmental and cultural devastation, activism may be more and more essential. In this catalogue and other publications, Demos has commented on the growing resistance, citing examples such as Liberate Tate, Standing Rock, and Blockadia. He opens a compelling conversation about activism and art, ethics and aesthetics.[21]

Also concerned with rebellion, justice, and peace are artists Jennifer Allora and Guillermo Calzadilla, creators of the sculpture *The bird of Hermes is my name, eating my wings to make me tame*. Hermes was a Greek deity, the god of transitions and boundaries. As a messenger and protector of travelers, he has access to all realms of the world, including Hades. Represented here as a bird, he has a body built from a Special Operations helmet, a surveillance camera, and other battlefield accessories (page 137). The sacrifice of his wings is a gesture of peace, a message of self-control to bring safety to the world. Such restraint from conflict is sorely needed.

IMAGINARY FUTURES

Just as blind optimism risks lubrication of existing forms of power, an equally blind pessimism risks stunting the collective capacities required to oppose them.

—Rory Rowan, "Extinction as Usual? Geo-Social Futures and Left Optimism"

Visions of the future are daunting. Environmental catastrophe is already here and has already made its mark on the future. Geologist and artist Trevor Paglen writes: "On the time scale of atmospheric processes, anthropogenic transformation to Earth's atmosphere will influence the climate and weather systems for tens of thousands of years. Furthermore, troves of nuclear waste stockpiled deep within Earth from the Gobi desert to New Mexico will guarantee that these sites exude poison for tens or even hundreds of thousands of years."[22] Timothy Morton brings the situation closer to home when he notes that "75% of the greenhouse gases in the atmosphere at this very moment will still be there in half a millennium. That is 15 generations away. It will take another 750 generations, or 25,000 years, for most of those gases to be absorbed into the oceans."[23]

Pessimism could reign, but many insist that optimism is crucial. "Optimism must be cultivated," writes Rory Rowan, "not despite worsening geo-social conditions, but precisely because of them. . . . Without a commitment to the enduring possibility of a better world, we simply resign ourselves, and the planet, to extinction as usual."[24]

Trevor Paglen, Allan Sekula, and Noelle Mason resist pessimism by bringing to light and sharing the misuse of technology. The artists are wary of militarization and the control of knowledge and are also suspicious of practices that weaken democracy under the guise of security. Within each of their works, the landscape serves as a veil, hiding secret and questionable maneuvers under the surface. Trevor Paglen's photograph focuses on sites of underwater communication cables used for surveillance purposes (page 141). Paglen found information from NSA whistle-blower Edward Snowden, who revealed where both the U.S. and U.K. governments routinely tap these cables to collect citizens' data. Paglen set out to pin and photograph their locations, enabling us to see the erosion of our privacy.

Allan Sekula's journeys took him to a CIA black site set in a beautiful landscape in Poland (page 143). These are sites where prisoners from the wars in Iraq and Afghanistan were illegally transferred. Outside of U.S. jurisdiction, black sites are known as secret spaces of extraordinary rendition and torture meant to block sight, knowledge, and life itself. *X-Ray Vision vs. Invisibility* by Noelle Mason is composed of three embroidered tapestries depicting infrared images of undocumented immigrants crossing the U.S./Mexico border (pages 144 and 145). Mason's work investigates the effects of vision technologies and the perception of undocumented immigrants and how they reinforce a neocolonial social and political relationship with Mexico.

Technology, humans, and nature are inextricably intertwined, but to what extent has been debatable. Eco-activist Vandana Shiva states that "living organisms, unlike machines, organize themselves" and "cannot be treated as simply 'biotechnological inventions,' 'gene constructs,' or 'products of the mind.'"[25] In contrast, scholar Donna Haraway celebrates cyborgs—hybrids of machines and organism—and champions the potential of transgenic research. The opposition has been referred to as a conflict between the Cyborg and the Goddess. Rory Rowan claims "a false dichotomy has been imposed between techno-critics and techno-utopians." He says that what is most important regarding technologies is to know what they do, "how they are used, by whom and to what end."[26]

Haegue Yang, Dornith Doherty, and Andrew Yang stir hope with new kinds of relationships emerging from nonhierarchical alliances and symbiotic attachments. They seamlessly relate technological systems and economies with biological systems, culture, hybridity, and the uncanny. Haegue Yang's sculpture *Ornamental Mountains and Seas—Monster and Cloud* dispels dichotomies of past/future, technical/natural, and human/nonhuman (pages 146 and 147). Yang draws inspiration from China's oldest book of mythology, bringing together fact and fiction including rituals, medicine, geographies, hybrid and fantastic creatures and people. Yang utilizes electricity as a metaphor for the potential connections between people and ideas across time and history.

Like Haegue Yang, Doherty creates work that is held between past and future. She takes X-ray photographs of the plants and seeds safeguarded in the major seed banks around the world. The X-ray camera records what is invisible to the human eye and renders life and time on both a macro and micro scale (page 151). Her work represents both the possible collapse and the potential rebirth of multispecies. The need for seed banks points to our imperfection as guardians of the Earth. It does, however, reflect Rory Rowan's urge to forgo perfection and live *with* and *through* environmental change in the search for *betterment*.[27] He mirrors the approaches of Donna Haraway's book *Staying with the Trouble* and the multiauthored book *Arts of Living on a Damaged Planet.*

Well-being and harmony are defining characteristics of *Buen Vivir,* the indigenous South American notion of the good life. *Buen Vivir* translates to "living in plentitude and knowing how to live in harmony with the cycles of Mother Earth. Life and history are in balance with every form of existence in a state of permanent respect."[28] The subject of well-being is not about the individual, but the individual in the social context of their community and in a unique environmental situation. *Buen Vivir* is related to other indigenous belief systems throughout South America, as well as to Western political philosophy.

Andrew Yang's films reflect harmony with the universe. Looking at the cosmos engenders memories and fantasies in the interviews Yang stages with Ellen Yang, his mother and a professor of psychology, and Jeff Odisha, a professor of astrophysics (pages 148 and 149). With them, Yang explores the relationship between humans and the Milky Way—both, on different scales, celestial bodies in the greater universe. They discuss life-giving sources, the patterns visible on the Earth and in the skies, and the amazing idea that the universe is comprehensible—that we can ask questions and get answers. Odisha has a feeling of well-being when he sees what is beyond human.

Based on her work as an anthropologist working in South America, Marisol de la Cadena theorizes about the commons. For her, common goods belong to everybody and cannot be exploited by the interests of multinational corporations or states. Those living in the commons have the capacity to resist, think, and act together while still acknowledging and respecting those with whom they differ. No one is alone, but all can be separate. Paul Ricco states that existence is relational and shared. Sharing in separation is the praxis of coexistence—of being together.[29]

In conclusion, one may still ask what worlds are possible for a vibrant future. To live within Tim Morton's haunting universe of hyperobjects, we must be attuned to vast forces and systems intricate beyond our ability to perceive or comprehend. Considering Isabelle Stengers's call for attention, we may hear the music of these perplexing and potent forces—the cosmos, black holes, and climate change. Listening to our planet, we may see and experience the world in new ways. In the spirit of theorist Gilles Deleuze, we may understand that we exist in a perpetual state of "flux, always 'becoming' as part of interconnected assemblages."[30] We may behold our planet and its inhabitants, human and nonhuman, with a new and grateful regard. Artists ignite our awareness and will not allow us to forget or ignore the dire political and environmental crisis we face. They recognize the damage we have inflicted on our planet yet still refuse to deny hope and change. We may have a dark cloud to disperse, but we must own this world and not despair. Artists show that we can resist, protest, and share our common and uncommon worlds with humans and other life forms alike. By embracing optimism and seeking the *Buen Vivir,* we can help make the world not perfect, but certainly better.

NOTES

1 Laura Ogden et al., "Global Assemblages, Resilience, and Earth Stewardship in the Anthropocene," 2013, http://coweeta.uga.edu/publications/10973.pdf 2013.

2 Carol Armstrong, *Women Artists at the Millennium* (Cambridge: MIT Press, 2008), 208.

3 Isabelle Stengers, *In Catastrophic Times: Resisting the Coming Barbarism* (London: Open Humanities Press, 2015), 24.

4 Timothy Morton, "Nonlocality," *Arcade: Literature, the Humanities, & the World,* http://arcade.stanford.edu/blogs/nonlocality.

5 The essay titled "Suicide Narcissus" by Hamza Walker can be found at www.renaissancesociety.org/publishing/11/suicide-narcissus/.

6 J. Hillis Miller, "Reading Paul de Man While Falling into Cyberspace," in *Twilight of the Anthropocene Idols,* ed. Thomas Cohen, Claire Colebrook, and Miller (London: Open Humanities Press, 2016), 188, 190.

7 Ibid., 7.

8 Jane Bennett, *Vibrant Matter: A Political Ecology of Things* (Durham, NC: Duke University Press, 2010), x.

9 T. J. Demos, "Decolonizing Nature: Making the World Matter," 2016, https://tjdemos.sites.ucsc.edu/wp-content/uploads/sites/374/2016/08/Demos-World-of-Matter.pdf.

10 Liam Downey, Eric Bonds, and Katherine Clark, "Natural Resource Extraction, Armed Violence, and Environmental Degradation," 2010, www.ncbi.nlm.nih.gov/pmc/articles/PMC3169238/.

11 Miller, "Reading Paul de Man While Falling into Cyberspace," 182, 187.

12 Ben Panko, "Humans Have Bogged Down the Earth with 30 Trillion Metric Tons of Stuff, Study Finds," *The Age of Humans: Living in the Anthropocene,* 2016, www.smithsonianmag.com/science-nature/humans-have-bogged-down-earth-30-trillion-metric-tons-stuff-new-report-finds-180961365/.

13 As quoted in Heather Davis and Etienne Turpin, "Art and Death: Lives between the Fifth Assessment and the Sixth Extinction," in *Art in the Anthropocene: Encounters among Aesthetics, Politics, Environments and Epistemologies* (London: Open Humanities Press, 2015), 5.

14 Geulda Voien, "The Remarkable Story of a Rebel Artist, Her Mysterious Death and Cult Resurgence," November 2015, http://observer.com/2015/11/three-decades-after-her-sordid-death-ana-mendietas-work-is-finally-getting-its-due/.

15 Steel Stillman, "In the Studio: Huma Bhabha," *Art in America,* November 2010, www.artinamericamagazine.com/news-features/magazine/huma-bhabha/2010.

16 Vandana Shiva, "Women and Biodiversity Feed the World, Not Corporations and GMOs," *Common Dreams*, 2015, www.commondreams.org/views/2015/05/20/women-and-biodiversity-feed-world-not-corporations-and-gmos.

17 Alex Blasdel, "'A Reckoning for Our Species': The Philosopher Prophet of the Anthropocene," 2017, www.theguardian.com/world/2017/jun/15/timothy-morton-anthropocene-philosopher.

18 Marisol de la Cadena, "Uncommoning Nature," *e-flux journal 56th Venice Biennale*, 2015, http://supercommunity.e-flux.com/authors/marisol-de-la-cadena/.

19 Eduardo Kohn, *How Forests Think: Toward an Anthropology beyond the Human* (Berkeley: University of California Press, 2013), 16.

20 Cyril Mychalejko, "Ecuador's Constitution Gives Rights to Nature," *Upside Down World,* 2008, http://upsidedownworld.org/archives/ecuador/ecuadors-constitution-gives-rights-to-nature/.

21 T. J. Demos, "Accumulation: The Great Transition: The Arts and Radical System Change," *e-flux architecture*, www.e-flux.com/architecture/accumulation/122305/the-great-transition-the-arts-and-radical-system-change/.

22 Trevor Paglen, "The Ethics of Deep Time," in *Speculation, Now: Essays and Artwork,* ed. Vyjayanthi Venuturupalli Rao with Prem Krishnamurthy and Carin Kuoni (Durham, NC: Duke University Press in association with the Vera List Center for Art and Politics, The New School, 2014), 70.

23 Blasdel, "A Reckoning for Our Species."

24 Rory Rowan, "Extinction as Usual? Geo-Social Futures and Left Optimism," *e-flux journal 56th Venice Biennale,* 2015, http://supercommunity.e-flux.com/authors/rory-rowan/.

25 Vandana Shiva, "Women and Biodiversity Feed the World, Not Corporations and GMOs," *Common Dreams,* 2015, www.commondreams.org/views/2015/05/20/women-and-biodiversity-feed-world-not-corporations-and-gmos.

26 Rowan, "Extinction as Usual?"

27 Ibid., 15.

28 T. J. Demos, *Decolonizing Nature: Contemporary Art and the Politics of Ecology* (Berlin: Sternberg, 2016), 24.

29 Davis and Turpin, "Art and Death," 21.

30 Helen Stuhr-Rummereim, "Women Who Make a Fuss—Isabelle Stengers & Vinciane Despret," *Full Stop: Reviews. Interviews. Marginalia,* www.full-stop.net/2014/04/17./reviews/helen-stuhr-rommereim/women-who-make-a-fuss-isabelle-stengers-vinciane-despret/2014.

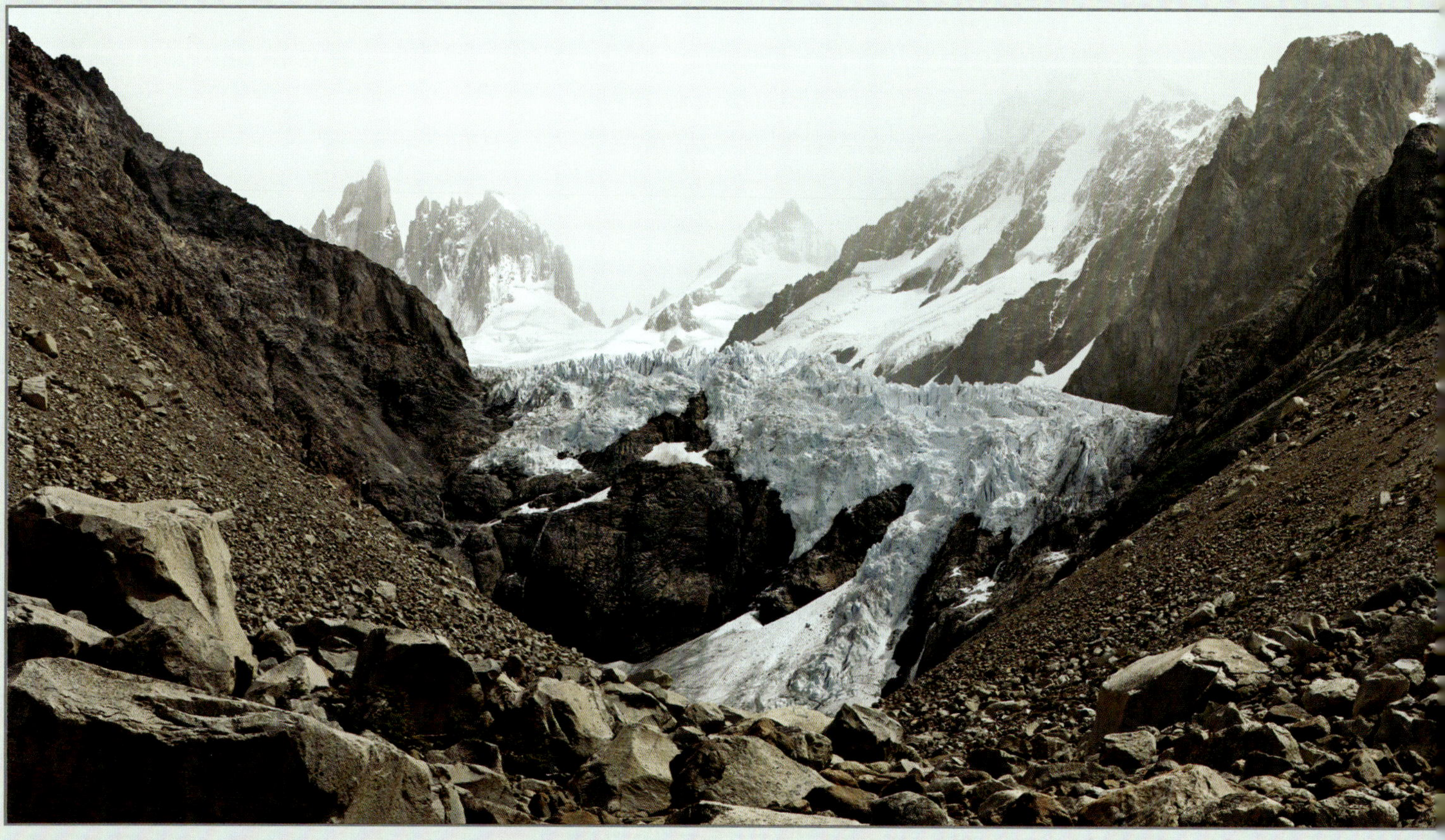

Frank Thiel
Piedras Blancas

THE ETHICS OF DEEP TIME

Trevor Paglen

Over the last two hundred years, humans have reconstructed their relationship to time. The late eighteenth century saw the discovery of geologic, or *deep,* time when James Hutton and other early geologists examined rock formations and concluded that Earth was far older than the six thousand years calculated by biblical scholars. The discovery of deep time was followed by the invention of absolute time. Before railroads and telegraphs revolutionized transportation and communication, vastly contracting the effective distance between disparate locales, each town and city kept its own time. Noon was whenever the sun was overhead. The railroads changed all of that: Beginning in 1840 in England, a system of uniform time was established and spread across the globe over the following decades. By the turn of the twentieth century, the world's clocks were synchronized with one another. Time was made uniform; human activities were coordinated to the artificial backdrop of a ticking second hand on a centralized clock.

With the reinvention of time came the reconfiguration of space. As time became absolute, space became frangible—a phenomenon Marx famously called "the annihilation of space by time." The ability to distort space and time became a central vehicle for capitalist accumulation and military dominance. On the capitalist side, altering the length of the workday and increasing turnover times through automated manufacturing, efficiency in transportation, just-in-time production, and high-speed financial transactions led to increased profits. On the military side, advances in speed through railway transportation, autobahns, communications infrastructure, and remote imaging translated into strategic advantages. The space-time constructions and annihilations that characterized the nineteenth and early twentieth centuries have continued uninterrupted through the twentieth and twenty-first.

The contemporary period, however, is also haunted by a human reconfiguration of time. Humans have not only distorted the time and space of everyday life and lived experience, but they have invaded the deep time of geologic processes and even the cosmic time of planets, stars, and galaxies. On the time scale of atmospheric processes, anthropogenic transformation of Earth's atmosphere will influence the climate and weather systems for tens of thousands of years. Furthermore, troves of nuclear waste stockpiled deep within the Earth from the Gobi Desert to New Mexico will guarantee that these sites exude poison for tens or even hundreds of thousands of years. Human activities have transformed the chemical makeup of the atmosphere and created bizarre strata in Earth's geologic record.[1]

Humans' spatiotemporal footprint extends even further into the future than the deep time of geomorphology, and farther across space than the confines of our planet. Human activities, it turns out, have also produced a cosmic archaeological record and a galactic footprint. The solar system is punctuated by a handful of machines, including the Stardust space probe, engaged in a long arcing orbit around the Sun, and the Chinese Chang'e-2 spacecraft, parked at a Lagrange point 1.5 million kilometers from Earth. Moreover, hundreds of geosynchronous communications satellites in stable orbit, 36,000 kilometers from Earth, form a man-made ring around the planet. All of these machines will glide through the solar system until the Sun becomes a red giant in approximately 5 billion years. A much smaller group of machines—the two Pioneer and Voyager spacecraft along with the New Horizons probe—will leave the solar system entirely to spend eternity wandering among the stars. While the remnants of human civilizations on Earth's surface will eventually be pulverized by erosion, volcanism, glaciation, and tectonics, the machines in distant Earth orbits and those on much farther trajectories may prove to be the longest-lasting material artifacts of the contemporary movement.

When we think about all the ways humans have transformed their environment, we tend to think about anthropogenic transformations of Earth's surface and its consequences for the present and near future. When we think about time, we tend to understand it on scales familiar to our everyday experiences. We worry about the effects of fiscal policy over the course of a few years or, at best, concern ourselves with climate change over a few decades. But humans have made equally great interventions into the deep time of geology and even the cosmic time of the galaxy. Geologic time and cosmic time are so far removed from our everyday experience that to even consider them seems fantastical. Nonetheless, the transformation of deep space-time comes with ethical responsibilities that we have failed to acknowledge. Can we imagine, for example, a "human rights" framework that extends far beyond individual human subjects to flora and fauna, or even minerals and geomorphic processes (both anthropogenic and "natural")? Can we imagine democratizing the production of time itself? What's at stake, quite literally, is the future of everything.

This text was first published in Vyjayanthi Venuturupalli Rao, Prem Krishnamurthy, and Carin Kuoni, eds., *Speculation, Now: Essays and Artwork* (Durham, NC: Duke University Press, in association with the Vera List Center for Art and Politics, The New School, 2014).

NOTES

1 Interestingly, a thin layer of radioactive fallout from atmospheric nuclear explosions has altered the radiocarbon signature of the present. Archaeologists in the distant future using radiocarbon dating techniques on contemporary artifacts will conclude that we existed nearly five hundred years later than we did. From the perspective of future radiocarbon dating, we are living in a period of five hundred "missing" years.

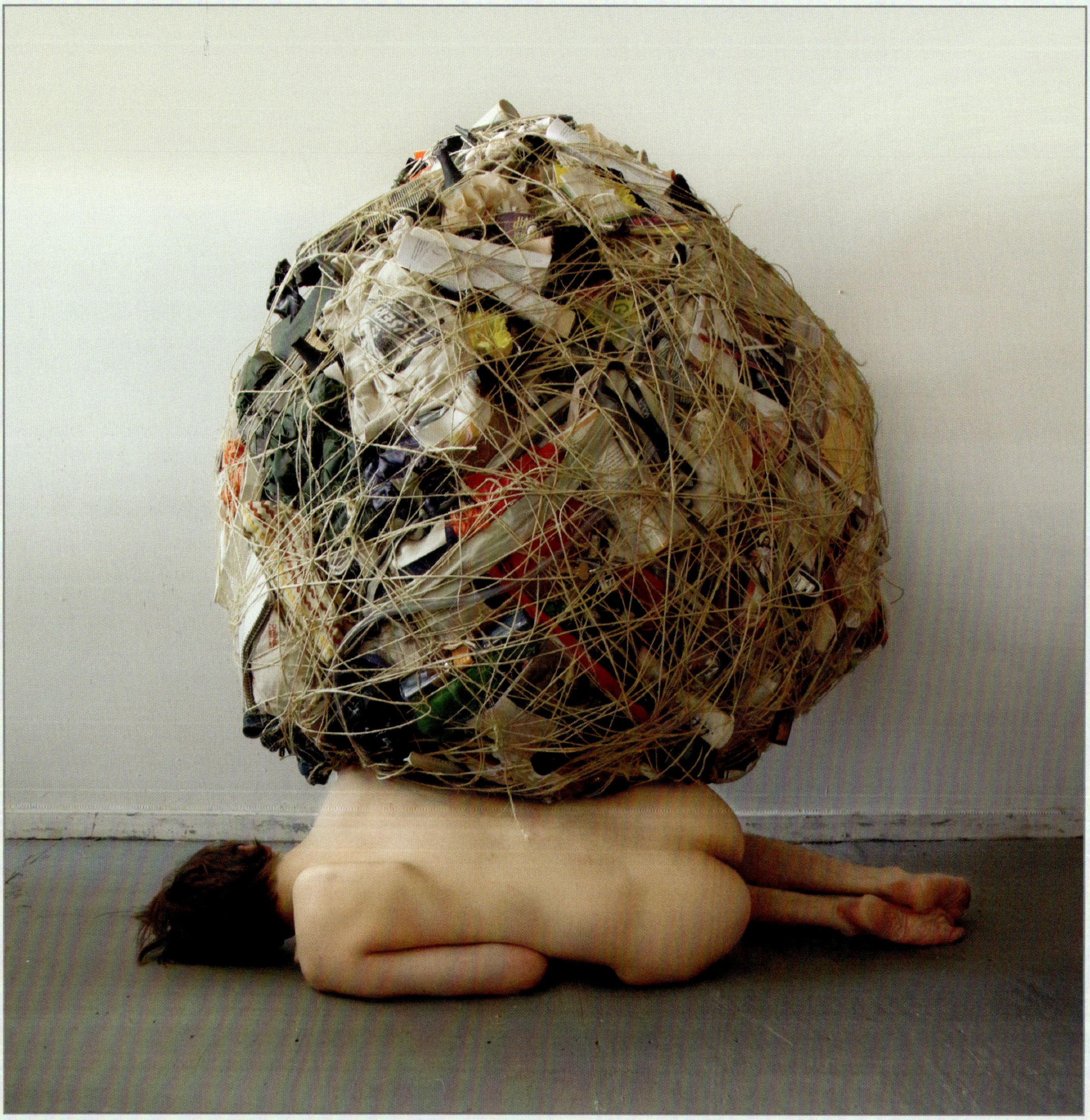

Mary Mattingly

Life of Objects

A WORLD OF OUR MAKING

T. J. Demos

In her recent book *Staying with the Trouble,* Donna Haraway suggests off-handedly that Burning Man—the neopagan festival celebrated annually in Nevada's Black Rock Desert—and more specifically its iconic figure, may be the most emblematic image of the Anthropocene.[1] The Man, a wooden sculpture standing a hundred feet tall, is a monument of verticality celebrating the human beings who made it, designed to be consumed by fire in a consumerist mass spectacle, with images disseminated widely on social media by the festival's many tech-savvy and IT-industry participants. It's an apt metaphor for a fossil-fueled and techno-utopian modernity, as well as for its disturbing implications. Complex and sometimes contradictory, Burning Man expresses triumphant anthropocentrism, neo-Prometheanism, and anti-authoritarian anarcho-primitivism, in addition to suicidal tendencies, cataclysmic climate breakdown, and an overheated and destroyed world. Still, the catastrophe that is the Anthropocene—threatening the end of life as we know it—really overwhelms any proposal for an adequate image or accurate representation. The events characterizing the end of the nearly twelve-thousand-year-old Holocene, at once climatological and geobiological, as well as sociopolitical and techno-economic, are simply too vast, complex, and momentous to conceptualize or represent.

Others suggest that all is not lost: it's possible yet to save ourselves from the fate of Burning Man. We might still create a "Good Anthropocene." This is the proposition of the California-based Breakthrough Institute, supported intellectually by the likes of Stewart Brand, the founder and former editor of the *Whole Earth Catalog*, and French sociologist-philosopher Bruno Latour. If we now face a new geological era wherein "human activities," over the long course of the Industrial Revolution and the Great Acceleration of post–World War II technological modernity, have become the central drivers of Earth's natural systems—anthropogenic climate disruption being the most obvious example—then the current challenge is how to harness that power for the good, ultimately becoming responsible for the monster we've created.[2] Even here, the monstrous Earth, the planet of the Anthropocene, is a human-distorted perversion of nature, revealing the roughly hewn constructedness of a dysfunctional "natureculture" without hyphen, in this case a horrific hybrid that is unnatural as much as inhuman or all-too-human, portending life's precariously modified future without historical analogue. Indeed, Latour likens environmentally transformed Earth to a contemporary Frankenstein, our new and unfolding creation that, for him, we cannot now abandon.[3]

The implication is that in order to avoid self-destruction, we need to care for that Frankenstein, meaning not hesitate from using whatever means at our disposal to prevent runaway climate breakdown—the global warming, melting ice, rising seas, desertification, extreme drought, habitat destruction, mass species extinction, and ocean acidification that bodes gravely for our near future. What the Breakthrough Institute and Latour mostly have in mind is the rejection of any hesitation in deploying further technological manipulation of Earth's systems to mitigate climate disruption. We must now willfully control climatological systems, they argue, in order to prevent further global warming. It's as if, for them, environmental transformation isn't necessarily negative; for, with it, we have the opportunity to create a new Eden on Earth, whereby humans will assume the role of divine creator. Indeed, Brand fanned the flames of just this sort of ambition decades ago with his 1960s motto for the *Whole Earth Catalog:* "We are as gods and might as well get good at it."

We're talking geoengineering—the large-scale recalibration of nature's global environment, primarily through technologies of solar radiation management (for instance, distributing aerosols in the planet's stratosphere to reflect surface-heating sunlight) and carbon capture (collecting the greenhouse gases from the atmosphere and storing them underground or in the ocean). In a way, it represents the transformation of the world into a giant design assemblage or expanded biotech architecture of human creation. But there are manifold problems. Many critics contend the proposals won't work, and never on the necessary scales to have any effect. If they do work at all, we risk becoming dependent on them, necessitating further, ongoing modulations. Geoengineering may also bring unintentional consequences in the Global South, such as disastrously altering monsoon seasons in India or intensifying drought in sub-Saharan Africa, imperiling millions or even billions. As well, there is no global governance or regulation for the practice, which devotes precious resources to cosmetic mitigation without addressing the causes of climate disruption. That said, these reservations are not stopping institutions such as Harvard University from carrying out the world's first geoengineering experiments in the field, funded to the tune of $20 million.[4] Such experiments only reveal the problems of our current technocracy, highlighting its elite scientism and ungoverned engineering practice, emerging from and enforcing global politico-economic inequality, antidemocratic processes, and unregulated experimentation—all of which could bring catastrophic results to those who have little responsibility for causing climate disruption in the first place.

With these conceptualizations and practices in mind, the Anthropocene emerges as an ideological discourse of choice for current climate governance, a geological-political instrument that allows those who wield it to negotiate or suspend contradictions. It's a narrative that selectively frames geological history (often ignoring histories of capitalism, and their relation to imperialism and slavery), diagnoses our present within that framework, and consequently provides selectively chosen routes toward a predetermined future. With it we opportunistically frame our transfigured environmental situation and reassure ourselves that those responsible are adequately addressing the situation. But if the Anthropocene thesis defines the crisis and also provides solutions, then it does so according to its own set of biases and within definite limits: to address climate change, we can focus only on techno-fixes and market-based mechanisms. Renewable energy is acceptable, but only within the system of green growth that doesn't threaten fossil-fuel interests. Under no circumstances can we consider alternatives that involve transforming ourselves instead of altering Earth's climate. The mantra of "system change, not climate change" promoted by activists and ecosocialists is off the table, even while conflict about the conventional approaches has been expressed at all the recent UN climate conferences.[5] Yet system change may very well be the only option that offers any credible hope of creating a livable future. System change entails reinventing our economic conditions of existence and thinking beyond the terms of our dominant capitalist paradigm, in which everything is up for sale—the air we breathe, the water we drink. According to this radical approach, the problem isn't technological or a simple matter of overshoot but rather a consequence of our growth-obsessed political economy. The concept of the Anthropocene, in its dominant expressions, helps to suppress and thereby manage this comprehensive and systemic perspective.

It's not that there are no critical attempts to mobilize the Anthropocene thesis against its technocratic tendencies. Consider the inspiring work of Anna Tsing, Donna Haraway, even Latour, and many others, where the term lends support to important theoretical and empirical research into the conditions of postanthropocentric multispecies ecologies, indigenous decolonial practices, and more egalitarian and sustainable socioeconomic systems.[6] Zoe Todd has asked what it would mean to indigenize the Anthropocene, detaching it from what Nick Mirzoeff has called the "white supremacy scene," designating a long unfolding history of Western racial capitalism, state violence, and climate transformation.[7] These writers seek to challenge the bounded individualism, regressive social connotations, and disavowal of the disproportionate environmental causes and effects—the fact that those with the fewest resources and least responsibility for the causes will be most negatively impacted by climate breakdown—that are otherwise tied to the Anthropocene, as well as to delink the term from the corporate-state-military complex. If the language of the Anthropocene continues to gain traction, then that will occur despite the ferocious critique the discourse has received by many of these writers.[8] Yet the techno-scientific and engineering logic, massively supported by major research institutions from Harvard to Stanford, appears to have the upper hand in defining the conceptualization of the Anthropocene, no doubt in part because the hegemonic economic system is least threatened by their approach.

Another option is to act against the term itself, challenging its use and theorization.[9] If we're indeed now living in the Anthropocene—and it looks like the International Union of Geological Sciences will officially endorse the term, following the recommendation of its Anthropocene Working Group—then we must put all our efforts into escaping it and coming out the other side as soon as possible. How? By abandoning anthropocentric practices, rethinking our economic system, pursuing low-impact energy systems and infrastructure, and reinventing democratic governmental politics beyond corrupting corporate interests. We need to think critically about non-Malthusian and equitable population reduction, embrace multispecies ethics and relational being, and prioritize ecological values that support flourishing biodiversity and functional ecosystems over economic values that privilege short-term profits and growing inequality. We must learn to live well with others and invent new stories, images, and sounds that allow us to transform our values in the most fundamental ways. That urgency is part of a new ethico-political imperative formed around climate justice, and traditional calls for artistic freedom cannot escape it.

Art is indeed key here, especially innovative modes of creativity appropriate for our current epoch, ones transcending obsolete Holocene thought patterns, perceptions, and sensibilities. What would an art critical of—and importantly offering an alternative to—techno-utopian geoengineering be? What is an aesthetics of degrowth, drawdown, and ethical depopulation? What is collective creativity beyond capitalism's competitive individualism, institutions of wealth accumulation, and possessive patronage? What is an art that opposes militarism and extractivism? If artistic autonomy has been prized within modernism, what happens to aesthetics when climate breakdown renders autonomy impossible?[10] What is an art of multispecies climate justice? What would it mean in cultural terms to decolonize nature, rescuing it from its neoliberal financialization? These questions are purposely open-ended, without any definitive answers, though there are multiple encouraging proposals, sources of aesthetic inspiration within the diverse history of the avant-garde, and a growing body of research and creative and critical practice addressing these very topics right now.[11]

"We must retain hope." It's a common refrain, spoken against all odds. To understand why, one must account for the economic interests invested in the petro-capitalist economy, which infuses government policymaking with the awesome financial resources of lobbying capital, preventing systemic transformation of our system from advancing beyond the failures of green capitalism, keeping conversation safely in the grips of climate denialism. It's difficult to retain or cultivate optimism under these circumstances, even a willed optimism that accompanies a pessimism of the intellect, as Antonio Gramsci had it during the years of German and Italian fascism. What are the psychological effects of the Anthropocene? The dominant ones include profound depression, experiential deflation, and psychic disarray. We're brought down by relational disconnection, the psychology of "pre-loss" one feels in advance of seemingly inevitable disaster (of species, forests, coasts, cities)—I'm reminded of Adrian Piper's prescient work that reads "*Everything will be taken away,*" written over human faces wiped clean, emptied of any and all subjectivity. Many are tempted by fatalism and nihilism, leading to political apathy and immobility. Can these soul-destroying emotions be turned around?

"We must embrace a despair that unflinchingly acknowledges the bleak future that will be created by climate change," Chris Hedges writes.[12] Such a view finds confirmation in recent scientific reports on our climate outlook, for instance in journalist David Wallace-Wells's investigation of how the future appears from an objective scientific viewpoint. Considering the worst-case scenario assuming no interruption to present global production and growth, we gaze upon an unstoppable cascade of unimaginable tipping points, leading to an uninhabitable Earth and the end of civilization as we know it within the next hundred or so years. That future is characterized by heat-related environmental transformation, with temperatures raised 5–10 degrees Celsius: the end of easily available food following agricultural failure; climate plagues released from millennia-old melting ice, threatening biological annihilation; unbreathable polluted air and poisoned oceans; and massive economic collapse and corresponding sociopolitical inequality and violence, including wide-scale military conflict, owing to these manifold eventualities.[13] The closest environmental precedent for our situation is the Permian-Triassic mass extinction event that occurred 252 million years ago, known as the Great Dying. Ninety-seven percent of all life on Earth expired owing to a carbon-warmed environment. Compared to that, Wallace-Wells notes: "We are currently adding carbon to the atmosphere at a considerably faster rate; by most estimates, at least ten times faster. The rate is accelerating." Given that the author was swiftly accused of irresponsible alarmism, fact-stretching sensationalism and catastrophism, one wonders whether such unblinking future-modeling is constructive. Is it, in fact, debilitating and counterproductive? Wallace-Wells has since doubled down, providing an annotated version of the essay to support its claims with interviews of credible scientists and links to further scholarly research.[14]

"The future of humanity is now in peril," Hedges observes. "At best, we can mitigate the crisis. We cannot avert it. We are fighting for our lives."[15] But what's the point? Why struggle at all, and why struggle to save a world that is unjust and violent? Hedges's answer: "We must see in any act of resistance, even if it appears futile, a moral victory." I'm in agreement. Even if environmental activism appears to have no appreciable political effect (consider the twenty-five-year-plus history of ineffectual UN climate change negotiations, accompanying the steady rise of atmospheric greenhouse gas), we can only continue to struggle. Silence is death, as ACT UP activists used to say. We are ethically bound. We may experience despair, but we must remain undeterred. Hedges is not convinced that resistance will inevitably lead to nothing; rather, his is an ethical argument for the necessity of continued insurrection against an unjust and destructive system (of which climate breakdown is only one part), above and beyond any practical considerations. That doesn't mean he has no hopes: "If we do not rapidly build militant movements of sustained revolt, movements willing to break the law and attack the structures of the corporate state, we will join the 99.9 percent of species that have vanished since life first appeared on earth." Indeed, there is still much that can be done to alter the disastrous future some plot out, to mitigate its worst effects, to initiate a massive transformation of our political and economic regime, to limit the impacts of further unnecessary environmental catastrophe. We can still create the basis for a just and sustainable future.

Where is the art that inaugurates the systemic transformation of our values? Where is the art that will carry us beyond the Anthropocene?

Reading the news, one might understandably conclude that our present priorities lie elsewhere than in environmental concerns—I'm thinking of the urgent struggles against white supremacy, neofascism, police brutality, economic inequality, militarism and the threat of nuclear war, and a thoroughly corrupt presidential administration. Consider also those fighting for Black Lives Matter, LGBTQ rights, Indigenous resurgence, equality and justice for all, redistributive economics, grassroots democratization, and postcapitalist alternatives. If climate disruption is the greatest and yet most invisible threat facing human civilization, that doesn't mean that these struggles are somehow unrelated or of greater or lesser importance. The fact is they are all intertwined, and if we're to do anything about climate breakdown, then we need nothing less than a political revolution to enact meaningful environmental transformation, and that transformation cannot be only environmental.[16] That will indeed necessitate the power of social movements, but movements not limited to the fight against greenhouse gases or atmospheric carbon or the fossil fuel industry.[17] In strengthening our necessary alliances, we must cultivate our collective imagination for a different kind of world, one worth fighting for, one capable of motivating a movement of movements, of a kind never seen before. Not the world of institutional racism and xenophobia, hate and discrimination, austerity budgets, neoliberal privatizations, economic inequality, and antidemocratic politics with which we're already familiar. These are not worthy of sustainability. Why save that world? To show why we're revolting and what for—such a vision of climate justice can only be intersectionalist, and it will require nothing less than an emancipated creativity to give expression to its transformative values.

NOTES

1 Donna Haraway, *Staying with the Trouble: Making Kin in the Chthulucene* (Durham, NC: Duke University Press, 2016), 46.

2 See https://thebreakthrough.org/; and John Asafu-Adjaye et al., "An Ecomodernist Manifesto," Breakthrough Institute, April 2015, www.ecomodernism.org/s/An-Ecomodernist-Manifesto.pdf.

3 See Bruno Latour, "Love Your Monsters: Why We Must Care for Our Technologies as We Do Our Children," *Breakthrough* 2 (Winter 2012), https://thebreakthrough.org/index.php/journal/past-issues/issue-2/love-your-monsters. I take issue with the generalizing implications of the problematic term "human activities" in my recent book *Against the Anthropocene: Visual Culture and Environment Today* (Berlin: Sternberg, 2017).

4 Arthur Neslen, "US Scientists Launch World's Biggest Solar Geoengineering Study," *Guardian,* March 24, 2017, www.theguardian.com/environment/2017/mar/24/us-scientists-launch-worlds-biggest-solar-geoengineering-study.

5 See, for instance, the website of System Change Not Climate Change: https://systemchangenotclimatechange.org/.

6 Among notable literature in the cultural and humanities sector, see Anna Tsing, Heather Swanson, Elaine Gan, and Nils Bubandt, eds., *Arts of Living on a Damaged Planet: Ghosts and Monsters of the Anthropocene* (Minneapolis: University of Minnesota Press, 2017); Haraway, *Staying with the Trouble;* Bruno Latour, *Facing Gaia: Eight Lectures on the New Climatic Regime* (London: Polity, 2017); and Heather Davis and Etienne Turpin, eds., *Art in the Anthropocene: Encounters among Aesthetics, Politics, Environments and Epistemologies* (London: Open Humanities Press, 2015).

7 Zoe Todd, "Indigenizing the Anthropocene," in *Art in the Anthropocene;* Nicholas Mirzoeff, "It's Not the Anthropocene, It's the White Supremacy Scene, or, the Geological Color Line," in *After Extinction,* ed. Richard Grusin (Minneapolis: University of Minnesota Press, 2018).

8 Haraway's being the most definitive. See *Staying with the Trouble,* especially her ferocious summary of objections to the Anthropocene on page 49.

9 For more on this argument, see Demos, *Against the Anthropocene.*

10 See the special issue of *South Atlantic Quarterly,* April 2017, edited by Bruce Braun and Sara Nelson, dedicated to "Autonomia in the Anthropocene"; and my own *Decolonizing Nature: Contemporary Art and the Politics of Ecology* (Berlin: Sternberg, 2016).

11 My most recent attempt at addressing these questions—focusing on the indigenous opposition to the Dakota Access Pipeline at Standing Rock, the autonomous zone in France called the Zad, and the movement for institutional liberation (from fossil fuel sponsorship)—is my essay "The Great Transition: The Arts and Radical System Change," *e-flux,* April 12, 2017, www.e-flux.com/architecture/accumulation/122305/the-great-transition-the-arts-and-radical-system-change/. See also the work of the Center for Creative Ecologies, which I direct: https://creativeecologies.ucsc.edu/.

12 Chris Hedges, "We Can't Fight Climate Change if We Keep Lying to Ourselves," Truthdig, June 19, 2017, www.truthdig.com/articles/we-cant-fight-climate-change-if-we-keep-lying-to-ourselves/.

13 For a further report, see Darh Jamail, "Scientists Warn of 'Biological Annihilation' as Warming Reaches Levels Unseen for 115,000 Years," Truthout, July 31, 2017, www.truth-out.org/news/item/41425-biological-annihilation-trillion-ton-icebergs-warming-levels-unseen-for-115–000-years.

14 David Wallace-Wells, "The Uninhabitable Earth," *New York Magazine,* July 9, 2017, http://nymag.com/daily/intelligencer/2017/07/climate-change-earth-too-hot-for-humans.html.

15 Hedges, "We Can't Fight Climate Change."

16 Fred Magdoff and Chris Williams write, "In order to replace capitalism with an ecological society we need a revolution." See their book *Creating an Ecological Society: Toward a Revolutionary Transformation* (New York: Monthly Review Press, 2017).

17 That is, counter to the position of Bill McKibben's war against nature, "A World at War: We're under Attack from Climate Change—and Our Only Hope Is to Mobilize Like We Did in WWII," *New Republic,* August 15, 2016, https://newrepublic.com/article/135684/declare-war-climate-change-mobilize-wwii; the work of 350.org; and the Climate Mobilization, www.theclimatemobilization.org/.

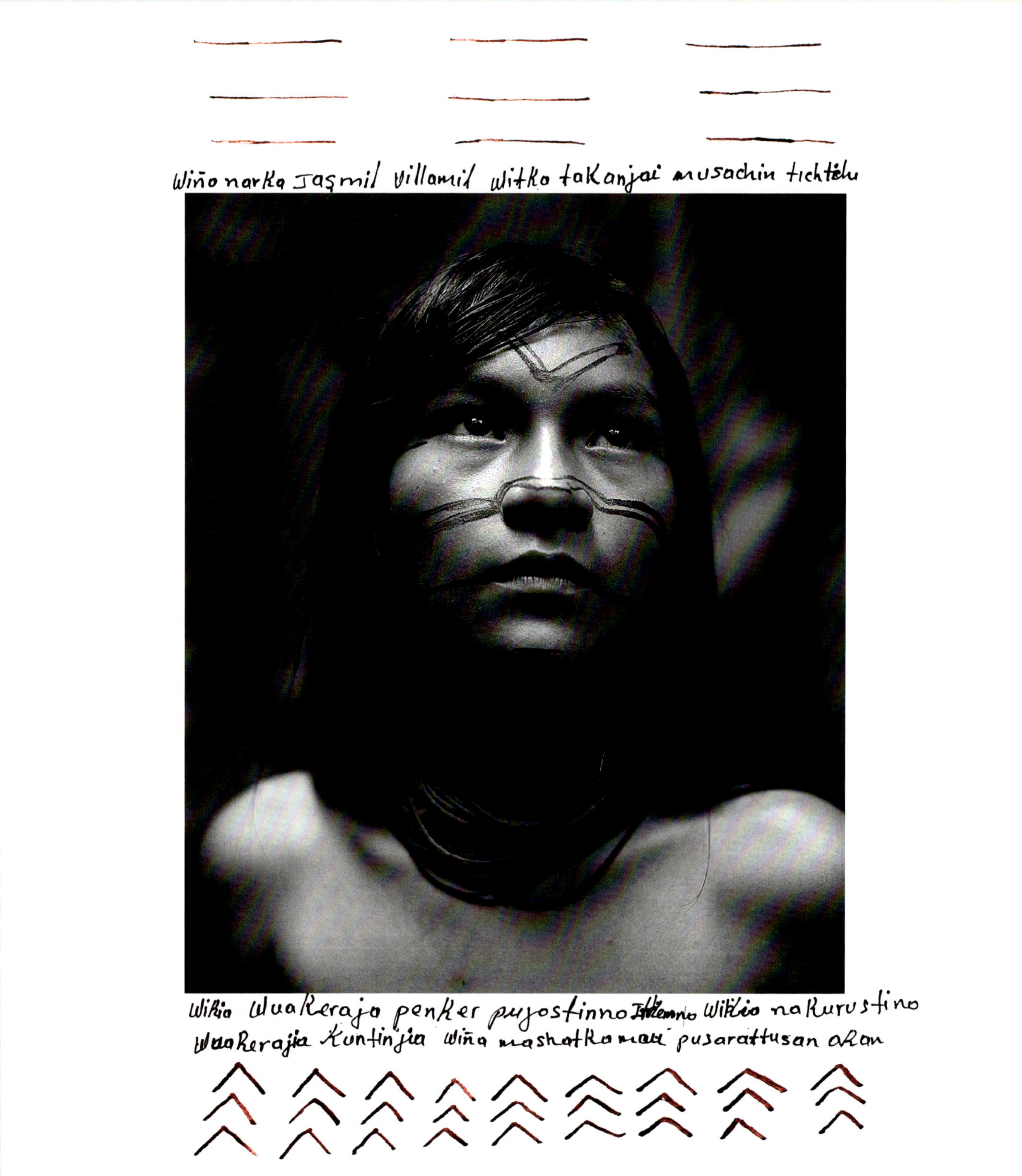

Felipe Jácome

Hasmil

UNCOMMONING NATURE

Marisol de la Cadena

On June 5, 2009, at dawn, a violent confrontation took place between police forces and a large group of Peruvian citizens declaring themselves as belonging to the Awajun-Wampis Indigenous groups. The police objective was to break up a blockade at a major highway near the town of Bagua in the Amazonian lowlands of northern Peru. The Awajun-Wampis had taken control of the highway at a place called La Curva del Diablo (Devil's Curve) as part of a general strike that started on April 9 of that same year, organized by several Amazonian Indigenous groups. They were protesting a series of legislative decrees conceding their territory to oil exploration without abiding by the Indigenous and Tribal Peoples (ILO) Convention No. 169, which requires that governments consult inhabitants of territories that corporations may approach for exploration and exploitation. Therefore, the protestors declared, the concession was illegal. The clash between police officers and the Awajun-Wampis yielded more than thirty deaths. On June 19 of that year, against the will of then president Alan García, the Peruvian Congress canceled the decrees. The state ordered the arrest of a number of Indigenous leaders, among them Santiago Manuin Valera, the prominent Awajun-Wampis leader. At the moment of the writing of this piece they face thirty-three murder-related charges. During his testimony on April 10, 2014, Manuin said:

> **The government is taking away our territory, the territory of the Awajun-Wampis people, so that we become dependent on its [form of] development. The government never asked: Do you want to develop? They did not consult us. We responded: "Cancel the legislative decrees that affect our existence as a people." Instead of listening to our complaint, the government wanted to punish us—other peoples surrendered, we did not. The government ordered our forced eviction.**

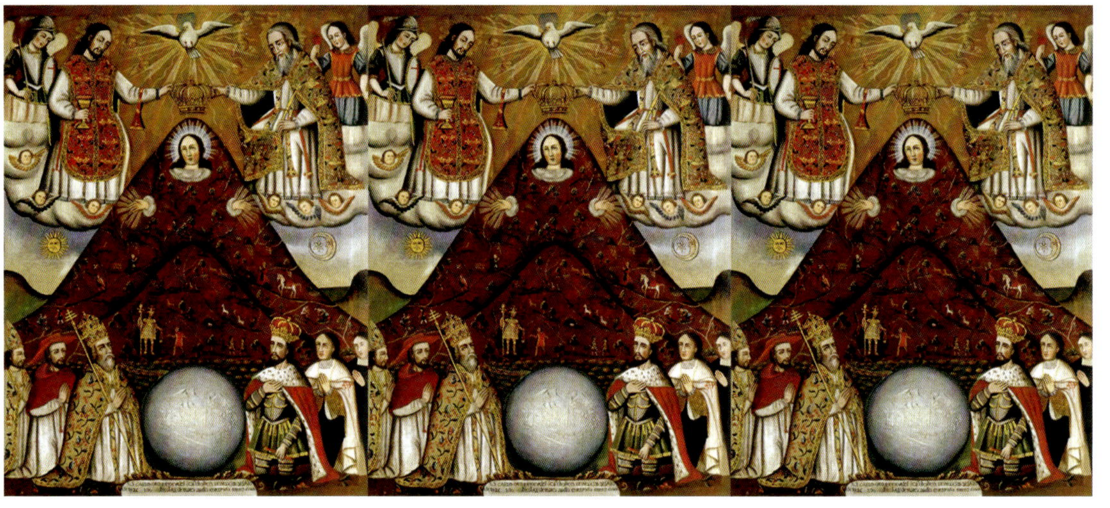

Anonymous, *Virgen-Cerro*, c. 1730. Museo de la Casa Nacional de Moneda, Potosí. The painting represents an Earth-being that is also a mountain, occupied by the Virgin and guarded by the Church, from where the Devil might have been expelled.

The event is part of what I am calling the "anthropo-not-seen": the world-making process through which heterogeneous worlds that do not make themselves through the division between humans and nonhumans—nor do they necessarily conceive the different entities in their assemblages through such a division—*both* obey that distinction (because they are obliged to do so) *and* exceed it (as they continue to practice the worlds without the division, thus also disobeying the obligation). Dating from the fifteenth century in what became the Americas, the anthropo-not-seen was, and continues to be, the process of destruction of these worlds *and* the impossibility of such destruction. It might very well represent the first historical apocalypse: the will to end many worlds that produced the *one-world* world and its excesses.

Scholars have discussed the Anthropocene as a transformation of humanity into a geological force capable of affecting, and possibly destroying, what we currently understand as the world. The anthropo-not-seen has been sustained since its early beginnings by a human moral force—and the unseen part of its destructive dynamic can be found in how this force has been considered constructive. Counterintuitively, the "not-seen" part of the world does not refer only to the anthropos—"the one who looks up from the Earth"—and is capable of destroying what refuses to be made in its image.

Exceeding this destruction, the anthropo-not-seen includes more-than-human assemblages, both in the usual sense (that is, they may include humans and nonhumans) and in the sense that these categories (human and nonhuman) are *also* inadequate to grasp such compositions, which, as said above, may not become through these categories. The assemblages of the anthropo-not-seen may be translated as "articulated collectives" of nature and humans, yet may also express conditions of "no nature, no culture."

The anthropo-not-seen was, and continues to be, a war waged against world-making practices that ignore the separation of entities into nature and culture—*and* the resistance to that war. The antagonism was clear in the seventeenth century: Christian clerics walked the Andes from Colombia to Argentina and Chile "extirpating idolatries" that the friars conceived as "devil-induced worship." Extirpation required dividing entities into God-created nature (mountains, rivers, forests) and humans, and saving the soul of the latter. The invention of modern politics secularized the antagonism: the war against the resistance to distinguishing nature from humanity silently continued in the name of progress and against backwardness, the evil that replaced the devil. Incipient humans became the object of benevolent and inevitable inclusion, enemies that did not even count as such. Until recently, that is.

The War Is Not Silent Anymore (But It Continues Undeclared)

The expansion of markets for minerals, oil, and energy, as well as for new technologies that allow for their quick and profitable extraction, stimulate what appears to be an unprecedentedly unstoppable—and massive—corporate removal of resources in places formerly marginal to capital investment. The construction of infrastructure (necessary to send the resources to market) sponsored by central financial institutions like the IMF and the World Bank, along with new regional financial entities like the Latin American Development Bank, has made even the most remote territories objects of financial investment. The reach of the current destruction of Indigenous worlds is historically unparalleled; the anthropo-not-seen (the destruction of worlds and resistance to it) has acquired a scope and speed that early extirpators of idolatries and nineteenth-century explorers (turned rubber- and sugar-plantation investors) would envy.

Overlapping with environmental devastation and converging with Anthropocenic forces at the planetary level, the transformation of territories into grounds for investment has met with strong local opposition and forceful disagreement—transforming the silent war into a relentless demand for politics that reveals, to paraphrase and tweak Jacques Rancière, the presence of many worlds being forced into one. Leveling a mountain to open a mine, drilling into the subsoil to find oil, damming all possible rivers, and razing trees to build roads and railroads that connect the Pacific and Atlantic Oceans translates, at the very least, into the destruction of networks of emplacement that make local life possible. Among other demands,

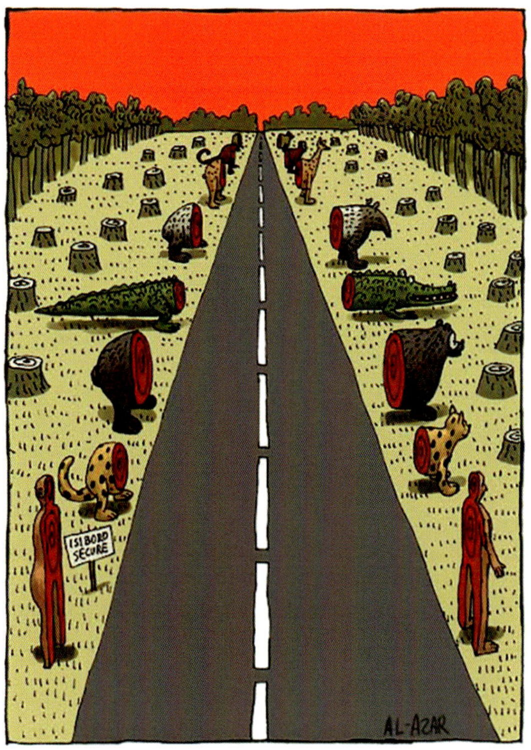

The cartoon *Paving Bolivia* shows the road across TIPNIS, which stands for "Territorio Indígena y Parque Nacional Isiboro Sécure."

local worlds—labeled indigenous or not—defy the monopoly of modern practices in making, inhabiting, and defining nature. With their hopes for economic growth at stake and the sovereignty over their territorial rule threatened, nations waver between rejecting the proposal for politics that local worlds extend and ending the silent war to wage it overtly—always in the name of progress. The 2009 confrontation in La Curva del Diablo is emblematic of the war becoming public: those who oppose the transformation of universal nature into resources and oppose the possibility of the common good as the mission of the nation-state are seen as the nation-state's enemies, who deserve prison at the very least.

Conceptualized through the anthropo-not-seen, the war is, however, peculiar. Defending themselves, worlds whose sacrifice progress demands have publicly revealed their practices through television stations and newspapers. Thus, the idea that nature—as the alleged grounds for the common good—is not only that, has come to the attention of the public (and faced majoritarian derision). For example, warning about the destruction of its world, the Awajun-Wampis leadership has described their relationship to the Amazon rain forest as one of siblings: "The river is our brother, we do not kill our brother by polluting and throwing waste on it." Kinship transforms rivers, plants, and animals into entities that financial capital, infrastructure, and contamination can kill rather than "merely" destroy or deplete. As ubiquitous as the war, these revelations slow down the translation of those entities into universal nature. The one-world world that Christianity and modernity collaboratively built and sustained is perhaps being challenged by an unprecedented degree of publicity for the first time since its inauguration five hundred years ago. This possibility needs to be cared for.

Uncommoning Nature: Or, a Commons through Divergence

Analogous to the Awajun-Wampis' claim of kinship with the forest, in a dispute about petroleum extraction in a site called Vaca Muerta (Argentina), a Mapuche group declared, "Our territories are not 'resources' but lives that make the Ixofijmogen of which we are part, not its owners."

In contrast, developers from Neuquén defined Vaca Muerta as one of the states included in the alleged hydrocarbons deposit: "Vaca Muerta is an immense *páramo* [a barren, cold plateau]. A desert that extends beyond what the eyes can see. . . . It is a hostile territory that shelters enough energy to make Argentinians self-sufficient and even export gas and oil to the world." The stark contrast suggests that the dispute over the extraction of petroleum is also a dispute over "the partition of the sensible" into universal nature and culturally diversified humanity, to paraphrase Rancière and Bruno Latour, respectively.

Emphasizing the inherent relationality between local entities (humans and other-than-human beings), the dispute questions the universality of the partition: what is enacted as humans and nature is *not only* enacted as such.

John Law calls this the capacity for *both/and* (rather than *either/or*). The interruption of the universal partition is a political and conceptual worlding event; what emerges through it is not a "mix" of nature and human. Being composed as humans *with* nature—if we maintain these categories of being—makes each more. Entities emerge as materially specific to (and with!) the relation that inherently connects them. An example located in the Andes of Cuzco: The materiality that relates modern humans *and* mountains is different from that which makes *runakuna* (the local Quechua word for people) *with* Earth-beings—entities that are also mountains.

The processes questioning the universality of partitioning the sensible into universal nature and humans, of course, do not require *runakuna* with Earth-beings. Here is another example: In the northern Andes of Peru, a mining corporation plans to dry out several lagoons to extract copper and gold from some and to throw mineral waste into others. In exchange, reservoirs with water capacity several times that of the lagoons would be built. Opposing the plan, environmentalists argue that the reservoirs will destroy the ecosystem of the lagoons, a landscape made of agricultural land, high-altitude wetlands, cattle, humans, trees, crops, creeks, and springs. The local population adds that the lagoons are *their* life: their plants, animals, soils, and trees. Families *are with* that specific water, which cannot be translated into water from reservoirs, not even if more water is provided, as the mining corporation promises to do. It would not be the *same* water, which they defend as "guardians of the lagoons." People have died in this making-public of another instance of the war against those who oppose the translation of nature into resources. Yet the guardians of the lagoons have never said that the water is a being. It is local water, and as such, nature, yet it is untranslatable to H_2O.

An iconic "guardian of the lagoons" is a peasant woman whose property the corporate mining project wants to buy to fully legalize its access to the territories it plans to excavate. The woman refuses to sell—even for what is most likely an amount of money she will not see in her lifetime. Countless times, the national police force has attacked her, her family, and even her animals; as I was writing this piece, the police destroyed the woman's crops. The property has been under siege for more than three years now. "I fight to protect the lagoon" has been one of her responses. And, asserting attachment to place, she adds: "I am not going to stop; they will disappear me. But I will die with the land." Like Bartleby, the legal copyist in Herman Melville's short story who refused to write copies, she "would prefer not to" sell; yet she is not politically a-grammatical (cf. Gilles Deleuze, *Essays Critical and Clinical,* 1998), at least not in the usual sense of politics.

Within the grammar that separates humans and universal nature, this woman can be interpreted as defending the ecosystem: an environmentalist, and thus an enemy (and a fool), or an ally (and a hero), depending on who speaks. In both cases, she is a subject in relation to an object. However, the "refusal to sell" may express a different relation: one from which woman-land-lagoon (or plants-rocks-soils-animals-lagoons-humans-creeks-canals!) emerge inherently together: an ecological *entanglement with* each other in such a way that pulling them apart would transform them into something else.

Refusing to sell may also forestall the transformation of the entities just mentioned into units of nature or the environment, for they are part of each other. The woman's refusal would thus enact locally an ecologized nature of interdependent entities that simultaneously coincides, differs, and even exceeds—also because it includes humans—the object that the state, the mining corporation, *and* environmentalists seek to translate into resources, whether for exploitation or to be defended. Thus seen, she is a-grammatical to the subject and object relation—or, she is *not only* an environmentalist.

Occupying the same space (that "cannot be mapped in terms of a single set of three-dimensional coordinates"),[1] this complex heterogeneous form (universal nature, the environment, and what I am calling ecologized nature—or nature recalcitrant to universality) allows for alliances and provokes antagonisms.

Confronted with the mining company's proposal to dry up the lagoons, the water's local guardians and environmentalists have joined forces against the mining corporation. Yet their shared interest—to defend nature or the environment—is not only the same interest: Ecologized nature and universal nature exceed each other; their agreement is also underpinned by *uncommonalities.* This condition shapes a possibility for an alternative alliance—one that, along with coincidences, may include the parties' constitutive divergence—even if this opens up discussion of the partition of the sensible and introduces the possibility of ontological disagreement into the alliance. An oxymoronic condition, this alliance would also house hope for a *commons* that does not require the division between universal nature and diversified humans: a commons constantly emerging from the uncommons as grounds for political negotiation of what the interest in common—and thus the commons—would be.

Instead of the expression of shared relations, and stewardship of nature, this commons would be the expression of a worlding of many worlds ecologically related across their constitutive divergence. As a practice of life that takes care of interests in common, yet not the same interest, the alliance between environmentalists and local guardians (of lagoons, rivers, forests) could impinge upon the required distribution of the sensible into universal nature and locally differentiated humans, thus disrupting the agreement that made the anthropo-not-seen and questioning the legitimacy of its war against those who question that distribution. The alliance would also queer the requirement of politics for sameness and provoke ontological disagreement *among those who share sameness*—inaugurating an altogether different practice of politics: one across divergence.

Marisol de la Cadena, "Uncommoning Nature," originally appeared in the "Apocalypsis" section of *e-flux journal* 65, "Supercommunity," on August 22, 2015. (This section of the issue was guest-edited by Pedro Neves Marques.)

NOTES

1 Annemarie Mol and John Law, "Complexities: An Introduction" in *Complexities,* ed. Law and Mol, 1–22 (Durham, NC: Duke University Press, 2001), 1.

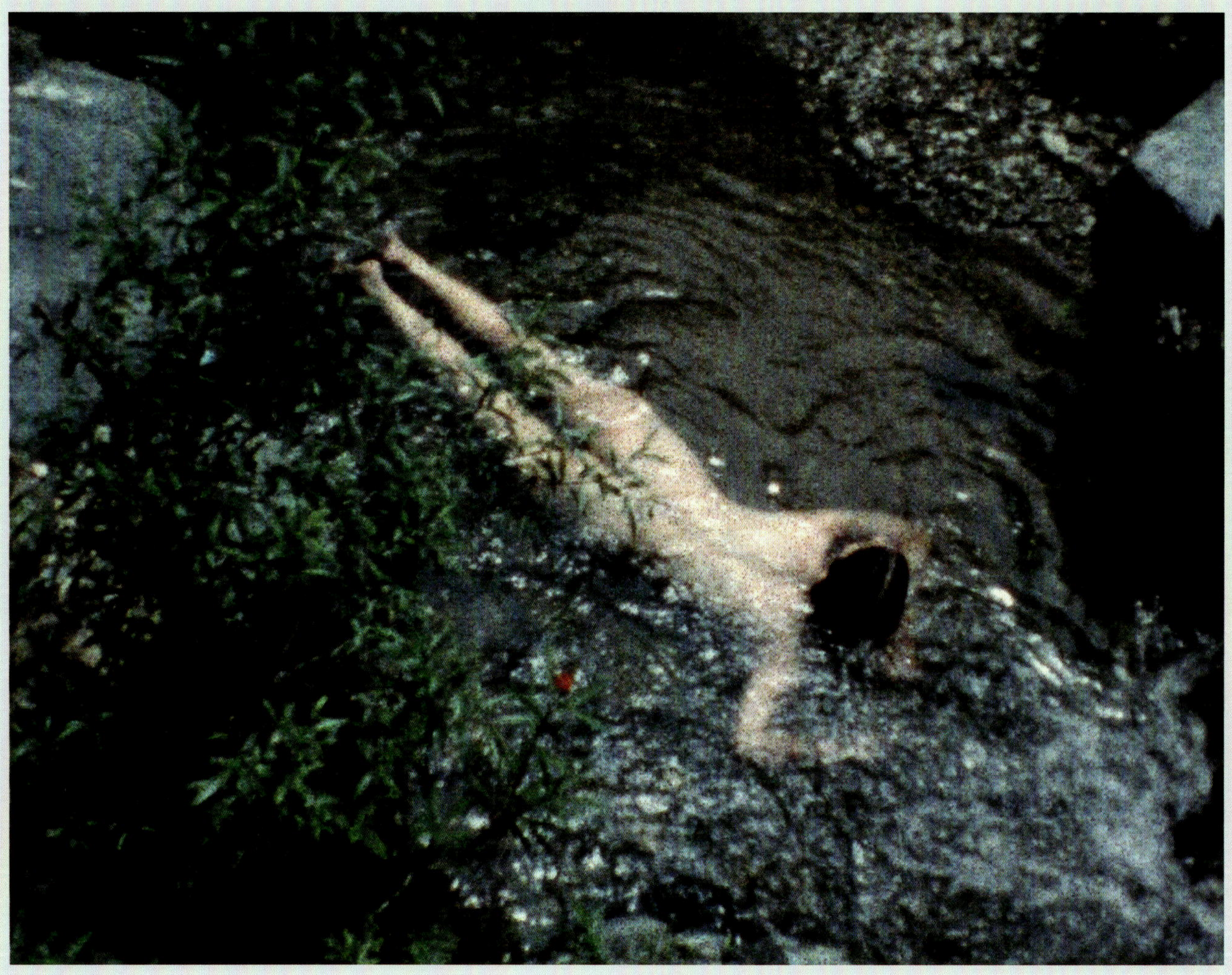

Ana Mendieta

Creek

FEMINIST COUNTER-APOCALYPSE

An Ethical Proposal for the Anthropocene

Joanna Zylinska

At a time when the dominant political and ecological discourses readily embrace the rhetoric of the crisis, is it possible to go beyond the "structures of mourning" when envisaging *the world to come?*[1] What conceptual and aesthetic tropes can we draw on to accomplish this? Can art and other forms of creative engagement be more than mere vessels for exploring the sorry state of the here and now? This essay has been conceived as a conceptual supplement to the exhibition *The World to Come: Art in the Age of the Anthropocene*, which engages with what has become a defining concept of our times: the Anthropocene. Against the background of the poetic figuration of a *feminist counter-apocalypse,* it outlines an affirmative ethical proposal in response to the various crises of our globalized postindustrial world.

The Anthropocene—posited as a new geological epoch in which human influence on the geosphere and the biosphere has been irreversible—has become a new epistemological filter through which we humans see ourselves. It has also triggered the production of multiple images and narratives about ourselves and the world around us. Apocalyptic imagery that seems to have been borrowed from the book of Revelation frames many of the current issues associated with the new epoch. We are thus confronted with images of "the blackening of the sun" as a result of fossil fuel use, of "heaven falling unto the earth" in the form of land erosion due to mining, and of lands such as the Solomon Islands and the Maldives being "moved out of their places" due to the rising ocean levels.[2] Yet the apocalyptic tropes that underpin the Anthropocene narrative are recurrent throughout Western and non-Western cultural history: from premodern religious texts that include the *Epic of Gilgamesh* and the book of Revelation (aka the Apocalypse of St. John), through to contemporary cultural productions such as Margaret Atwood's dystopian novels *The Handmaid's Tale* and *MaddAddam,* and TV series such as *Survivors* and *The Walking Dead.* Critic Frank Kermode has pointed out that "apocalypse and the related themes are strikingly long-lived," while theologian Catherine Keller has gone so far as to suggest that "we stand . . . in an unfinished history of apocalyptic finalities."[3]

At the same time, the apocalyptic narrative has acquired a new lease of life after becoming associated with the Anthropocene. The beginning of the Anthropocene epoch is variously dated to the early days of agriculture, the launch of the Industrial Revolution in the eighteenth century, and the Great Acceleration of population growth and energy use in the years after 1945. Human and nonhuman extinction, as well as the destruction of life as we know it on our planet, loom as the endpoint of this epoch. The Anthropocene conveys an ambivalent attitude toward its foundational concept, the *anthropos:* while predicting the demise of humans as a species, it simultaneously appoints the human as the key agent of "deep history," capable of wielding destructive power on a geological scale. The apocalyptic narrative of the Anthropocene thus has an ontological dimension: it brings forth a temporarily wounded yet ultimately redeemed human, who can conquer time and space by rising above the geological mess "he" has created. Indeed, this ostensibly individuated human is actually a masculinist subject, who achieves power and status by way of sacrificing sexual and biological difference. Disavowing his kinship with women and those of nonbinary gender—along with animals, microbes, and fungi—the masculinist *anthropos* separates from "nature" to emerge standing proud. This disavowal is a condition for the preservation of his self-belief and self-appointed authority, allowing him continued "dominion over the fish of the sea, and over the fowl of the air, and over the cattle, and over all the earth, and over every creeping thing that creepeth upon the earth."[4]

In response to the apocalyptic tenor of the dominant discourse of the Anthropocene, with its uniform structure of subjectivity, its power ambitions, and the gender assumptions behind it, I want to outline an alternative microvision: the prospect of a feminist counter-apocalypse. A feminist counter-apocalypse would take seriously the current geopolitical unfoldings while also rethinking our relations *to* and *with* our planet precisely *as relations.* Relationality, I suggest, offers a more compelling model of subjectivity. Instead of positing a human subject who is separate from the world he (*sic*) inhabits and in which he can make interventions, it acknowledges *the prior existence of relations* between clusters of matter and energy that temporarily stabilize for us humans into entities—on a molecular, cellular, and social level. The relational model of subjectivity, involving a critical transfer of scientific ideas into a cultural context by feminist scholars such as Donna Haraway and Karen Barad,[5] challenges the de facto masculinist subject who disinterestedly looks at the world as his possession and playground. Recognizing that we are *of* the world, relational subjectivity also presents instances of differentiation between subjects and objects as ethico-political tasks for the human. These tasks involve having to account for asymmetries of relations, making "agential cuts" to the arrangements of the world,[6] and trying to establish fairer and more just relations.

The concept of a feminist counter-apocalypse I am outlining here builds on the work of Catherine Keller, for whom "A 'counter-apocalypse' recognizes itself as a kind of apocalypticism; but then it will try to interrupt the habit. . . . If counter-apocalypse reveals anything, it does so in ironic mimesis of the portentous tones of the original—with which it dances as it wrestles."[7] One author who has attempted to cut the *anthropos* of the Anthropocene down to size while also imagining new ways of living in the Anthropocene's shadow is Anna Lowenhaupt Tsing, author of *The Mushroom at the End of the World*. "Following a mushroom,"[8] Tsing retraces the material and economic organization of life on our planet by highlighting the relational ecologies developed from and around the fungi species called matsutake, both in the forest and on the market. A delicacy in Japan, matsutake is relatively rare, which is why it needs to be sourced from places as remote as Oregon and Yunnan, China, thus establishing a global network of growth, labor, and exchange. This socioeconomic network is woven into the already existent micro-network of fungi ecologies that traverse our soil and air.

Tsing's book is set against the horizon of what she terms "capitalist ruin": the aftermath of anthropogenic climate change coupled with the collapse of the dream of industrial progress. Yet, rather than just lament the passing of the world as we (or at least some of us) know it, she sets off in search of life among the debris. The socioeconomic context of her exploratory pursuit is provided by the situation of matsutake pickers in the forests of Oregon: a mixture of Southeast Asian immigrants from Cambodia, Laos, and China, as well as white Americans who have opted out, willingly or by turn of fate, of "what liberals think of as 'standard employment.'"[9] Reflecting on the precarious lives of the pickers, Tsing also lends an ear to the precarity of ecologies, of various scales, in which they operate. She then extends this idea of precarity, understood as "life without the promise of stability,"[10] from the situation affecting those placed outside privileged—or at least stable—socioeconomic circumstances to the structuring condition of life in postindustrial capitalist economies. In a tone similar to that of Italian philosopher Franco "Bifo" Berardi in his analysis of the radically destabilized nature of employment in the era of semiocapitalism ("the contemporary regime of production in which capital valorization is based on the constant emanation of information flows"),[11] Tsing recognizes that increasing numbers of people, in both the Global North and the Global South, are exposed to precarious existence.

Precarity encompasses not only phenomena such as the increasing insecurity of the labor market but also environmental threats on the level of individual species threatened with extinction, as well as on the level of whole regions or even ecosystems. Yet Tsing challenges the traditional view of precarity as "an exception to how the world works" and proposes that we instead accept precarity as "the condition of our time."[12] This suggestion must not be mistaken for a sign of political resignation or withdrawal —a peaceful embracing of life among the postindustrial ruins, driven by a naïve desire to reconnect with nonhuman others such as forests, fungi, and microbes. Instead, it is a deeply ethical proposal that redrafts the stand-alone (and traditionally male) subject of ethics as always already relational, multiple, and strange to itself. Such a subject does not have to open itself to others because it is already invaded, or contaminated, by them. However, it does have to undertake the effort of grasping this relationship as potentially mutually constitutive and hence entailing a call to responsibility for others. This responsibility for others and the willingness to be vulnerable to them should not, of course, be reduced to just being "nice" to other people or pets, or accepting any encounter or intrusion passively—be it with fungi or cancer cells. Rather, it entails the task of recognizing that entanglement with others is not just a matter of our acceptance or goodwill because it precedes the emergence of the human sense of self.

Such a non-normative ethics in which we are not told what to do but rather faced with a call to responsibility nevertheless entails a minimal injunction to embrace cross-species coexistence and collaborative survival. What is at stake in this call for embracing human-nonhuman relations is by no means a development of a flat and banal world model in which everything is connected with everything else—or deciding, as some may derisively claim, whether "I" am more (or less) important than a mushroom. Instead, what is really at stake here is the possibility of cutting down to size the supposedly unique human "I" by showing that this "I" is already, literally, made up of others.[13] But this possibility also needs to involve recognizing the ability on the part of those capable of adopting the human "I" pronoun as theirs to develop conscious ethical responses to this situation of ongoing material and ethical entanglement, beyond mere instinctive reactions to stimuli, and then being able to consolidate those responses into an ethical framework. Indeed, there is no way of unthinking ourselves out of our human standpoint, no matter how much kinship or entanglement with "others" we identify. It is also next to impossible to abandon our human mode of perception and suspend the material and epistemological subject-object divisions we humans introduce into the flow of matter (including our primary positing of what surrounds us and constitutes us as "matter")—notwithstanding the misguided (even if well-intentioned) attempts to think like a bat, walk like a sheep, or float like a jellyfish. Rather than fantasize about some kind of ontological "species switch," the ethical task for us humans is not only to see ourselves as contaminated but also to account for the incisions in the ecologies of life we make, for the differentiations and cuts we introduce and sustain, and for the values we give to the entities we have carved out of these ecologies with our perceptual and cognitive apparatus.

A feminist counter-apocalypse therefore unfolds from accepting the material condition of precarity, without submitting to the "portentous tones" of the precarity discourse. In parodying the Anthropocene as the Armageddon for the White Man, it also embraces the intensity and the drive for justice entailed by its affective setup. The feminist counter-apocalyptic framework creates a space for an ethical opening to the precarious lives and bodies of human and nonhuman others—including the male bodies and minds that have been discarded in the downsizing process of disruptive semiocapitalism. In doing so, it promises liberation from the form of subjectivity that is pinned to a competitive, overachieving, and overreaching masculinity. Through this, it prompts us to ask: If unbridled progress is no longer an option, what kinds of coexistences and collaborations do we want to create in its aftermath?

Isabelle Stengers's concept of Gaia could perhaps serve as another figuration for this mode of being in the world. Gaia is derived from interdisciplinary Earth systems thinking that adopts the dynamic interaction between the Earth's spheres—atmosphere, hydrosphere, geosphere, and biosphere—as its unit of analysis. Not to be mistaken for a peaceful coexistence of entities under the banner of an unreconstructed and benign "Nature," Gaia, at least in Stengers's use of this term, merely entails an attempt to shift the human observation point from the center of the action to its margins, while simultaneously reducing in scale, scope, and significance the outcomes of human activity—without relieving humans of the responsibility for the activities they do enact or participate in. Indeed, there is something rather demanding or even violent about Gaia, whose mode of appearance is that of an "intrusion,"[14] because it reminds us that the Earth, in all its "systems," is not arranged for our pleasure or benefit. In this sense, the notion of Gaia could be seen an alternative to the masculinist Anthropocene fantasy that ends up aggrandizing "Man" in the process. For Stengers, Gaia "makes the epic versions of human history, in which Man, standing up on his hind legs and learning to decipher the laws of nature, understands that he is the master of his own fate, free from any transcendence, look rather old. Gaia is . . . a ticklish assemblage of forces that are indifferent to our reasons and our projects."[15]

The adoption of this form of philosophical humility is only the first step, though. It needs to be followed up—according to Stengers, Tsing, and other counter-apocalyptic thinkers

—by embracing precarity as a political horizon against which the dream of infinite linear progress is presented as expired. For this horizon to be political rather than just aesthetically mournful, it needs to be inscribed with the aforementioned drive for justice. A political response arising out of this horizon may entail, after Stengers, working toward "the possibility of a future that is not barbaric,"[16] while also giving up on a fantasy of peaceful coexistence between individuals, species, or systems. Indeed, Tsing reminds us that opening the political horizon "to other beings shifts everything. Once we include pests and diseases, we can't hope for harmony; the lion will not lie down with the lamb. . . . The best we can do is to aim for 'good-enough' worlds, where 'good-enough' is always imperfect and under revision."[17] A feminist counter-apocalypse that reworks finalism as a structuring condition of being in the world, while also issuing a responsibility for our entanglements with and in it, presents itself as both a less tragic and less naïve response to the Anthropocene narrative.

I want to close by recognizing that, in modern times, art institutions are increasingly being challenged to offer their publics more than just self-contained aesthetic experiences. Curators as well as artists have taken on the task of repositioning such institutions as spaces for showcasing complex ethico-political issues in creative ways. Seen as part of a wider transformative—albeit nondidactic—project, art can help us, as suggested by philosopher Jacques Rancière, to reconfigure and redistribute the human sensible,[18] enabling us to perceive, experience, and engage with the world otherwise, especially in times of precarity. Yet it is important to recognize that these kinds of "sensory interventions" must not be confined to the walls of institutions that put crises on display: galleries, exhibition halls, museums, conference centers. To avoid anesthetizing ourselves to the threat by turning it into an artistic commodity, any creative figuration that is to work must be able to *seep through* institutional walls. This is why the feminist counter-apocalypse proposed here, born as it is *of* artistic sensibility, is intended as more than just a creative figuration: it is also a call to ethical responsibility for the world in the Anthropocene, and for the images and concepts we make of it. Unless we are prepared to take up this ethical call, the aesthetic of the Anthropocene, built of the familiar apocalyptic images and tropes, risks turning into an "anaesthetic,"[19] a dulling of the senses whereby we are unable to care any more because we have already seen it all.

NOTES

1 The phrase "structures of mourning" has been used by Tom Cohen and Claire Colebrook in their preface to *Twilight of the Anthropocene Idols,* by Cohen, Colebrook, and J. Hillis Miller (London: Open Humanities Press, 2016), 11.

2 Rev. 6:12–15. All citations are from the King James Version of the Bible, available at the University of Michigan Library Digital Collections, http://quod.lib.umich.edu/cgi/k/kjv/kjv-idx?type=DIV1&byte=5379618.

3 Frank Kermode, *The Sense of an Ending: Studies in the Theory of Fiction* (Oxford: Oxford University Press, 2000), 29; Catherine Keller, *Apocalypse Now and Then: A Feminist Guide to the End of the World* (1996; Minneapolis: Fortress, 2005), 2.

4 King James version of the Bible, Gen. 1:26.

5 See Donna Haraway, *The Companion Species Manifesto: Dogs, People, and Significant Otherness* (Chicago: Prickly Paradigm, 2003); and Karen Barad, *Meeting the Universe Halfway: Quantum Physics and the Entanglement of Matter and Meaning* (Durham, NC: Duke University Press, 2007).

6 Barad, *Meeting the Universe Halfway*, 140.

7 Keller, *Apocalypse Now and Then,* 19.

8 Anna Lowenhaupt Tsing, *The Mushroom at the End of the World* (Princeton, NJ: Princeton University Press, 2015), viii.

9 Ibid., 77.

10 Ibid., 2.

11 Franco "Bifo" Berardi, *Heroes: Mass Murder and Suicide* (London: Verso, 2015), 24.

12 Tsing, *The Mushroom at the End of the World*, 20.

13 I am grateful to Piotr Boćkowski for infecting me with fungal thinking.

14 Isabelle Stengers, *In Catastrophic Times: Resisting the Coming Barbarism,* trans. Andrew Goffey (London: Open Humanities Press, 2015), 58.

15 Ibid., 47.

16 Ibid., 25.

17 Tsing, *The Mushroom at the End of the World,* 255.

18 See Jacques Rancière, *The Politics of Aesthetics: The Distribution of the Sensible* (London: Continuum, 2014).

19 This idea comes from Nicholas Mirzoeff, "Visualizing the Anthropocene," *Public Culture* 26, no. 2 (2014): 223–24.

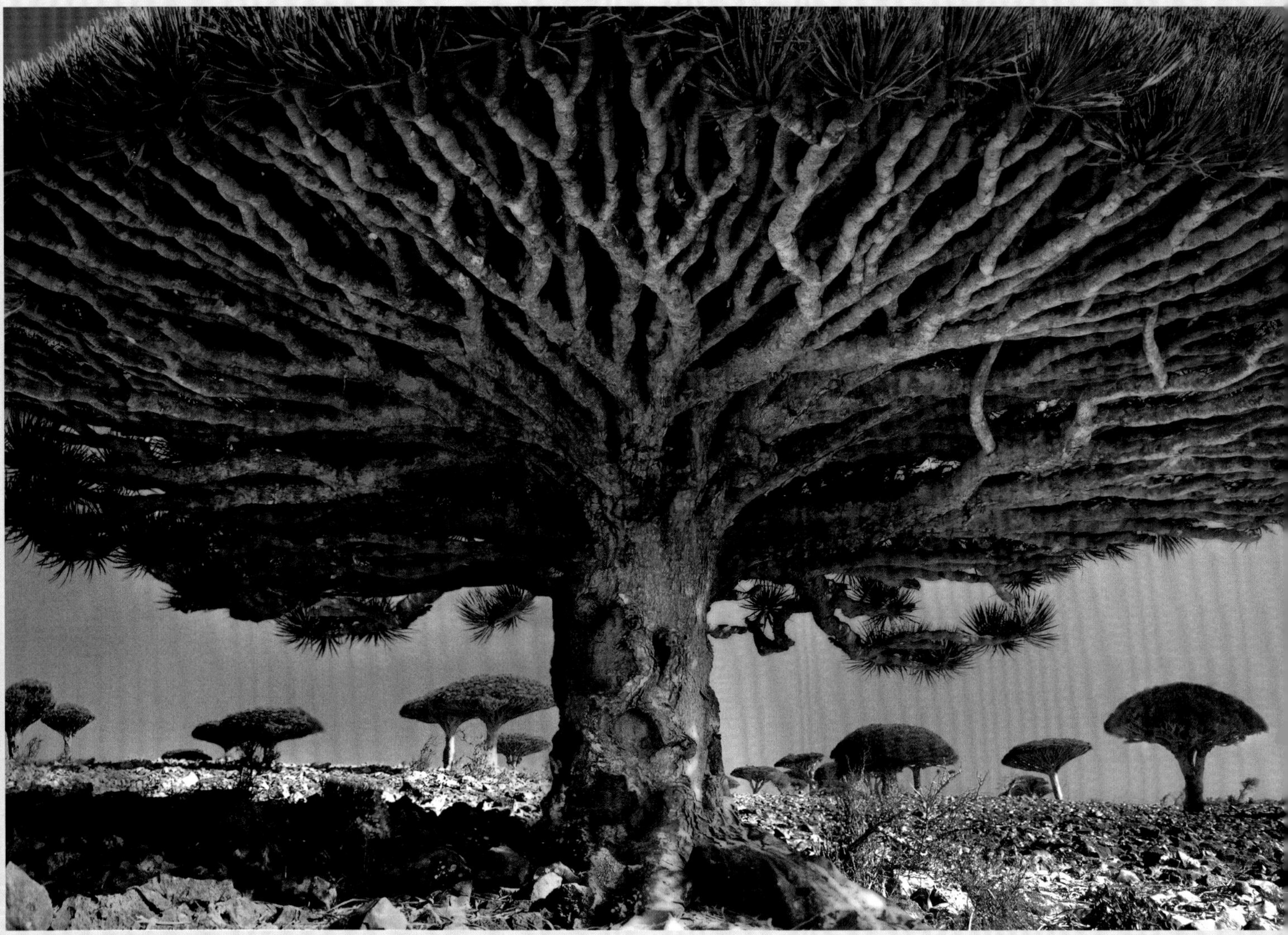

Beth Moon

Heart of the Dragon

HOW TO GROW LIVABLE WORLDS

Ten Not-So-Easy Steps

Natasha Myers

Step 1: Never Forget This: "We" Are Not "One"

Say it again. And again. We cannot forget to keep asking: precisely who is hailed by this *Anthropos,* that figure positioned at the helm of the Anthropocene? Anthropocenic rhetoric calls out "Man" as the agent of his own demise and simultaneously vaults him into position as the only viable savior of the planet: "We got ourselves into this mess. We alone can get us out." Even as Anthropocenic thinking attempts to call our attention to—and finally hold us responsible for—the egregious effects of our actions, it still figures humans as a singular figure, transcendent over and separate from some Edenic nature in peril. These narratives re-center rather than decenter Man as the agent with natural dominion over this planet's future.

Do not get distracted by the misplaced concreteness of scientific efforts to articulate the physical markers and temporal boundaries of a geological era made by humans. What we are witnessing is the apotheosis of five hundred years of colonial violence, extractive capitalism, white supremacy, and the hubris of human exceptionalism.[1] The Capitalocene and the Plantationocene are apt monikers to identify the forces that have long been at work terraforming the planet.[2] These destructive forces are propelled, not by all people, but by those particularly egregious ways of doing life modeled on self-aggrandizing Man.

Remember this: not all are hailed by this figure or form of life. Anthropocene worlds are built on slavery and dispossession, those Anthropo-not-seen[3] whose lives and lands continue to be spent in the accumulation of wealth by colonial and neocolonial powers. These are the people who remain targets of dispossession and attempted annihilation even (perhaps especially) today as capitalism gets into high gear in its efforts to "go green" and "save the world." Don't believe the hype of sustainability rhetoric.[4] The worlds built by colonialism and capitalism are unlivable for us all.

Step 2: Break This World to Make Other Worlds Possible

There is no way to "mitigate" Anthropocenic violence using Anthropocene logics. Refuse calls to *design for the Anthropocene.*[5] Such designs are precisely the "technological fixes" that will keep us locked into the same rhythms of extraction and dispossession.[6] Refuse to be lured into those climate change edutainment complexes, those gleaming glass, metal, and concrete infrastructures whose capital- and labor-intensive designs exquisitely expose the ruse of sustainability as an aesthetic maneuver grounded in Edenic visions of nature.[7] That is not the kind of green that will save us.

Yes, there are apocalypses already ongoing all around us. The decimation of the Boreal forest to extract bitumen on stolen indigenous land in Canada is one such apocalypse. But giving in to apocalyptic thinking is itself a kind of exit strategy, an easy out. Ruin porn thrives on this narrative of "a world without us."[8] The world will be better without people, right? Look around you to see how Anthropocenic thought catches you up in thrall of apocalypse and sets us all to work, furtively dreaming the end of times.[9] We must refuse the "tragic detumescence" of a narrative arc that is bent on pulling the entire planet toward unstoppable catastrophe.[10] Do not be swayed into thinking that this is how it has to go down, as if apocalypse is precisely what *will have been*.[11]

Resist this pull like your life depends on it. Yes, it's easier to dream the end of the world than the end of capitalism,[12] but the only way to thwart the momentum of the Anthropocene is to break capitalism and activate processes of decolonization.[13] And while it is clearly time to dismantle Anthropocene logic, there is no need to wait until the end of this world to begin to conjure livable ones. There are as yet other worlds in this world.[14] And there are, as yet, worlds to come. But which worlds will be livable? And what makes a livable world?

Step 3: Repeat This Mantra: We Are Not Alone. We Are Not Alone. We Are Not Alone.

Looking back at the past five hundred years of efforts to assert Man's independence from—and power over—nature, it is clear that we should never be trusted to act alone. Anthropocene thinking is so obsessed with Man's independence, with unilateral action and autonomy, that it forgets that there are other forces and powers among us, including those with significantly better skills in the realm of world-making and planetary-scale change. In some cases, these beings have billions of years more experience than us in terraforming livable worlds.

Step 4: Name Our Most Powerful Ally

Who made this planet livable and breathable for animals like us? Say it out loud: The photosynthetic ones. Photosynthetic organisms form a biogeochemical force of a magnitude we have not yet properly grasped.[15] More than 2 billion years ago, photosynthetic microbes spurred the event known today as the oxygen catastrophe, or the great oxidation. These creatures dramatically altered the composition of the atmosphere, choking out the ancient anaerobic ones with poisonous oxygen vapors. If we were to continue to fall into the trap of naming linear, time-bound eras after singular agents, we might be rattled to think that we are living in the wake of what should have been called the "Phytocene."[16]

Photosynthesizers like cyanobacteria, algae, terrestrial plants, and trees are utterly cosmic beings.[17] We think they can't move, but plants reach out across the cosmos, drawing the energy of the sun into their tissues so that they can work their terrestrial magic. Pulling matter out of thin air, plants are conjurers, and they teach us the most nuanced lessons about *mattering*. More powerful than any industrial plant, communities of photosynthetic creatures rearrange the elements on a planetary scale.[18] They know how to compose livable, breathable, and nourishing worlds. As they exhale, they compose the atmosphere; as they decompose, they matter the compost and feed the soil. Holding the earth down and the sky up, they sing in nearly audible ultrasonic frequencies as they transpire, moving massive volumes of water from the depths of the earth up to the highest clouds. They cleanse the waters. And for those caught up in the thrall of an economy that fetishizes carbon, perhaps the most important art these creatures practice is sucking up, with gusto, the gaseous carbon emissions we humans generate so abundantly.

To say that forests and marine microbes form the "lungs of the earth" is an understatement. They literally breathe us into being. All cultures turn around plants' metabolic rhythms. Plants are the substance, substrate, scaffolding, symbol, sign, and sustenance of political economies the world over. We must learn how to work with and for the plants so that we can be nourished and clothed and sheltered and pleasured and healed—without destroying the earth. These are the world-makers we need to heed if we hope to grow livable worlds. And our worlds will only be livable worlds when people learn how to *conspire with the plants*.

Step 5: Foment Plant/People Conspiracies to Root into the Planthroposcene

Repeat this again and again: *We are of the plants*. Now, if this is true, then the figure that should ground our actions is not the self-aggrandizing *Anthropos* so much as a strangely hybrid figure we could call *Planthropos*. And now try wrapping your mouth around this word until it rolls off your tongue with ease: *Planthroposcene*. (Yes, it's awkward and you will sound silly. But just give it a try.) The Planthroposcene names an aspirational episteme, not a time-bound era, one that invites us to stage new *scenes*[19] and new ways to see and seed plant/people relations in the here and now, not some distant future. And it is grounded in the wisdom of the ancient and ongoing radical solidarity projects that plants have already cultivated with their many people.

Rather than circumscribing the terrors we face now, the Planthroposcene is an invitation to root ourselves into a way of doing life that would break the frame of Anthropocene logic. The Planthroposcene acknowledges the joint and uncertain futures of plants and peoples and demands we change the terms of encounter so that we can become allies to these green beings. Thinking with Tim Choy and his powerful call to unite people in a *conspiracy of breathers,*[20] it is clear to me that we must learn not just how to collaborate, but how to *conspire* with the plants, to learn how to breathe with them.

Remember this: what is good for plants is good for everyone else. Get on their side. Consider yourself at their service. Get to know plants intimately and on their terms. And be sure to tap into their desires for forms of life that are not *for* us. Support their efforts to keep the earth cool and the waters cleansed. Give them space and time to flourish outside of capitalist extraction and the chemical violence of industrial agriculture. Remember: They need their pollinators. They need their fungal relations. They need their animal allies.

Above all, they need us to radically reconfigure how we stage our relations with them. Indeed, if plants are sun worshipers, perhaps we ought to be plant worshipers. A little reverence for the plants could go a long way. Invent rituals. Practice permaculture with the witches.[21] Start a local church for plant worship. Don't worry: reverence for plants doesn't mean you can't eat them. But it does mean it would be polite to thank them for their generosity. Just think: If you had to consult the plants to ask permission to use them, industrial agriculture, strip mining, clear-cutting, and the expanding concrete of urban sprawl would be inconceivable. Just ask, they will tell you.

Step 6: Decolonize Your Imagination

Does talking to plants sound crazy to you? Consider this: for millennia, and still to this day, people all over the world cultivate intimate relationships with plants. Many have come to know plants' powers and predilections, especially those whose lives and livelihoods get them tangled up with the plants and caught in their spiraling whorl. There are gardeners, farmers, hunters, healers, herbalists, cooks, artists, naturalists, foresters, scientists, and shamans all over the world who consider plants as sentient beings worthy of address. Lots of people hear plants sing.[22]

And at the same time, many people, perhaps even you, would think this is absurd. Sure, you read that story about plants in your Facebook feed: "Science has confirmed that plant roots have a kind of swarm intelligence . . ." But we don't need the disenchanting sciences of plant sensing to tell us what plant people have long known.[23] What we do need to do is make strange the disenchantment and skepticism we have inherited from those whose power was secured in part through sciences designed to invalidate all other ways of knowing the world. It was the colonizers, of course, who refused to believe local and Indigenous people's claims that the plants can sing.

Decolonization means giving stolen lands back to Indigenous peoples.[24] Decolonization demands that we all reckon with and dismantle the overt and covert ways in which settler states are structured on white supremacy and the erasure of existing land/body relations through fantasies of Terra Nullius. While you are doing that important work, don't forget that human exceptionalism is another colonial formation, one that violently evacuates the liveliness and sentience of the more-than-human world around us.

Perhaps a first step toward decolonization would require that we *detune* our colonial sensorium. To do this, we would need to upend everything we believed was common sense. Forget everything you thought you knew about the living world, especially what you believe is perceptible, imaginable, reasonable, legible, and meaningful. Refuse the disenchantments of a mechanistic science that renders more-than-human worlds in the form of alienable bits of life and death ready to be portioned off as property, resource, or commodity. Sideline colonial and capitalist moral economies that dictate what is good, valuable, and true—especially those that naturalize economic growth and extraction as the work that is proper to Man.

Refuse to discipline or deride the animisms of local and Indigenous cosmologies. Push back on every contortion or erasure or reduction of their knowledge that seeks to make their practices legible or commensurable or rational to science. Do not appropriate Indigenous knowledges, but do the work to make yourself receptive and responsive so that you can take these knowledges seriously. Make room. Make space. Remember: Indigenous knowledge keepers have the protocols, the know-how, and the responsibility to consult the plants.[25] Livable worlds need people who know how to talk to the plants.

Step 7: Vegetalize Your Sensorium

Once you have set in motion efforts to decolonize your common sense, it is time to *vegetalize your sensorium* so that you, too, can learn with and alongside the plants. As a coconspirator supporting their world-making projects, you will need to apprentice with them. What do plants want? What do plants know? What can a plant do? We do not yet know. But you could reach toward them with the openness of not knowing, and forget what you thought counts as knowledge.

Consider this: your sensorium, especially your senses of color, texture, taste, touch, and smell, is already articulated by plant life. Their forms inspire your aesthetics, entrain your habitus, and excite your imagination. From this perspective, it is clear that your senses are already *vegetalized.* And yet there is still much work do to learn how to extend your synesthetic sensorium to meet their lively worlds.

In order to awaken the latent plant in you, you will need to get interested in the things that plants care about. Though plants don't have eyes, ears, noses, or mouths, don't be fooled: they can see, hear, smell, taste, and feel.[26] Let their planty sensitivities inflect your own. Tune into the different ways they do time, learn to follow their tempos and rhythms. Pay attention to the ways they defy all-too-human notions of individuality, bodily integrity, subjectivity, and agency. Let the plants redefine what you mean by the terms "sensing," "sensitivity," and "sentience." Let yourself be lured by their tropic turns, and you will soon acquire freshly vegetalized sensory dexterities.

You can also activate the latent plant in you through incantations, hypnosis, meditation, or yoga. Try cultivating your inner plant through meditation.[27] If that doesn't work, let the plants work directly on you. Cannabis and Ayahuasca have been great allies for those seeking to palpate the sentience of the more-than-human world.[28] But above all, *involve* yourself with plant life.[29] Make space for plants to take root, and take the time to watch them grow. Linger among them and let their sentiences and sensibilities alter your perception, how you think, and how and what you know.

Step 8: Take Ecology off the Grid

Once you have decolonized your imagination and vegetalized your sensorium, the world will look and feel a lot different. You may begin to sense things you have never perceived before. You may get the feeling that you are being watched everywhere you go. Indeed, the plants and trees are not indifferent to you: they are paying very close attention to all the beings that ingather around them. They know how to lure you and their other coconspirators with force. Start with the plants, follow their inquisitive growth, their running roots and rhizomes, the widespread movements of their pollen and seeds, and an entire ecology of beings and becomings and comings undone will soon become perceptible. Get caught up in the *involutionary* momentum that propels these beings into one another's lives and you will soon start to perceive affective ecologies taking shape among the thicket of relations all around you.[30] Cultivate modes of attention that allow you to perceive what matters to the plants and their coconspirators. *Becoming* sensor, tune into this ecology of practices and practitioners.[31] Follow the push and pull, the attractions and repulsions, the happenings taking shape in and around the plants. Get a feel for the ways that plants practice their arts at the cusp of life and death.[32] With time you will begin to detune your colonial ecological sensorium, and new worlds will open up into view.

Develop protocols for an *ungrid-able ecology*—a mode of inquiry that refuses the colonialism, militarism, heteronormativity, and economization of life that grounds conventional ecology.[33] Resist desires for legibility and statistical generalizability. Refuse attempts to calculate an ecology's energetic efficiencies or apply cost-benefit analyses. Invalidate metrics that would parse ecological relations into mechanical parts. Break all automatic, prefabricated sensors.

Over time you will begin to forget what you used to think "nature" was; you will forget how you used to think life "worked"; and eventually you will forget, too, the naturalizing tropes that made you believe that living beings "work" like machines, or that forests perform "ecosystems services," or that "reproduction" and "fitness" were the only valuable and recordable measures of a life. Confront the colonial and capitalist desires of the ecological sciences. Say no to conventional ecology's exacting metrics that justify an extractive ecology indebted to expansion and dispossession. Beware of Anthropocene ecologies that reduce land-care practices to resource management. *Do ecology otherwise.*

Step 9: Garden against Eden

Forget everything you thought a garden was. And everything you thought a gardener was supposed to do.[34] Your job in the Planthroposcene is to stage plant/people conspiracies to keep this planet livable and breathable. Your primary commitment will be to support plant growth. Everywhere. Start by letting the plants grow where they want to: let them break through the concrete; root into every fissure and surface; grow through the holes in every fence. The Planthroposcene uproots the infrastructures of our Anthropocenic cities founded on Edenic desires of a nature tamed and contained by Man.[35] Give those old-order infrastructures back to the plants and the fungi; let them decompose. Wild urban plant growth certainly does portend the decline of Empire, but in the Planthroposcene, wild growth will not be read as a sign of ruin. Planthroposcenic cities will be designed to support plant life everywhere. Each surface will offer an affordance, a place for plants to root and grow and decompose. Perhaps one day you will conspire with the plants to grow your own home. Perhaps cities will grow themselves into cooling forests, brimming with nourishment. In the Planthroposcene, radical farmers like those at the Land Institute in Kansas will have succeeded in dismantling industrial agriculture by conspiring with the plants to bring back the plains, growing perennial grains in the form of regenerating grasslands. These lands will demand the return of the buffalo; they will resist erosion, retain water, activate soil microbes, and reject heavy machinery and chemical fertilizers.[36] In the Planthroposcene, the capitalist imperative to grow economies will be subverted and supplanted by the imperative to give plants the time and space they need to grow, to freely articulate relations with their allies, and express their fullest desires. Humans will have to cede their biopolitical powers over lands and bodies. We will no longer be in control.

Step 10: Make Art for the Planthroposcene

Refuse the aesthetics of ruin porn, which constrains our imaginations about wild growth to sites of cultural ruin, as if it is only in the wake of human extinction that plants can express their full, unfettered (read: monstrous) powers.[37] Cultivate, instead, a taste for Planthroposcene porn: art that keeps people in the game by staging intimate relations between plants and people; art that figures "nature as lover, not mother"; art that lures us into the realm of more-than-human pleasures.[38] Curate your own EcoSexual Bathhouse and make love with the plants.[39] Join Slovenian artist Špela Petrič and the *Plant Sex Consultancy* to design vibrators for lonely potted plants and flowers that have lost their pollinators.[40] Apprentice with Mexican artist Gilberto Esparza to design lively nomadic plant companions. Build the bodies of your planimal-machines from electronic waste harvested from the ruins of capitalism, and engineer them to draw their energy from bacterial life, so that when they suck up raw sewage downstream from toxic industrial flows, they can transform it into water that supports plants and their allies.[41] Whatever you do, conspire with the plants to make art like your life depends on disrupting the colonial common sense that would leave us all to die in the Anthropocene.

NOTES

1 See, for example, Zoe Todd, "Indigenizing the Anthropocene," in *Art in the Anthropocene: Encounters among Aesthetics, Politics, Environments and Epistemologies*, ed. Heather Davis and Etienne Turpin, 241–54 (London: Open Humanities Press, 2015); and Marisol de la Cadena, "Uncommoning Nature," in this volume.

2 See Donna Haraway, "Anthropocene, Capitalocene, Plantationocene, Chthulucene: Making Kin," *Environmental Humanities* 6 (2015): 159–65; and J. W. Moore, "The Capitalocene, Part I: On the Nature and Origins of Our Ecological Crisis," *Journal of Peasant Studies* 44, no. 3 (2017): 594–630.

3 De la Cadena, "Uncommoning Nature."

4 Duygu Kasdogan, "Potentiating Algae, Modernizing Bioeconomics: Algal Biofuels, Bioenergy Economies, and Built Ecologies in the United States and Turkey," Ph.D. diss., Graduate Program in Science and Technology Studies, York University, 2017.

5 Natasha Myers, "From Edenic Apocalypse to Gardens against Eden: Plants and People in and after the Anthropocene," in *Infrastructure, Environment, and Life in the Anthropocene,* ed. Kregg Hetherington (Durham, NC: Duke University Press, forthcoming).

6 Erik Swyngedouw, "Apocalypse Forever? Post-Political Populism and the Spectre of Climate Change," *Theory, Culture & Society* 27, no. 2–3 (2010): 213–32.

7 Natasha Myers, "Edenic Apocalypse: Singapore's End-of-Time Botanical Tourism," in *Art in the Anthropocene: Encounters among Aesthetics, Politics, Environments and Epistemologies,* ed. Heather Davis and Etienne Turpin, 31–42 (London: Open Humanities Press, 2015); Myers, "From Edenic Apocalypse to Gardens against Eden."

8 See, for example, Alan Weiseman's "The World Without Us," www.worldwithoutus.com/.

9 Swyngedouw, "Apocalypse Forever?"

10 Donna Haraway and Martha Kenney, "Anthropocene, Capitalocene, Chthulucene," in *Art in the Anthropocene: Encounters among Aesthetics, Politics, Environments and Epistemologies,* ed. Heather Davis and Etienne Turpin, 255–70 (London: Open Humanities Press, 2015).

11 Elizabeth A. Povinelli, *Economies of Abandonment: Social Belonging and Endurance in Late Liberalism* (Durham, NC: Duke University Press, 2011).

12 Fredric Jameson, "Future City," *New Left Review* 21 (2003): 65.

13 Start with indigenous scholars' approaches to decolonization. See, for example, works by Leanne Simpson on Indigenous resurgence and land-based pedagogy (*Dancing on Our Turtle's Back: Stories of Nishnaabeg Re-Creation, Resurgence, and a New Emergence* [Winnipeg: Arbeiter Ring, 2011]; and "Land as Pedagogy: Nishnaabeg Intelligence and Rebellious Transformation," *Decolonization: Indigeneity, Education & Society* 3, no. 3 [2014], http://decolonization.org/index.php/des/article/view/22170); Audra Simpson on decolonizing anthropology, Indigenous political sovereignty, and refusal (*Mohawk Interruptus: Political Life across the Borders of Settler States* [Durham, NC: Duke University Press, 2014]); Zoe Todd on Métis legal orders and land/body relations

("From a Fishy Place: Examining Canadian State Law Applied in the Daniels Decision from the Perspective of Métis Legal Orders," *TOPIA: Canadian Journal of Cultural Studies* 36, http://topia.journals.yorku.ca/index.php/topia/article/view/40398); and Glen Coultard on the politics of recognition in settler states (*Red Skin, White Masks: Rejecting the Colonial Politics of Recognition* [Minneapolis: University of Minnesota Press, 2014]).

14 Stuart McLean, "Blubberbomb," in *Between Matter and Method: Encounters in Anthropology and Art*, ed. Gretchen Bakke and Marina Peterson, 209–26 (London: Bloomsbury Academic, 2017).

15 Lynn Margulis, *Symbiotic Planet: A New Look at Evolution* (New York: Basic, 1999).

16 Natasha Myers, "Photosynthesis," 2016, Theorizing the Contemporary (cultural anthropology website), http://culanth.org/fieldsights/790-photosynthesis/. Dorion Sagan has recently called this the *Cyanocene* ("Beautiful Monsters: Terra in the Cyanocene," in *Arts of Living on a Damaged Planet: Stories from the Anthropocene*, ed. Anna Lowenhaupt Tsing, Heather Anne Swanson, Nils Bubandt, and Elaine Gan [Washington, DC: Island Press, 2016]).

17 Emanuele Coccia, *La vie des plantes: Une métaphysique du mélange* (Paris: Rivages, 2016).

18 Natasha Myers, "Photosynthetic Mattering: Rooting into the Planthroposcene," in *Moving Plants*, ed. Line Marie Thorsen, 123–29 (Rønnebæksholm, Denmark: Narayana, 2017).

19 See Anand Pandian, *Reel World: An Anthropology of Creation* (Durham, NC: Duke University Press, 2015).

20 Tim Choy, "Breathers Conspire—On Drawing Breath Together," paper presented at the Annual Meeting for the Society for Social Studies of Science, Barcelona, Spain, September 2016.

21 See https://earthactivisttraining.org/.

22 See Stephan V. Beyer, *Singing to the Plants: A Guide to Mestizo Shamanism in the Upper Amazon* (Albuquerque: University of New Mexico Press, 2009); and electro-acoustic performance artist Jo Simalay Alcampo's "Singing Plants Reconstruct Memory," www.josimalaya.com/.

23 Natasha Myers, "Conversations on Plant Sensing: Notes from the Field," in "Acting with Nonhuman Entities," special issue, *NatureCulture* 3 (2015): 35–66.

24 See Eve Tuck and K. Wayne Yang's important article "Decolonization Is Not a Metaphor," *Decolonization: Indigeneity, Education & Society* 1, no. 1 (2012): 1–40.

25 For more on Indigenous plant knowledge, see, for example, Robin Wall Kimmerer, *Braiding Sweetgrass: Indigenous Wisdom, Scientific Knowledge and the Teachings of Plants* (Minneapolis: Milkweed Editions, 2015); and Wendy Makoons Geniusz, *Our Knowledge Is Not Primitive: Decolonizing Botanical Anishinaabe Teachings* (Syracuse, NY: Syracuse University Press, 2009).

26 See, for example, Daniel Chamovitz, *What a Plant Knows: A Field Guide to the Senses* (2012; repr., New York: Scientific American/Farrar, Straus and Giroux, 2012). See Myers, "Conversations on Plant Sensing," for more on the contemporary sciences of plant sensing.

27 Natasha Myers, "Sensing Botanical Sensoria: A Kriya for Cultivating Your Inner Plant," Centre for Imaginative Ethnography, 2014, http://imaginativeethnography.org/imaginings/affect/sensing-botanical-sensoria/.

28 See, for example, Richard M. Doyle, *Darwin's Pharmacy: Sex, Plants, and the Evolution of the*

Noösphere (Seattle: University of Washington Press, 2011); Beyer, *Singing to the Plants*; and Piera Talin and Emilia Sanabria, "Ayahuasca's Entwined Efficacy: An Ethnographic Study of Ritual Healing from 'Addiction,'" *International Journal of Drug Policy* 44 (2017): 23–30, https://www.sciencedirect.com/journal/international-journal-of-drug-policy/vol/44/suppl/C.

29 On involvement and involutionary momentum, see Carla Hustak and Natasha Myers, "Involutionary Momentum: Affective Ecologies and the Sciences of Plant/Insect Encounters," *Differences* 23, no. 3 (2012): 74–118

30 Ibid.

31 See Isabelle Stengers, *Cosmopolitics I* (Minneapolis: University of Minnesota Press, 2010).

32 See Ayelen Liberona and Natasha Myers, *Becoming Sensor,* a synesthetic installation, Canadian Association of Theatre Researchers Annual Conference, The Great Hall, Toronto, May 28–30, 2017; and Natasha Myers, "Becoming Sensor in Sentient Worlds: A More-Than-Natural History of a Black Oak Savannah," in *Between Matter and Method: Encounters in Anthropology and Art,* ed. Gretchen Bakke and Marina Peterson (London: Bloomsbury Academic, 2017).

33 On economizations of life more generally, see M. Murphy, *Economizations of Life* (Durham, NC: Duke University Press, 2017); and on ecology, see Natasha Myers, "Ungrid-able Ecologies: Decolonizing the Ecological Sensorium in a 10,000 Year-Old *NaturalCultural* Happening," in "Science Out of Feminism," ed. Banju Subramaniam and Angela Willey, special section in *Catalyst: Feminism, Theory, Technoscience* 3, no. 2 (2017): 1–24.

34 For inspiration, see Lois Weinberger's plant-based artworks, www.loisweinberger.net/.

35 Myers, "From Edenic Apocalypse to Gardens against Eden."

36 See https://landinstitute.org/.

37 See, for example, the award-winning 2014 short animation *Wrapped*, which renders monstrous plants overtaking a depeopled New York City: https://vimeo.com/161599224.

38 See Annie Sprinkle's and Beth Stephens's eco-sexual projects at http://sexecology.org.

39 See http://helloponyexpress.com/.

40 See www.spelapetric.org/; and http://psx-consultancy.com/.

41 See www.plantasnomadas.com/.

Jennifer Allora and
Guillermo Calzadilla

Claudia Andujar

Sammy Baloji

Subhankar Banerjee

Huma Bhabha

Liu Bolin

Edward Burtynsky

Sandra Cinto

Elena Damiani

Dornith Doherty

Charles Gaines

Mishka Henner

Felipe Jácome

Chris Jordan

William Kentridge

Wifredo Lam

Maroesjka Lavigne

Eva Leitolf

Dana Levy

Yao Lu

Pedro Neves Marques

Noelle Mason

Mary Mattingly

Gideon Mendel

Ana Mendieta

Kimiyo Mishima

Richard Misrach

Beth Moon

Richard Mosse

Jackie Nickerson

Gabriel Orozco

Trevor Paglen

Abel Rodríguez

Allan Sekula

Taryn Simon

Nicole Six and
Paul Petritsch

Laurencia Strauss

Thomas Struth

Bethany Taylor

Frank Thiel

Sergio Vega

Andrew Yang

Haegue Yang

PLATES

Sea-level rise comes from the ice melt in Antarctica and Greenland, an expanding ocean, and a slowing Gulf Stream. Excess heat whips the waves of ocean water into storms and hurricanes that rip away rocks, earth, and the homes in which we live.

—Kerry Oliver-Smith

DELUGE

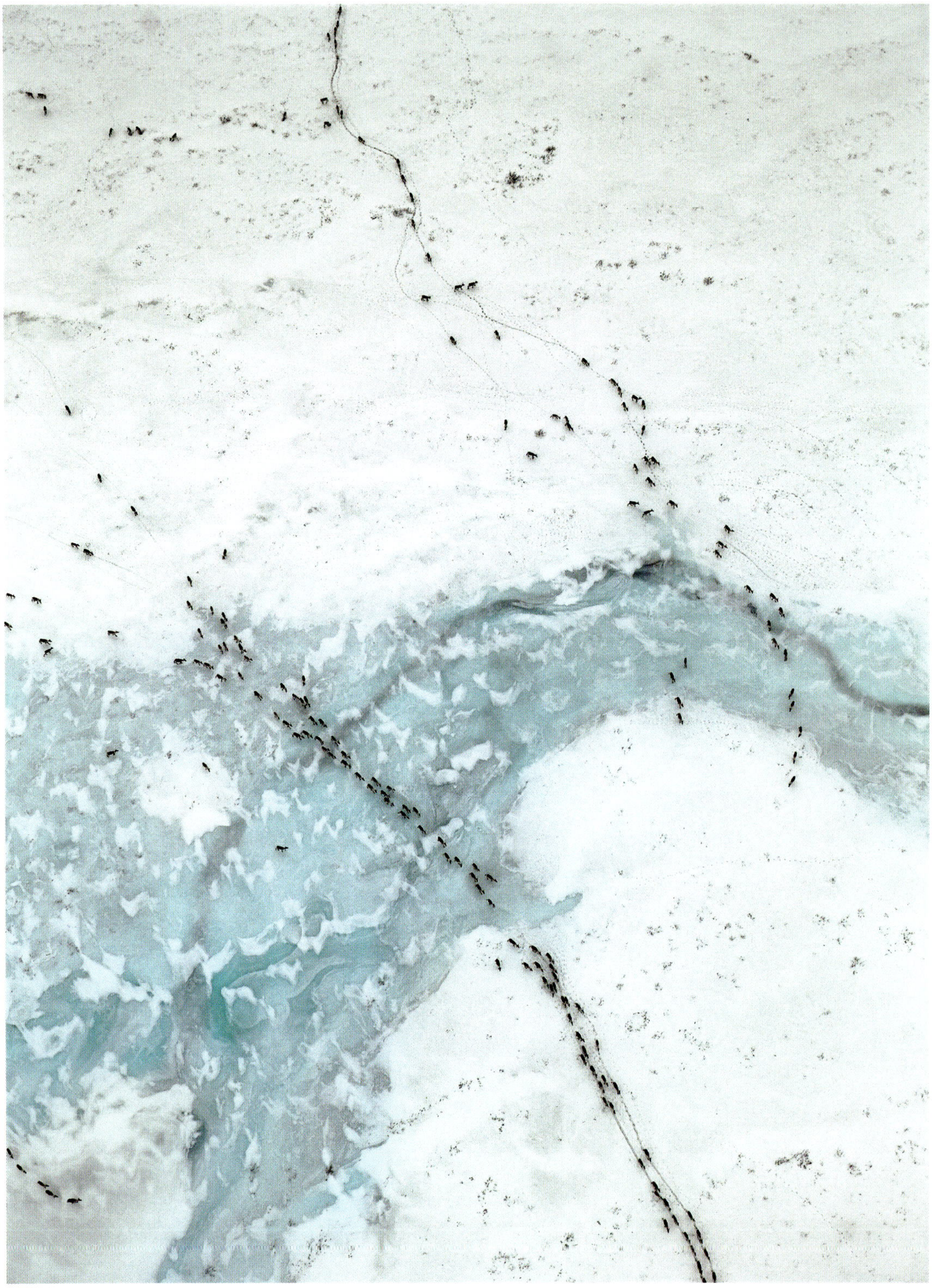

Subhankar Banerjee

American b. India, 1967

Caribou Migration

From the series *Oil and the Caribou*

2002

UltraChrome print

39¾ × 29¾ in. (100.9 × 75.5 cm)

Loan courtesy of Hood Museum of Art, Dartmouth College, Hanover, New Hampshire; purchased through the Charles F. Venrick 1936 Fund

Image courtesy of the artist

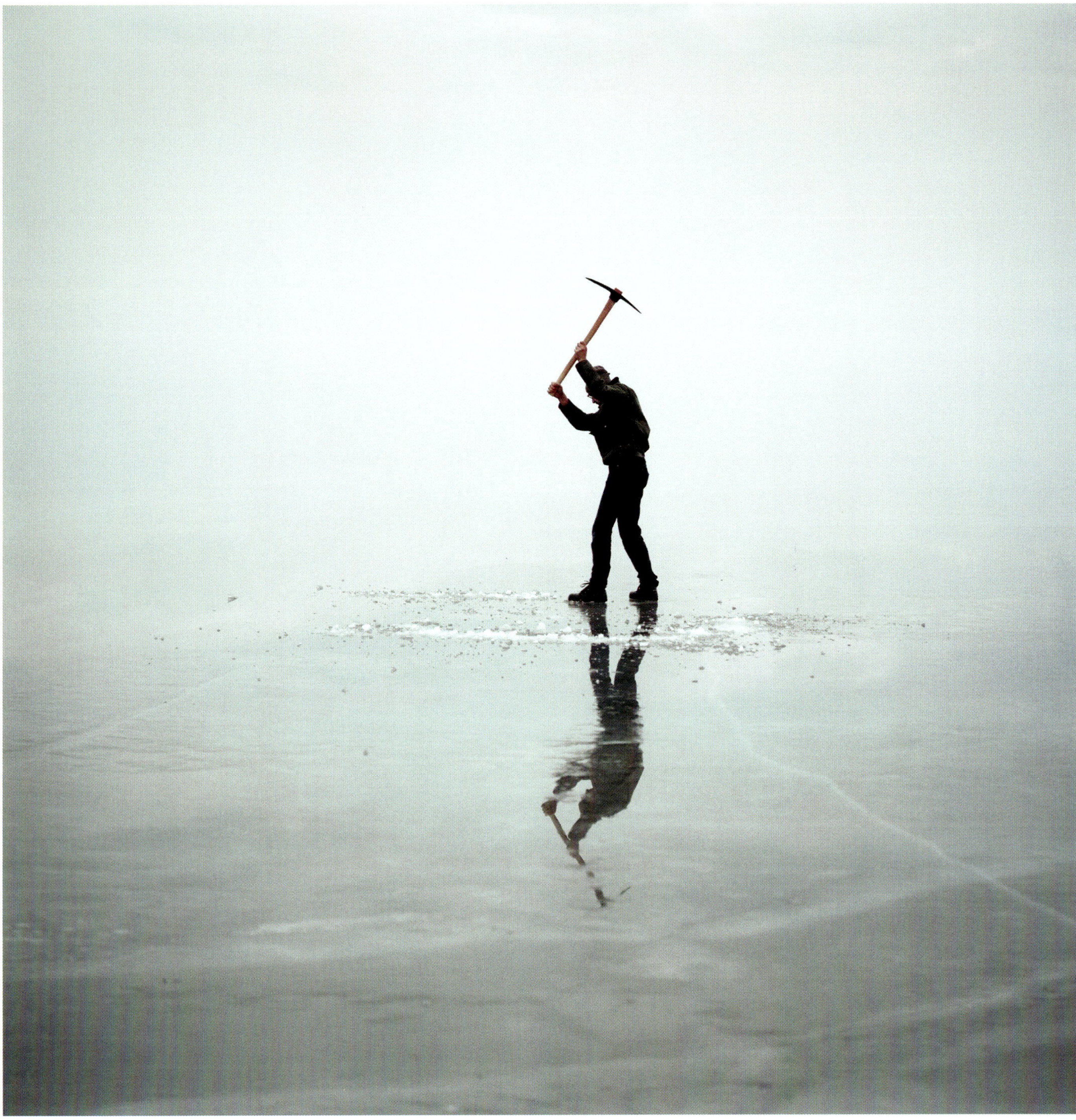

Nicole Six & Paul Petritsch
Austrian, b. 1971; Austrian, b. 1968
Spatial Intervention (1)
2002
Color video, 28 min.

Courtesy of the artists

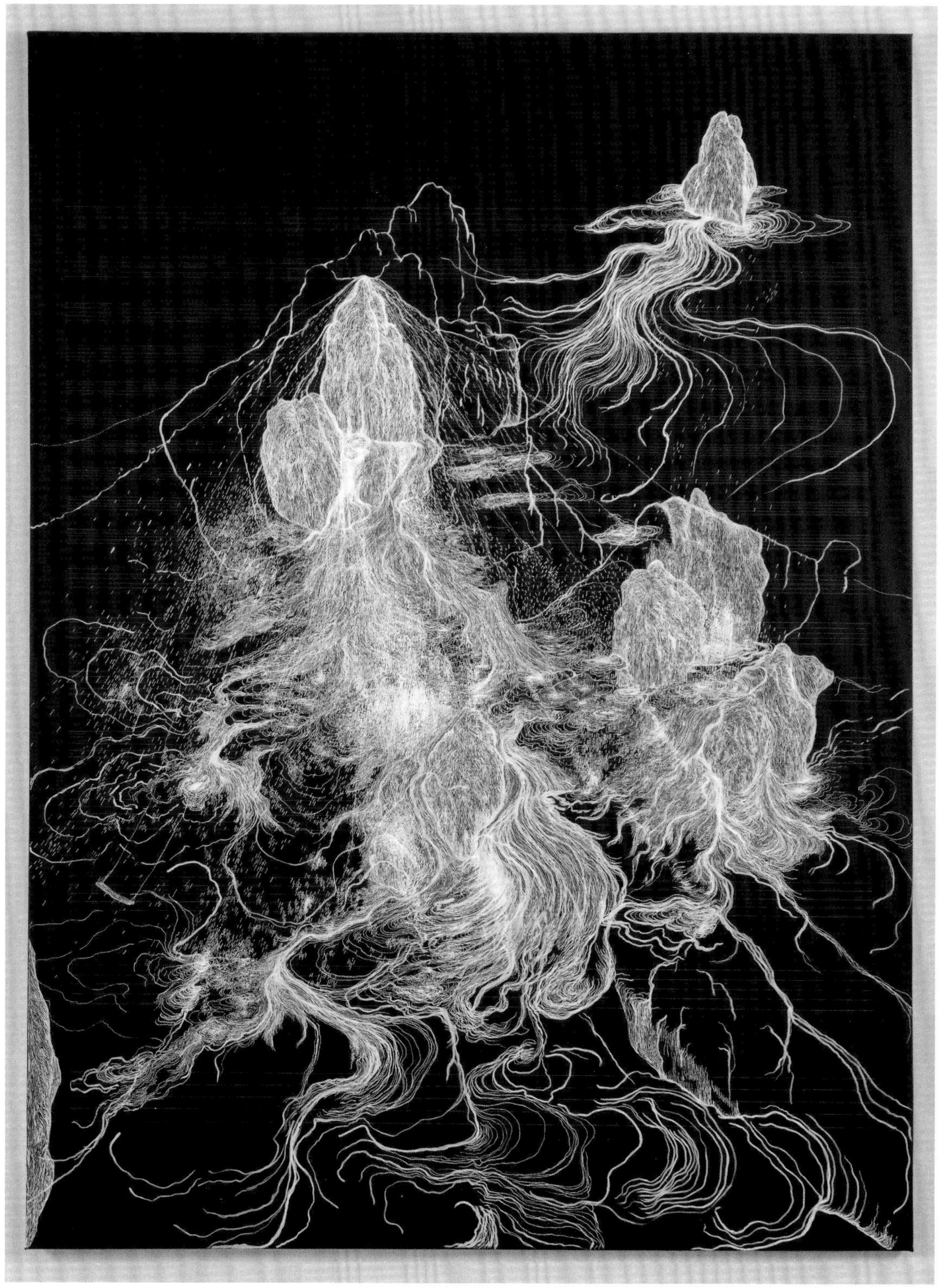

Sandra Cinto

Brazilian, b. 1968

Untitled

2015

Permanent pen and acrylic on canvas

78¾ × 59 in. (200 × 149.9 cm)

Courtesy of the artist and Tanya Bonakdar Gallery, New York

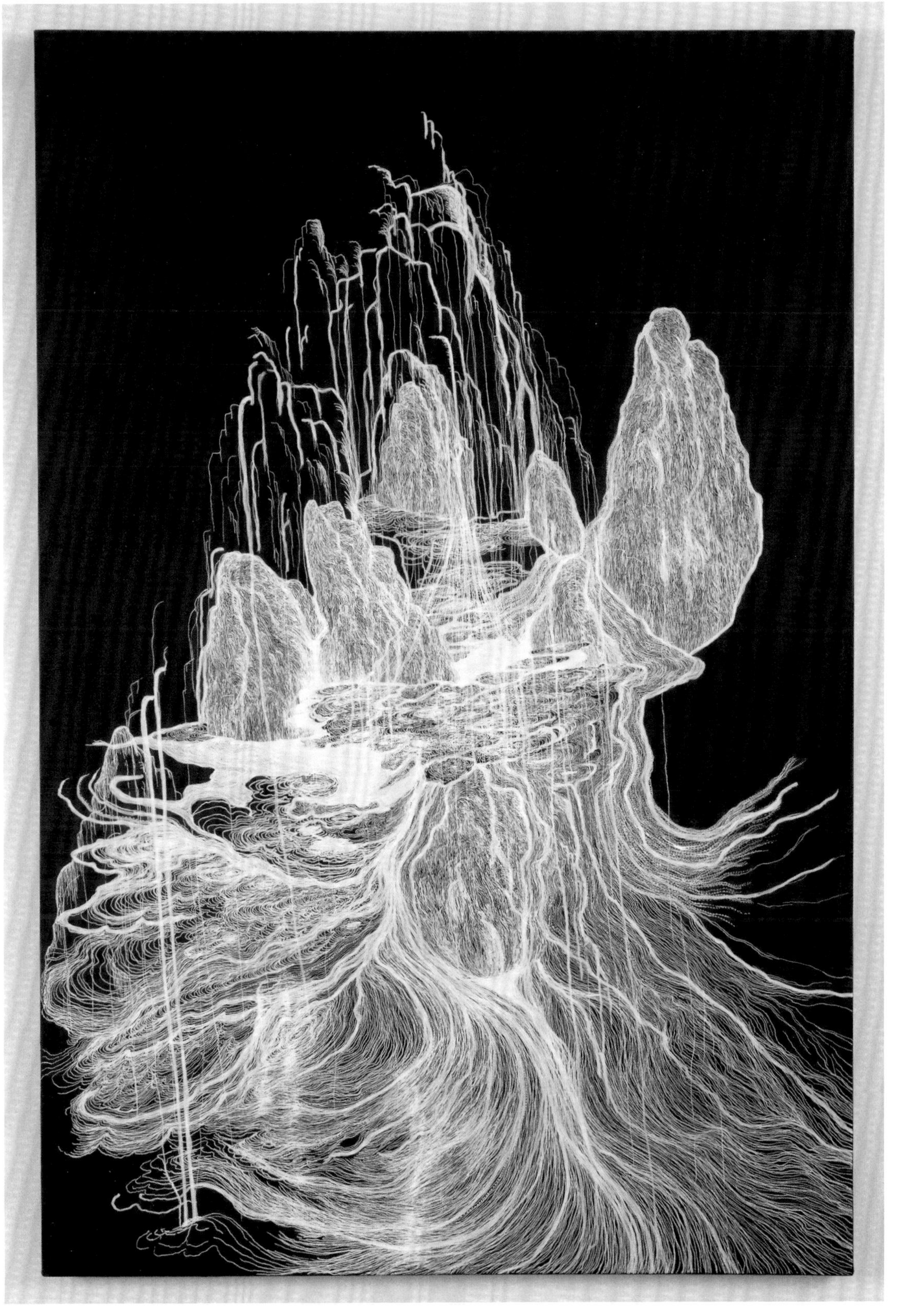

Sandra Cinto

Brazilian, b. 1968

Untitled

2015

Permanent pen and acrylic on canvas

60 × 40 in. (152.4 × 101.6 cm)

Courtesy of the artist and Tanya Bonakdar Gallery, New York

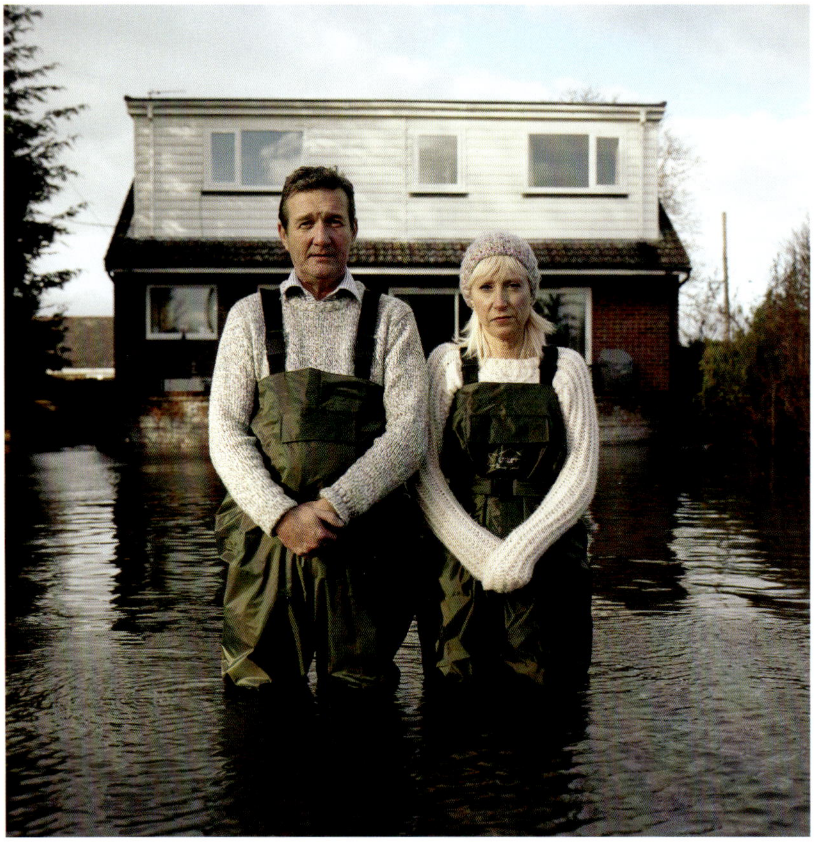

Gideon Mendel

South African, b. 1959

Jeff and Tracy Waters, Staines-upon-Thames, Surrey, UK, February 2014

From the series *Drowning World*

2014

Chromogenic print

27½ × 27½ in. (69.9 × 69.9 cm)

Courtesy of the artist and Axis Gallery, New York and New Jersey

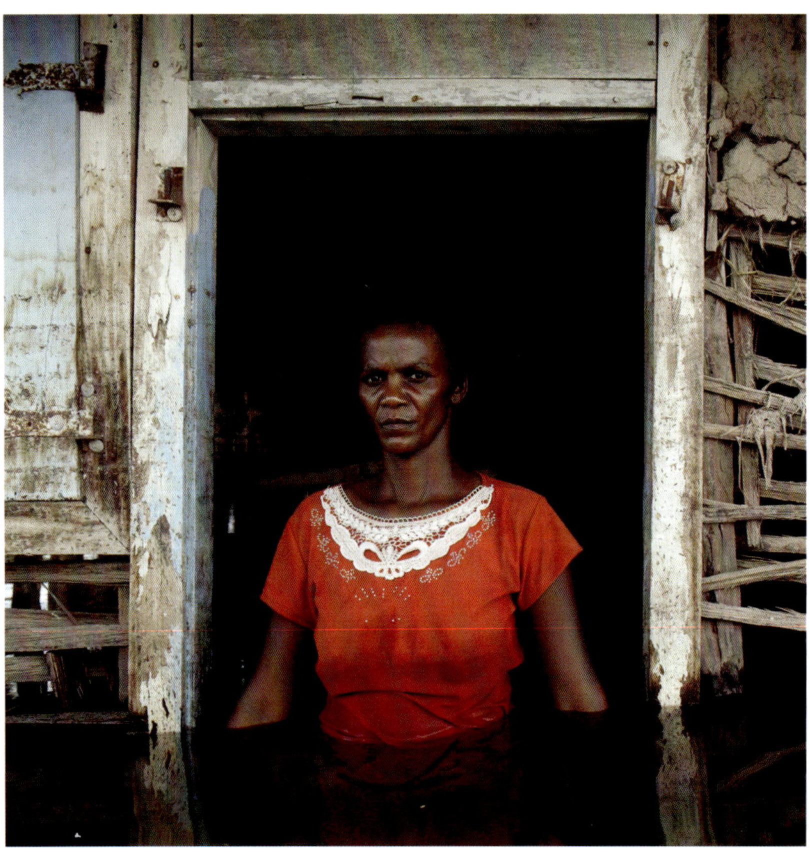

Gideon Mendel

South African, b. 1959

Adlene Pierre, Savanne Desolée, Gonaïves, Haiti, September 2008

From the series *Drowning World*

2008

Chromogenic print

27½ × 27½ in. (69.9 × 69.9 cm)

Courtesy of the artist and Axis Gallery, New York and New Jersey

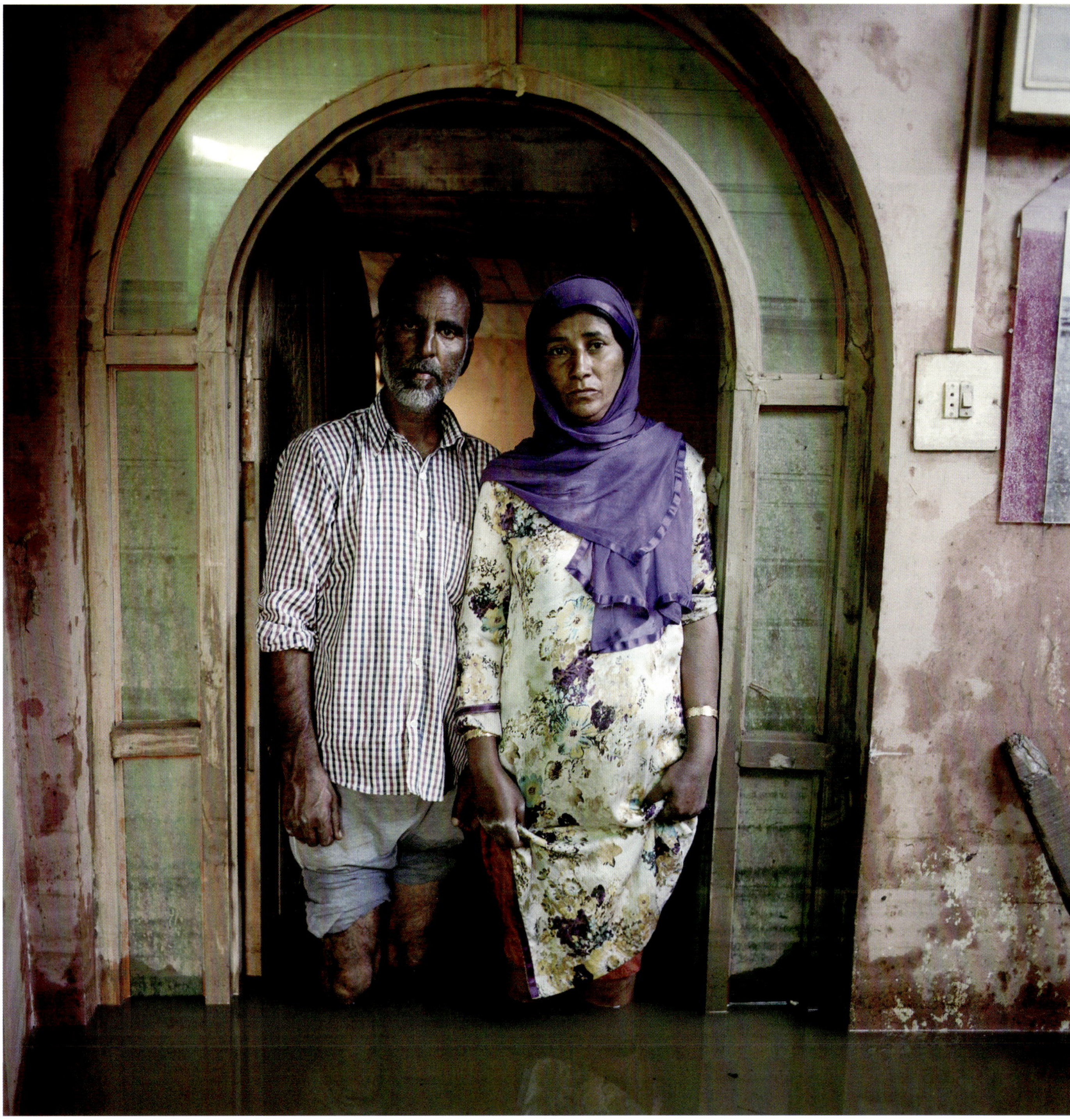

Gideon Mendel

South African, b. 1959

Mushaq Ahmad Wani and Shafeeqa Mushtaq, Jawahar Nagar, Srinagar, Kashmir, India, October 2014

From the series *Drowning World*

2014

Chromogenic print

27½ × 27½ in. (69.9 × 69.9 cm)

Courtesy of the artist and Axis Gallery, New York and New Jersey

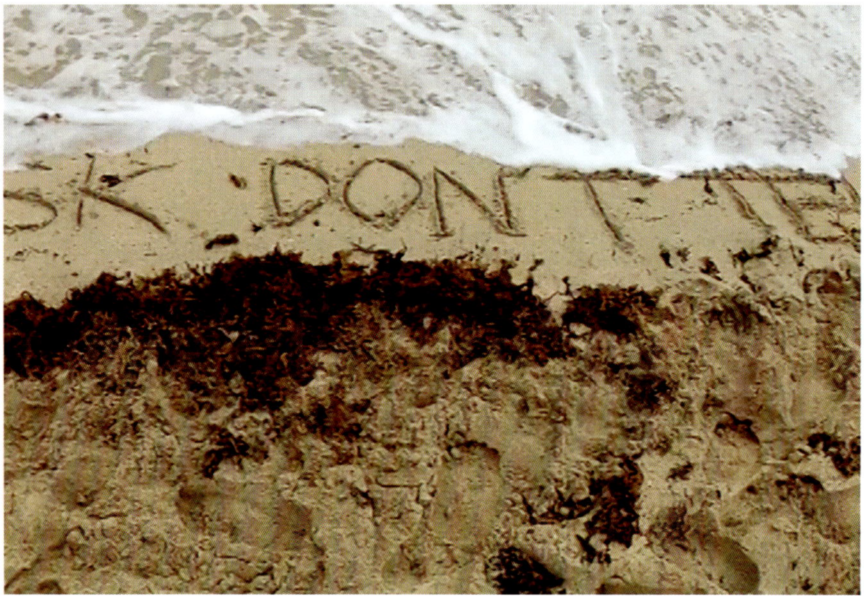

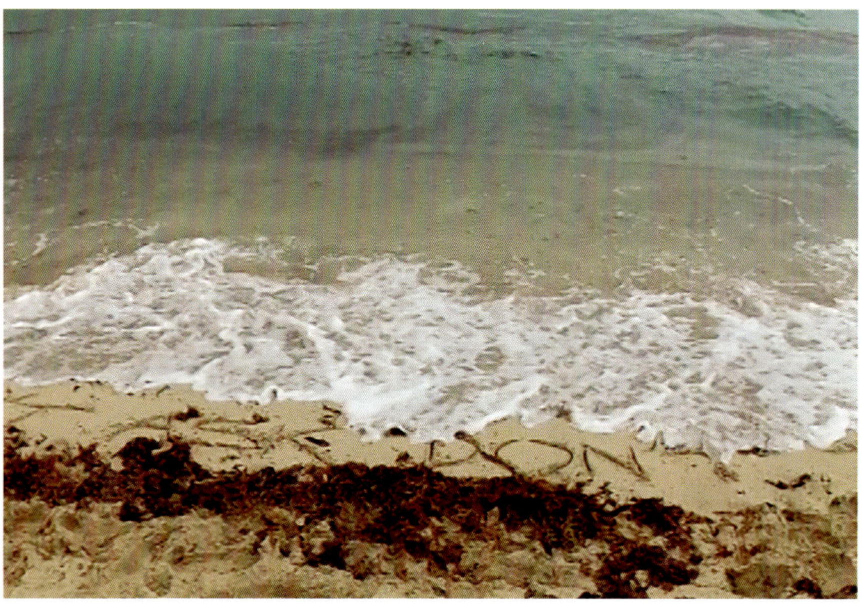

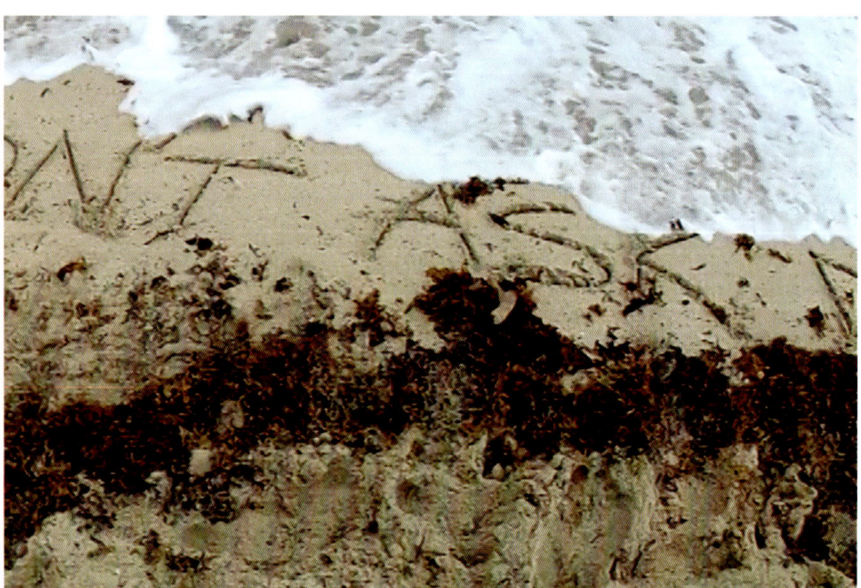

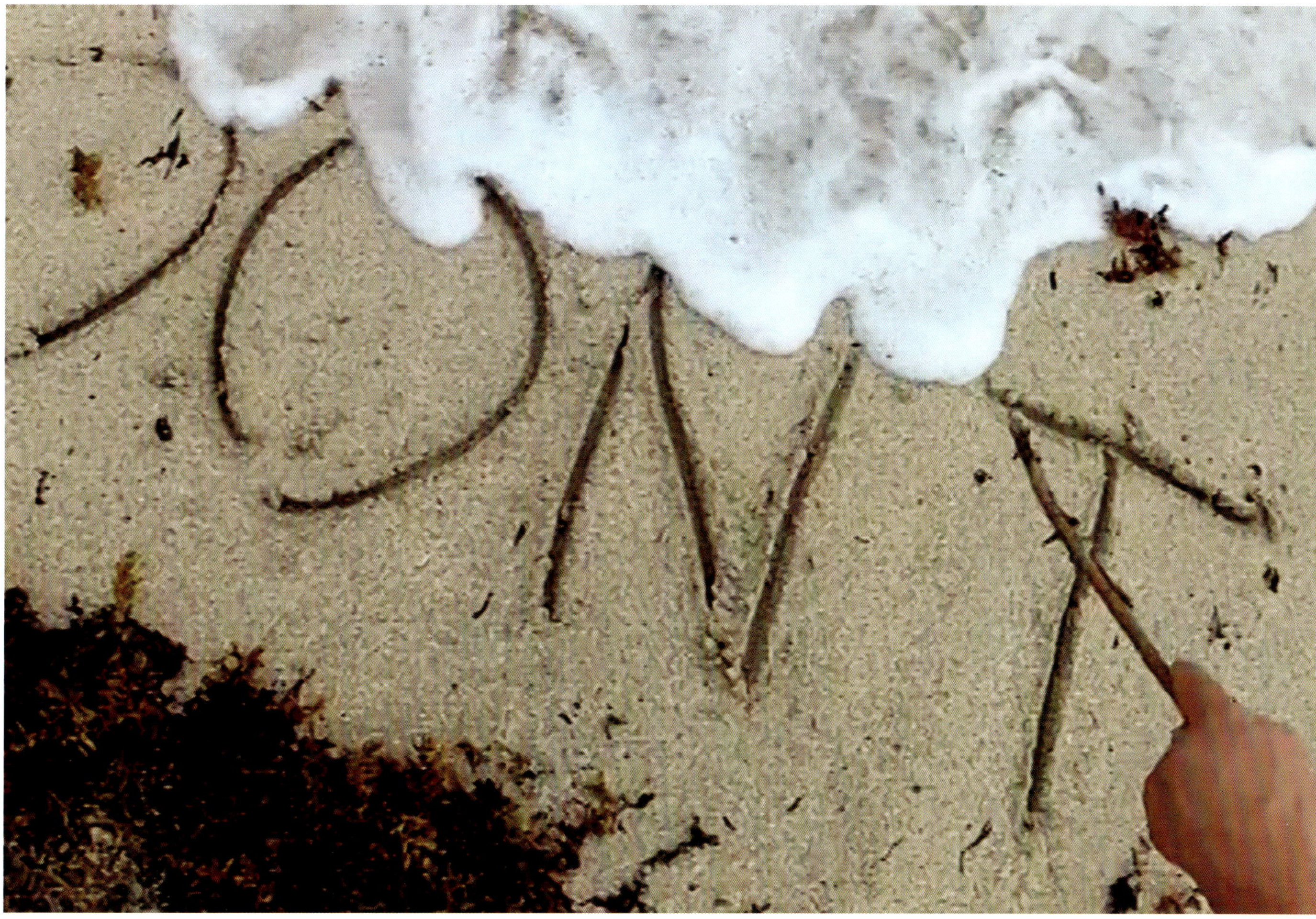

Laurencia Strauss

American, b. 1966

Shifting Zero: Don't Ask Don't Tell

2015

Color video, 10 min.

Courtesy of the artist

For the global assemblage of development initiatives, corporations, and financial institutions, matter exists only to be exploited and commercialized. —Kerry Oliver-Smith

RAW MATERIAL

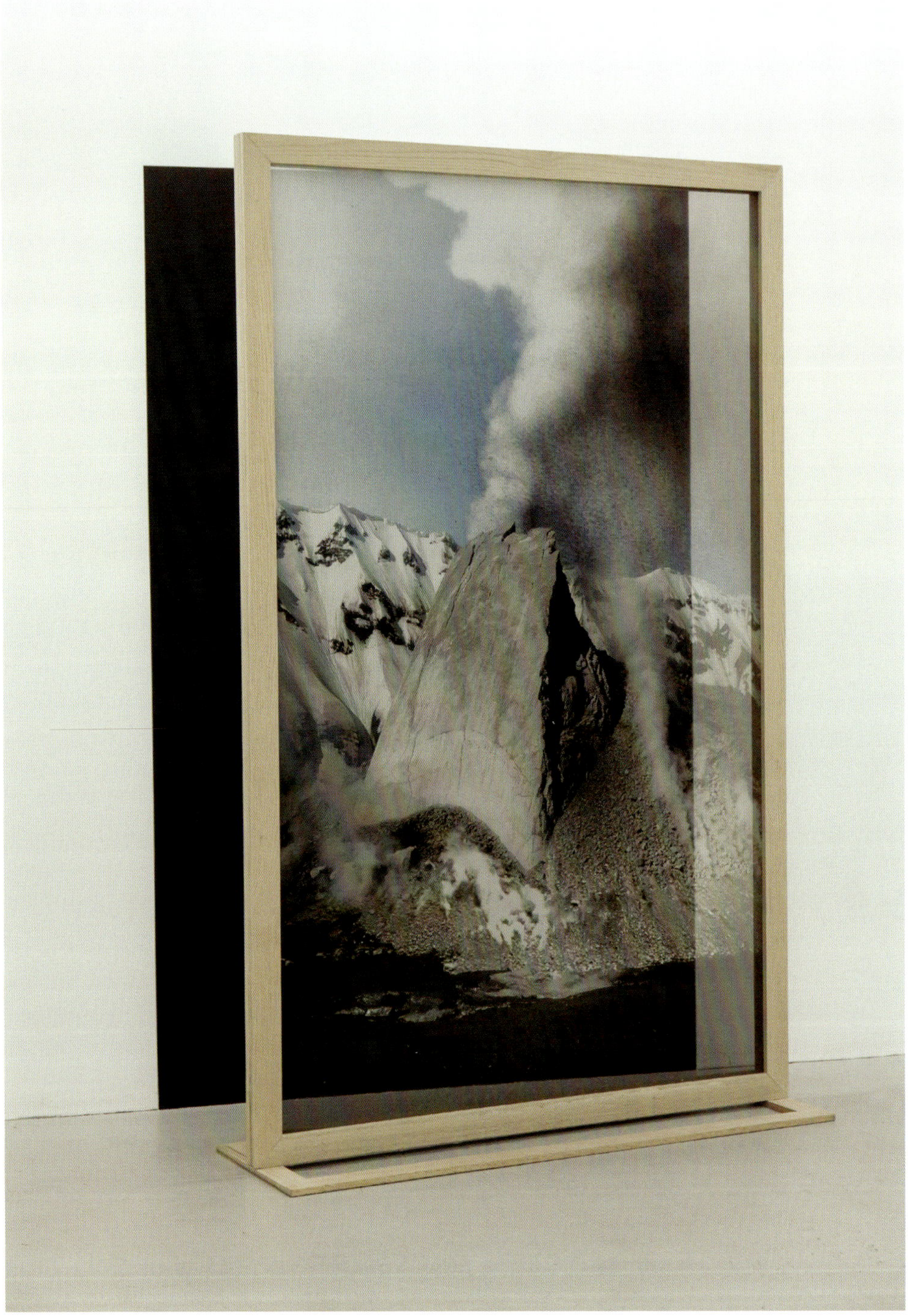

Elena Damiani

Peruvian, b. 1972

Fading Field N.9

From the series *The Fading Fields*

2015

Digital print on silk chiffon, wood structure, black paint on wall

73 × 56 × 15 in. (185.4 × 142.2 × 38.1 cm)

Loan courtesy of the collector, Cota Cohen

Image courtesy of the artist

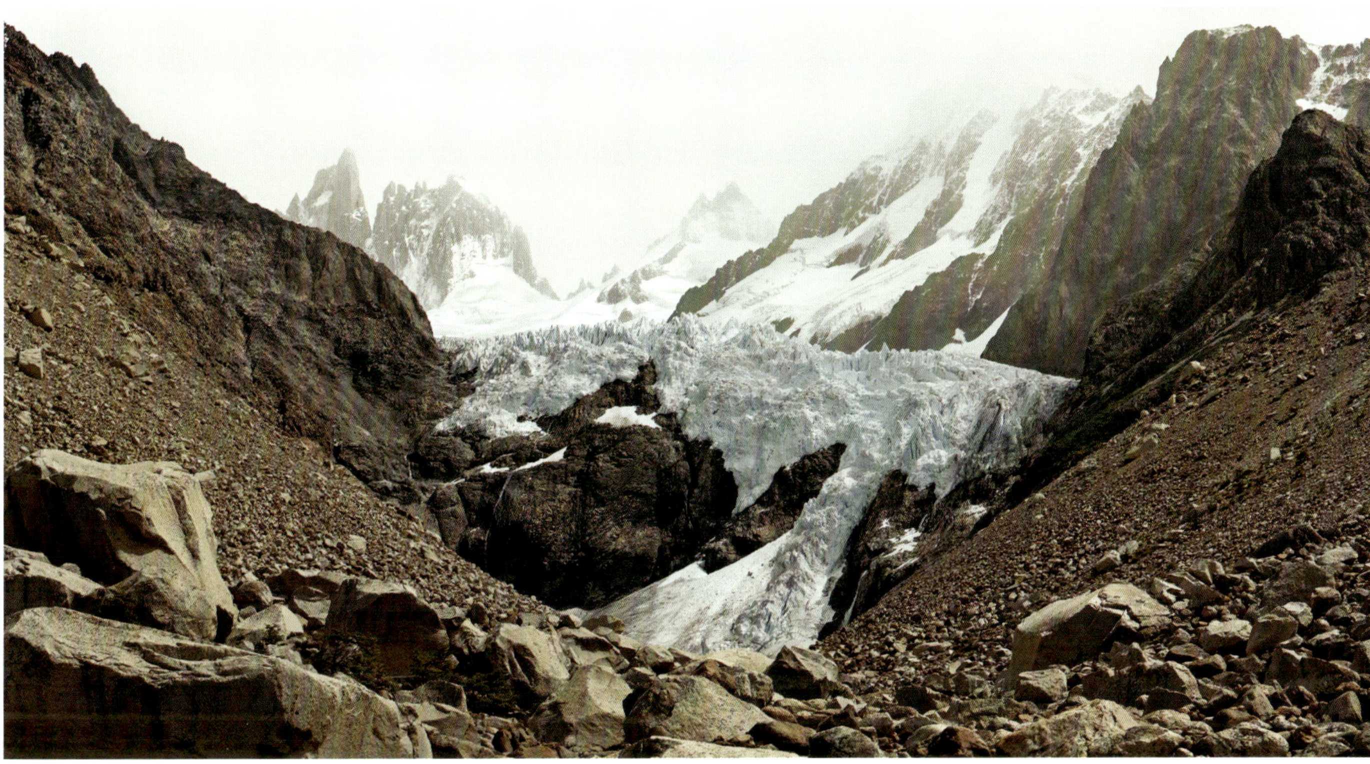

Frank Thiel

German, c. 1966

Piedras Blancas

2012–2013

Framed chromogenic print face mounted
to Plexiglas

Framed: 72½ × 126½ × 2⅜ in. (184.2 × 321.2 × 6 cm)

Edition of 5 with 2 Aps

Loan courtesy of Rodney M. Miller Collection, New York

Image courtesy of Sean Kelly, New York

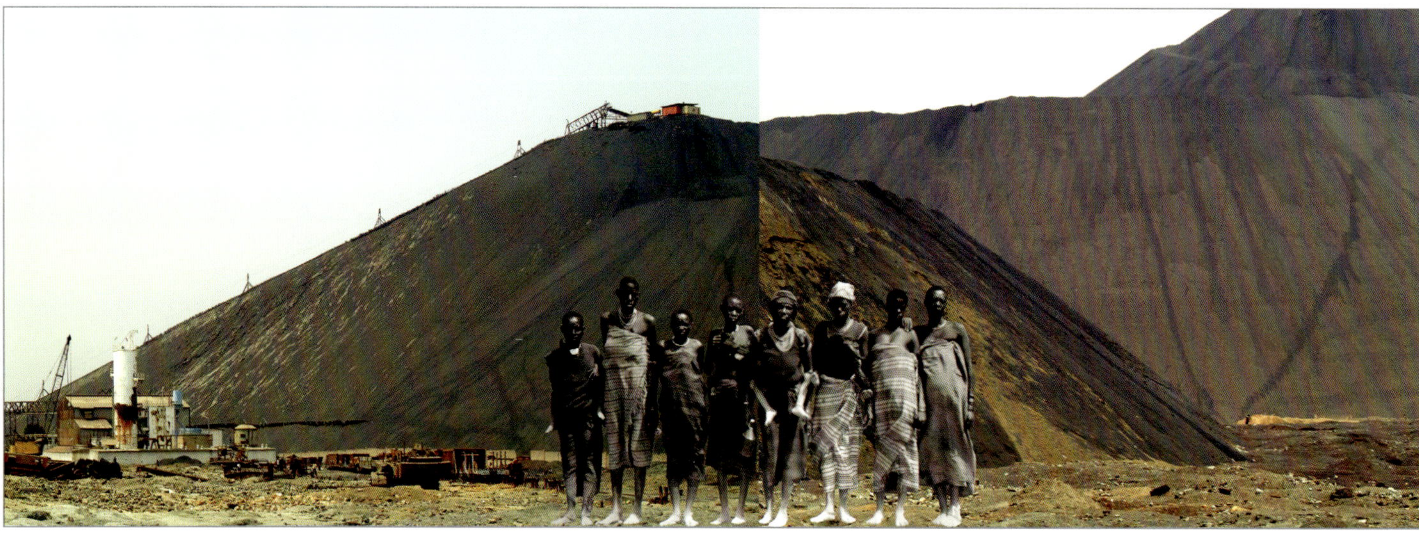

Sammy Baloji

Congolese, Democratic Republic of the Congo, b. 1978

Untitled 6

From the series *Mémoire*

2006

Archival digital photograph on satin matte paper

24 in. × 5 ft. 6¾ in. (61 × 169.5 cm)

Courtesy of the artist and Axis Gallery, New York and New Jersey

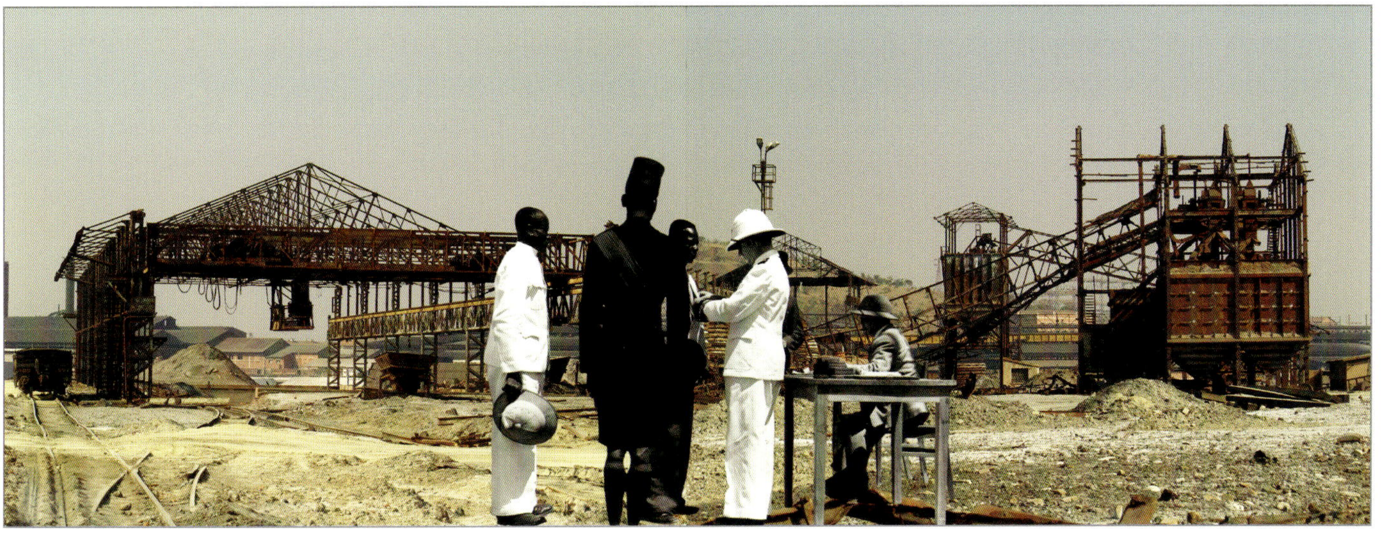

Sammy Baloji

Congolese, Democratic Republic of the Congo, b. 1978

Untitled 21

From the series *Mémoire*

2006

Archival digital photograph on satin matte paper

24 in. × 5 ft. 4½ in. (61 × 163.8 cm)

Courtesy of the artist and Axis Gallery, New York and New Jersey

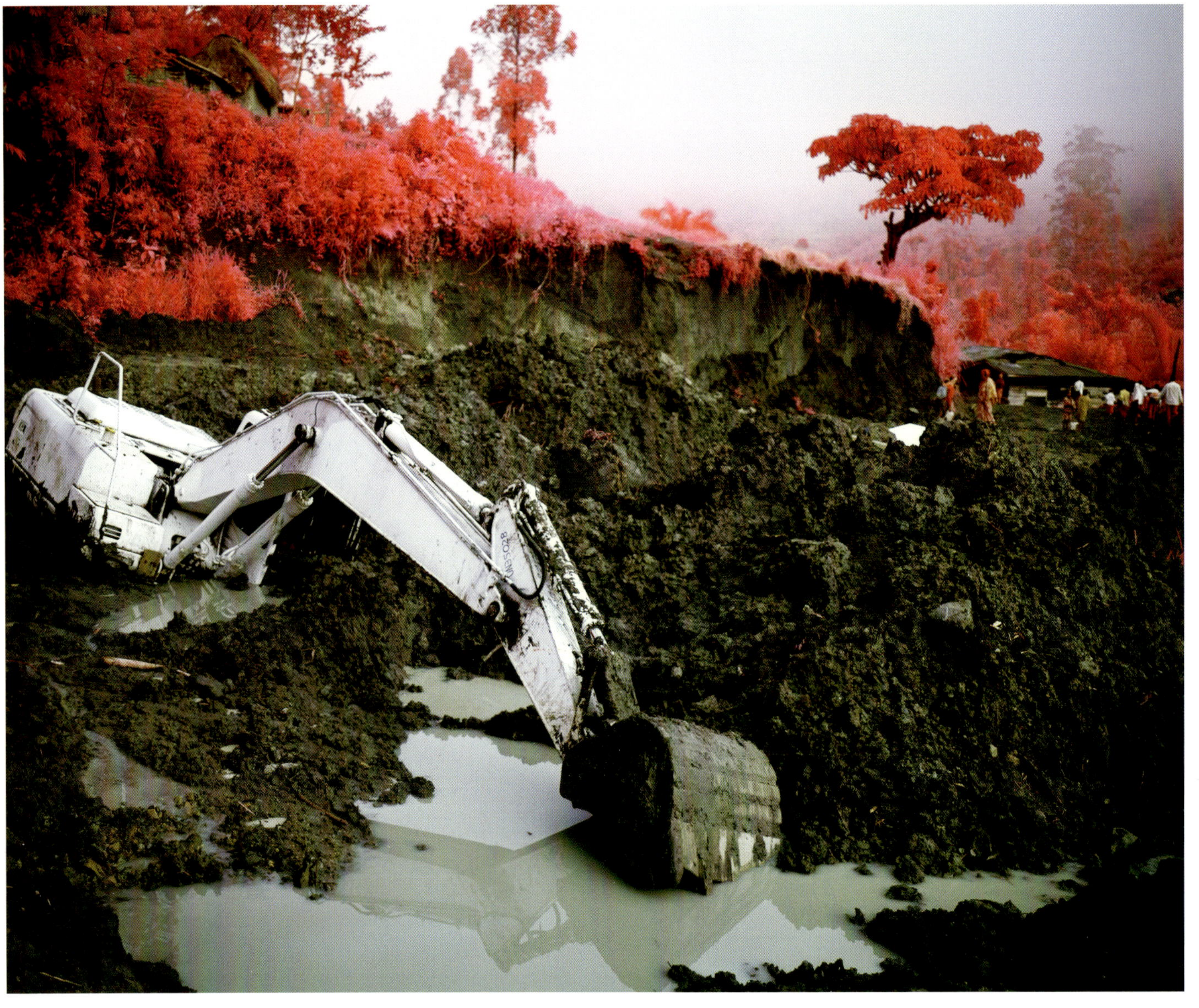

Richard Mosse

Irish, b. 1980

Stalemate

2011

Digital chromogenic print

48 × 60 in. (121.9 × 152.4 cm)

Courtesy of the artist and Jack Shainman Gallery, New York

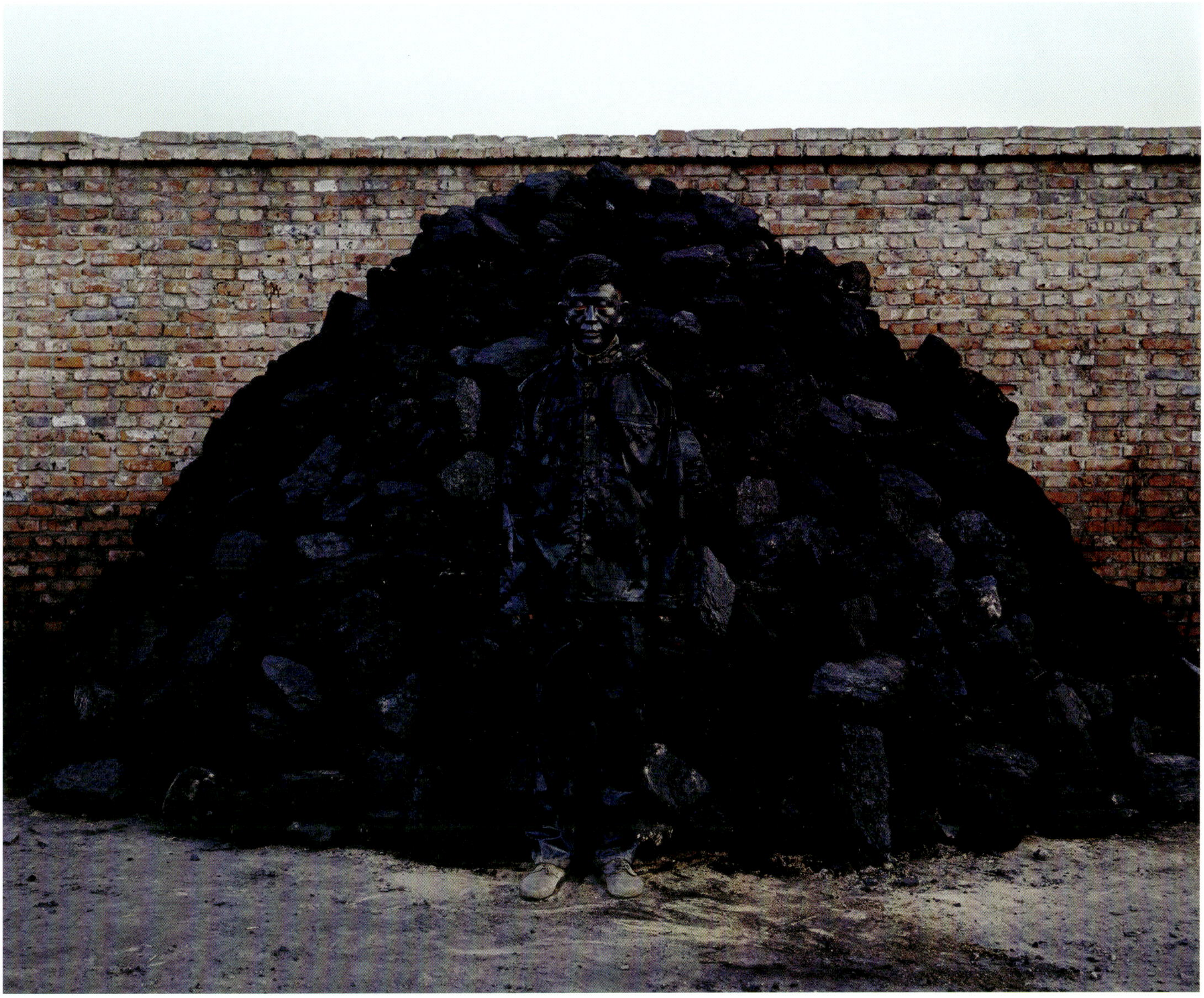

Liu Bolin
Chinese, b. 1973
Hiding in the City, No. 95, Coal Pile
2010
Chromogenic print
46½ × 59 in. (118.1 × 149.9 cm)
Loan courtesy of Eli Klein
Image courtesy of Eli Klein and the artist, © Liu Bolin

More than ever, nature is monetized as a human resource. Animal agriculture harms the Earth and transforms the human/animal connection to a consumer/commodity relationship.

—Kerry Oliver-Smith

CONSUMPTION

Allan Sekula

American, 1951–2013

Shipwreck and Worker, Istanbul

1998–2000

Cibachrome

34 × 50 in. (86.4 × 127 cm)

Harn Museum of Art collection

Museum purchase, gift of Michael A. Singer

2002.14

Photography by Randy Batista

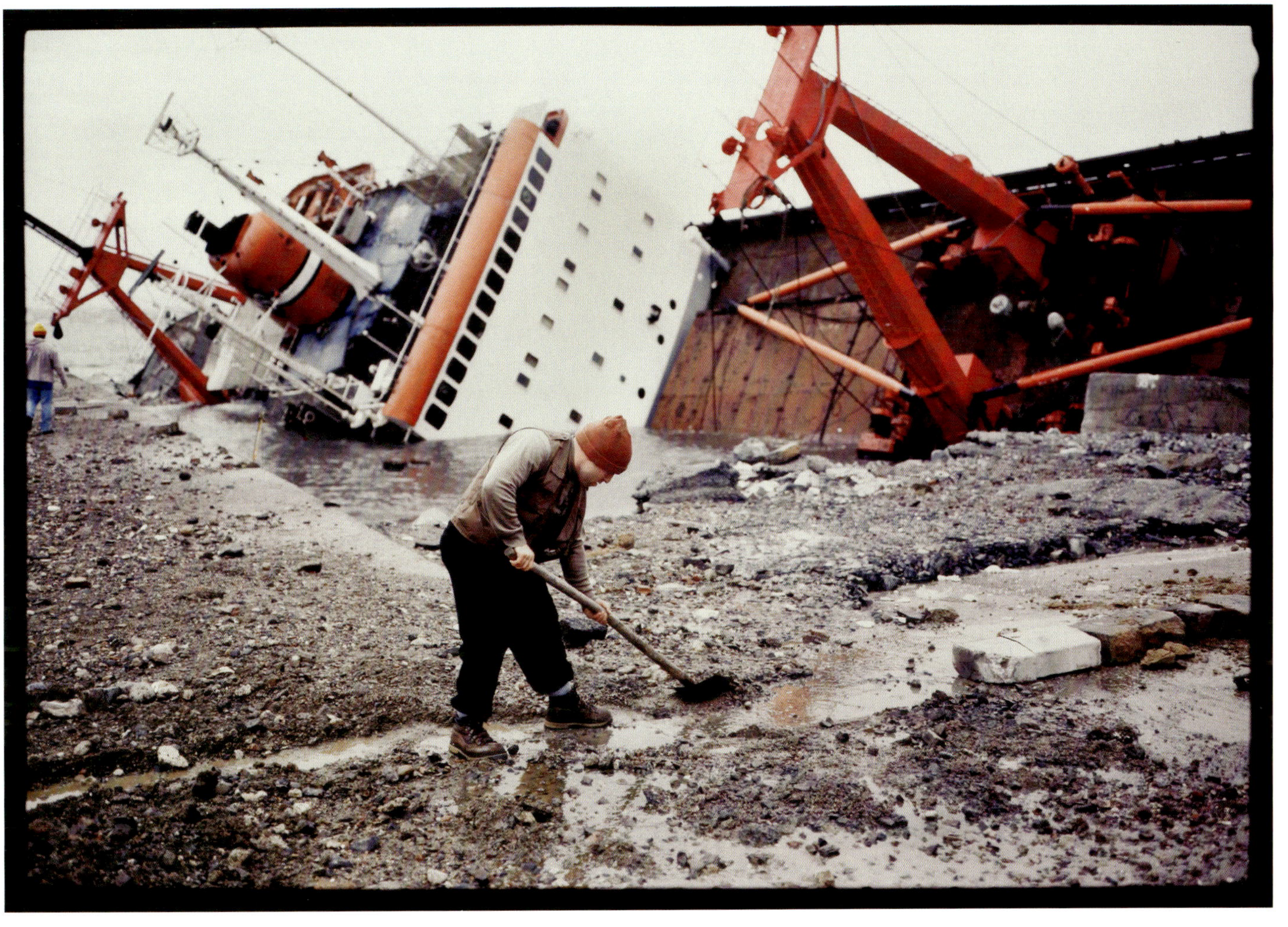

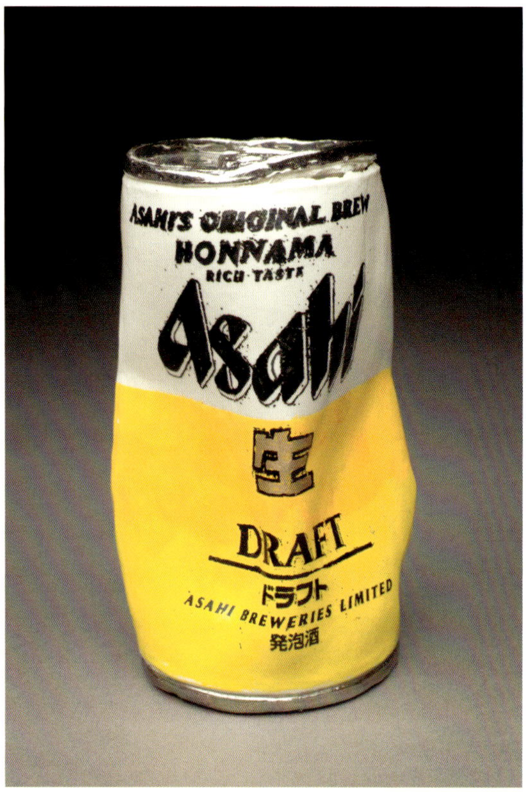

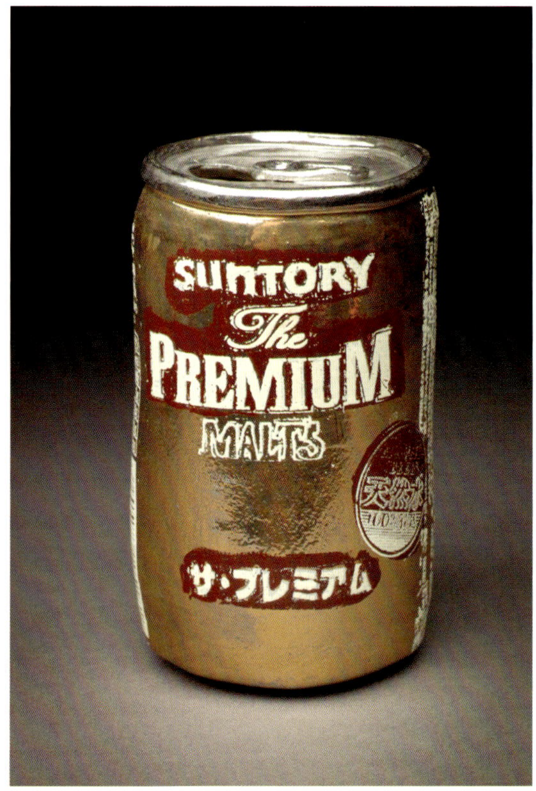

Kimiyo Mishima

Japanese, b. 1932

Akikan (Empty Can)

2012

50% stoneware, 50% clay. Mat-glaze sprayed over silk-screen transfer print fired at 1,270°C. Then portions hand-painted and fired at 200°C.

5⅛ × 2⅜ × 3 in. (13 × 6 × 7.6 cm)

Harn Museum of Art collection

Gift of the artist

2012.26.4

Photography by Randy Batista

Kimiyo Mishima

Japanese, b. 1932

Akikan (Empty Can)

2012

50% stoneware, 50% clay. Mat-glaze sprayed over silk-screen transfer print fired at 1,270°C. Then portions hand-painted and fired at 200°C.

5½ × 3 × 3⅛ in. (14 × 7.6 × 7.9 cm)

Harn Museum of Art collection

Gift of the artist

2012.26.5

Photography by Randy Batista

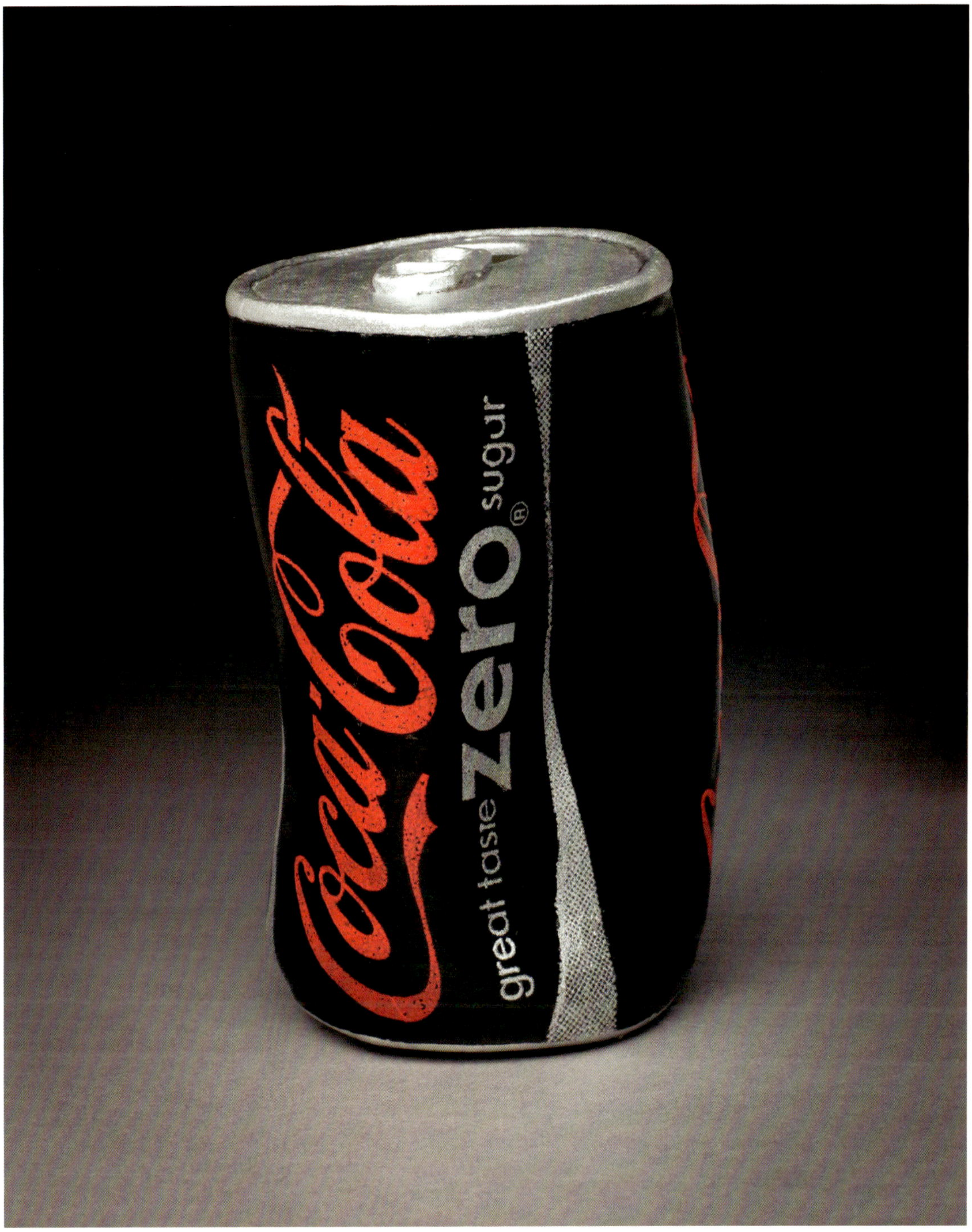

Kimiyo Mishima

Japanese, b. 1932

Akikan (Empty Can)

2012

50% stoneware, 50% clay. Mat-glaze sprayed over silk-screen transfer print fired at 1,270°C. Then portions hand-painted and fired at 200°C.

5⅜ × 3 × 3 in. (13.7 × 7.6 × 7.6 cm)

Harn Museum of Art collection

Gift of the artist

2012.26.3

Photography by Randy Batista

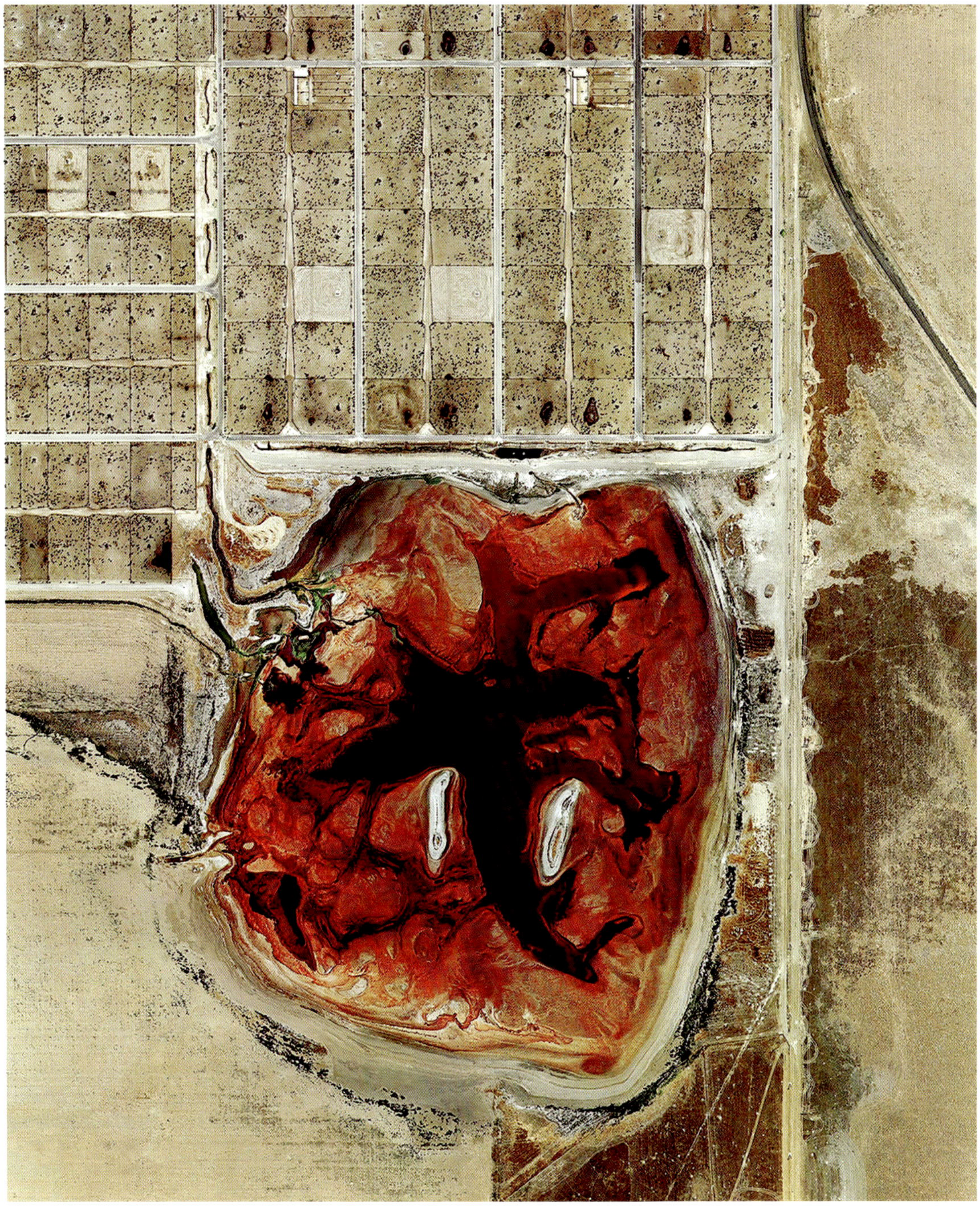

Mishka Henner

Belgian, b. 1976

Coronado Feeders, Dalhart, Texas, 2013

2013

Archival pigment print, photographed by satellites orbiting Earth

48 × 40⅛ in. (122 × 102 cm)

Loan courtesy of Bruce Silverstein Gallery, New York

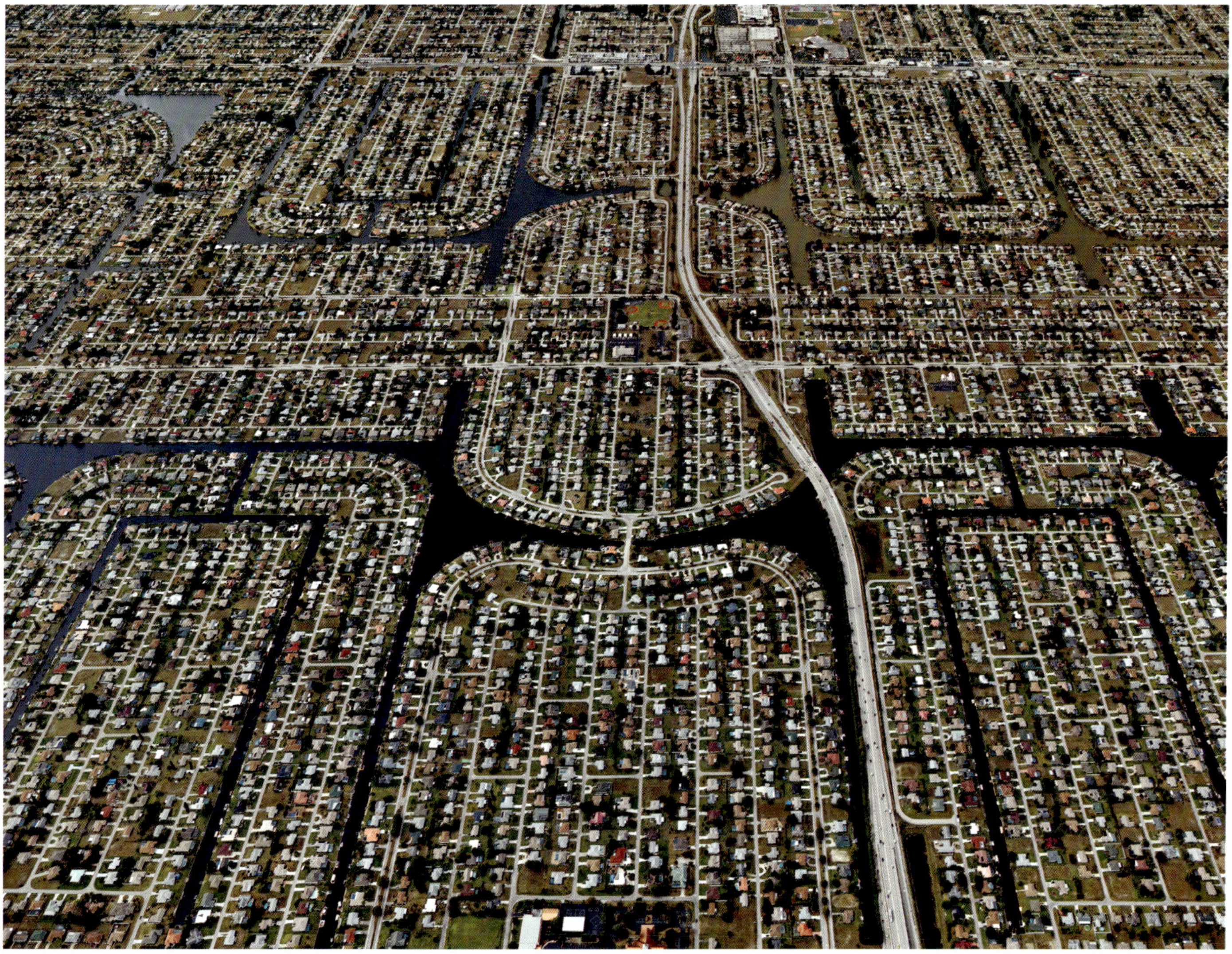

Edward Burtynsky

Canadian, b. 1955

Cape Coral, Florida #1, 2012

2012

Chromogenic print

30 × 52 in. (76.2 × 132.1 cm)

Loan courtesy of Howard Greenberg Gallery, New York

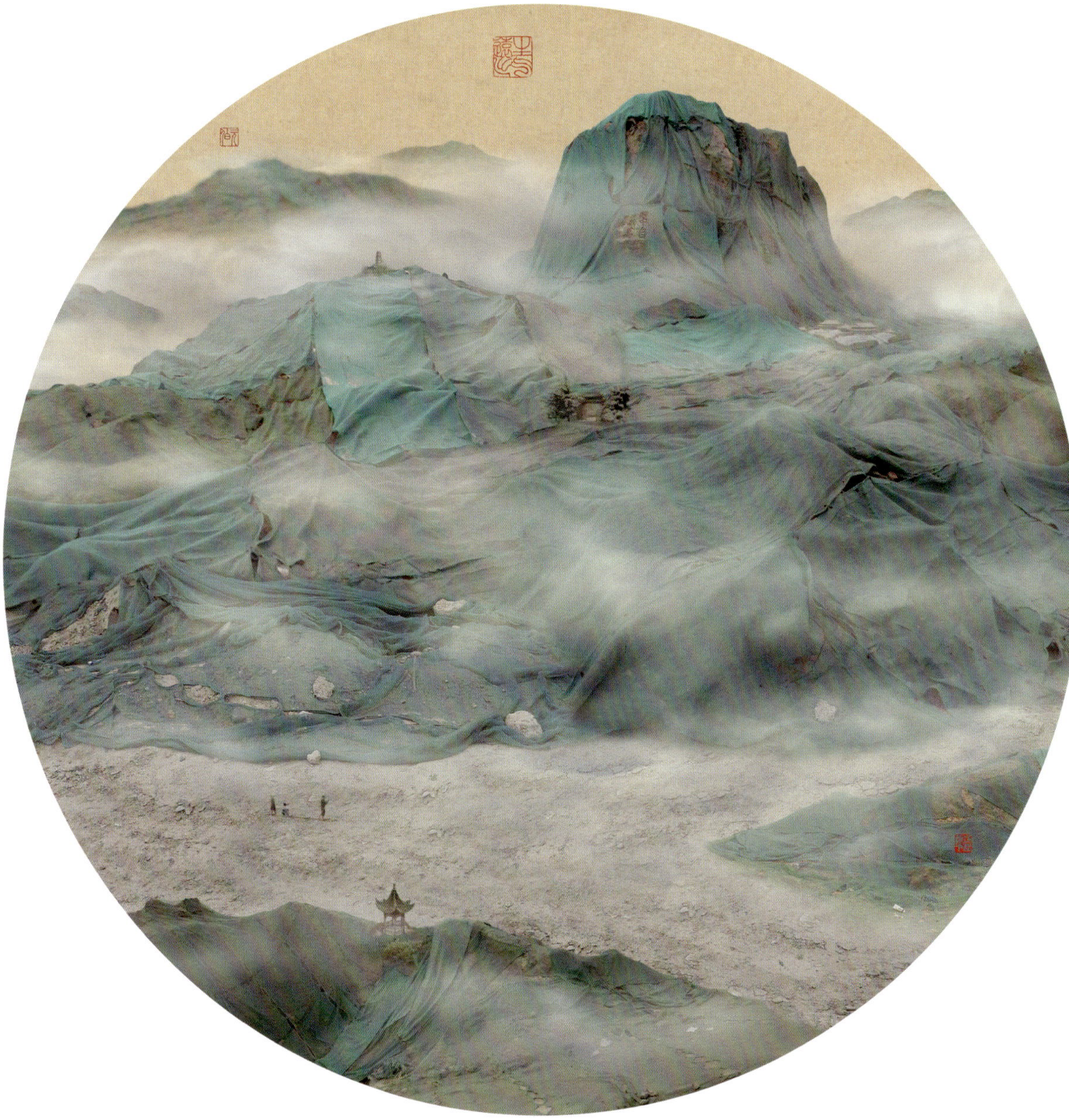

Yao Lu

Chinese, b. 1967

New Landscape Part 1–YL08 Overlapping Waves and Lush Trees

2007

Chromogenic print

31 × 31 in. (78.7 × 78.7 cm)

Loan courtesy of Bruce Silverstein Gallery, New York

Image courtesy of Bruce Silverstein Gallery, New York, and the artist, © Yao Lu

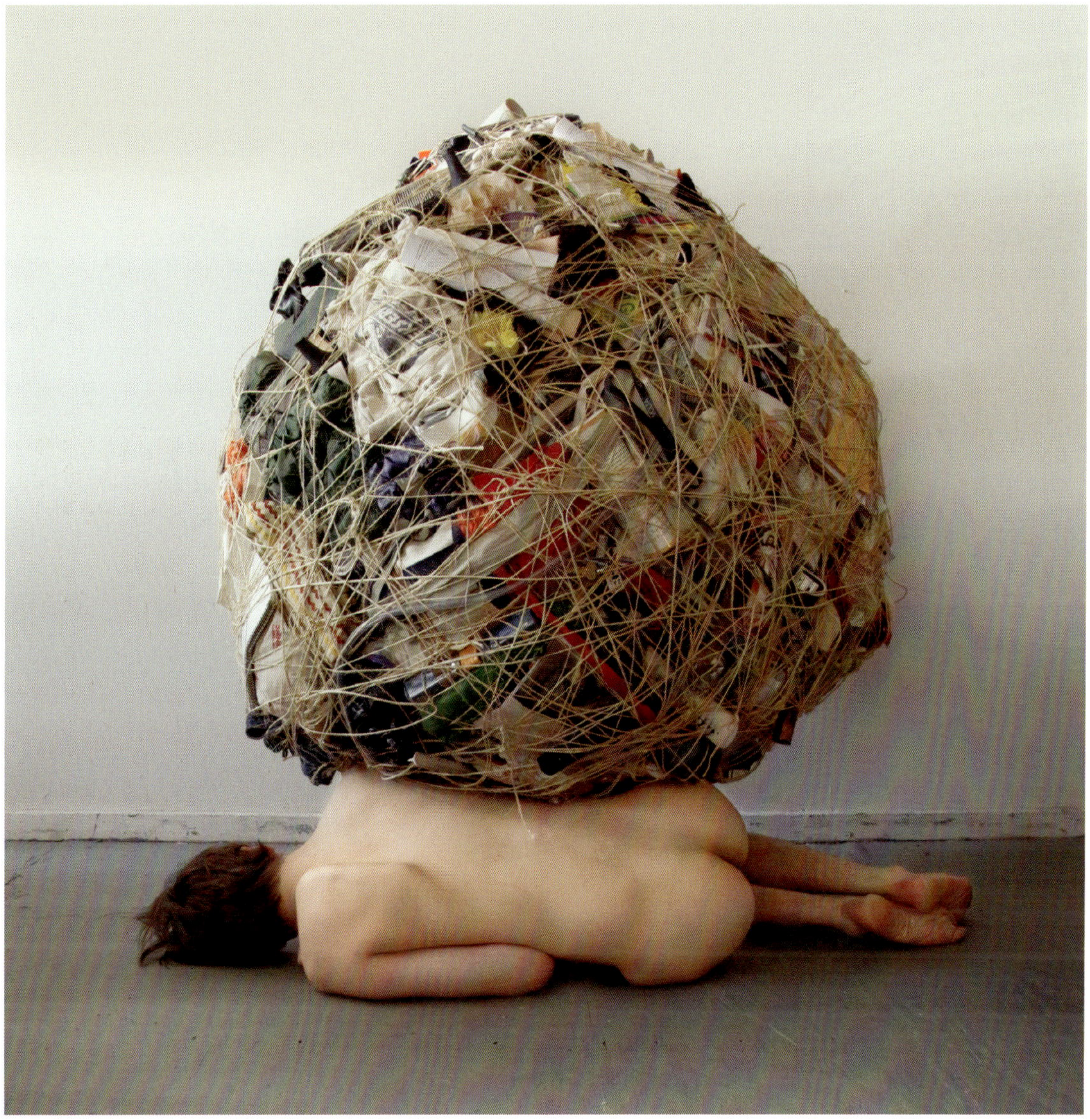

Mary Mattingly

American, b. 1978

Life of Objects

From the series *House and Universe*

2013

Chromogenic dye coupler print

40 × 40 in. (101.6 × 101.6 cm)

Loan courtesy of Robert Mann Gallery, New York

Ghosts remind us that we live in an

impossible present—a time of rupture,

a world haunted with the threat of extinction.

Deep histories tumble in unruly graves that

are bulldozed into gardens of Progress.

—Anna Lowenhaupt Tsing

EXTINCTION

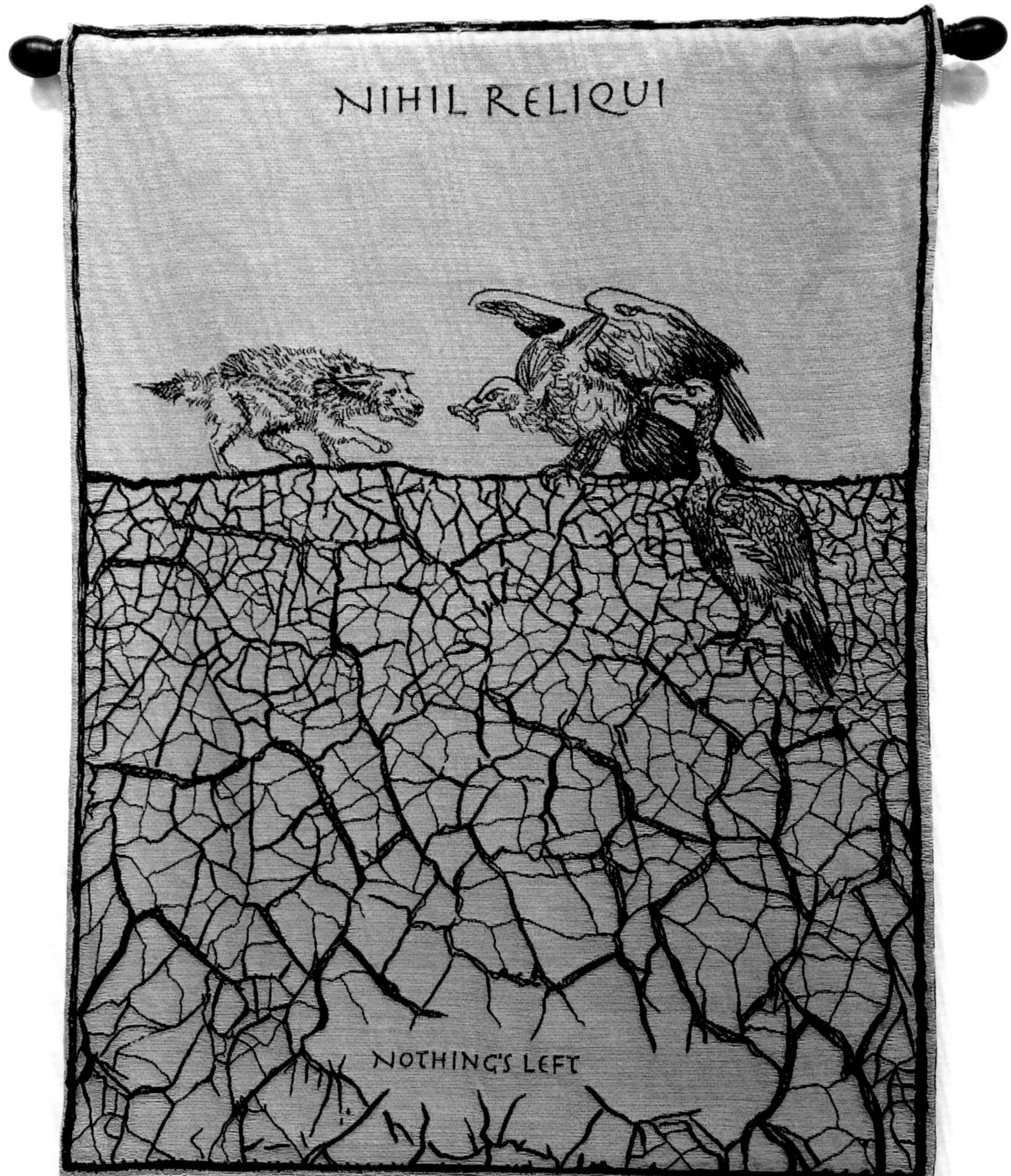

Bethany Taylor
American, b. 1969
NIHIL RELIQUI: NOTHING IS LEFT
2015
Emblematic jacquard woven tapestries
36 × 26 in. (91.4 × 66 cm)

Courtesy of the artist

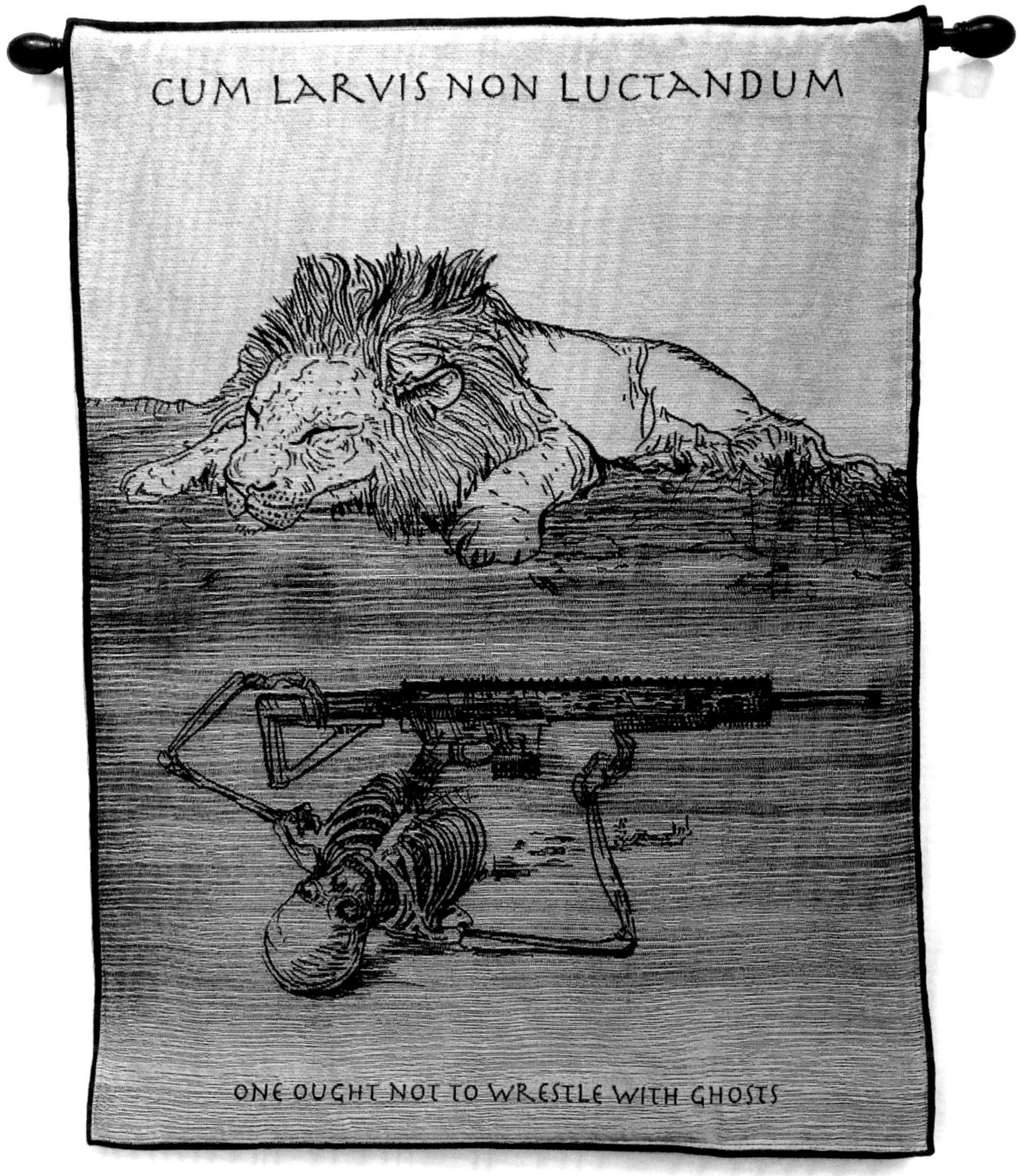

Bethany Taylor

American, b. 1969

CUM LARVIS NON LUCTANDUM: ONE OUGHT NOT TO WRESTLE WITH GHOSTS

2015

Emblematic jacquard woven tapestries

36 × 26 in. (91.4 × 66 cm)

Courtesy of the artist

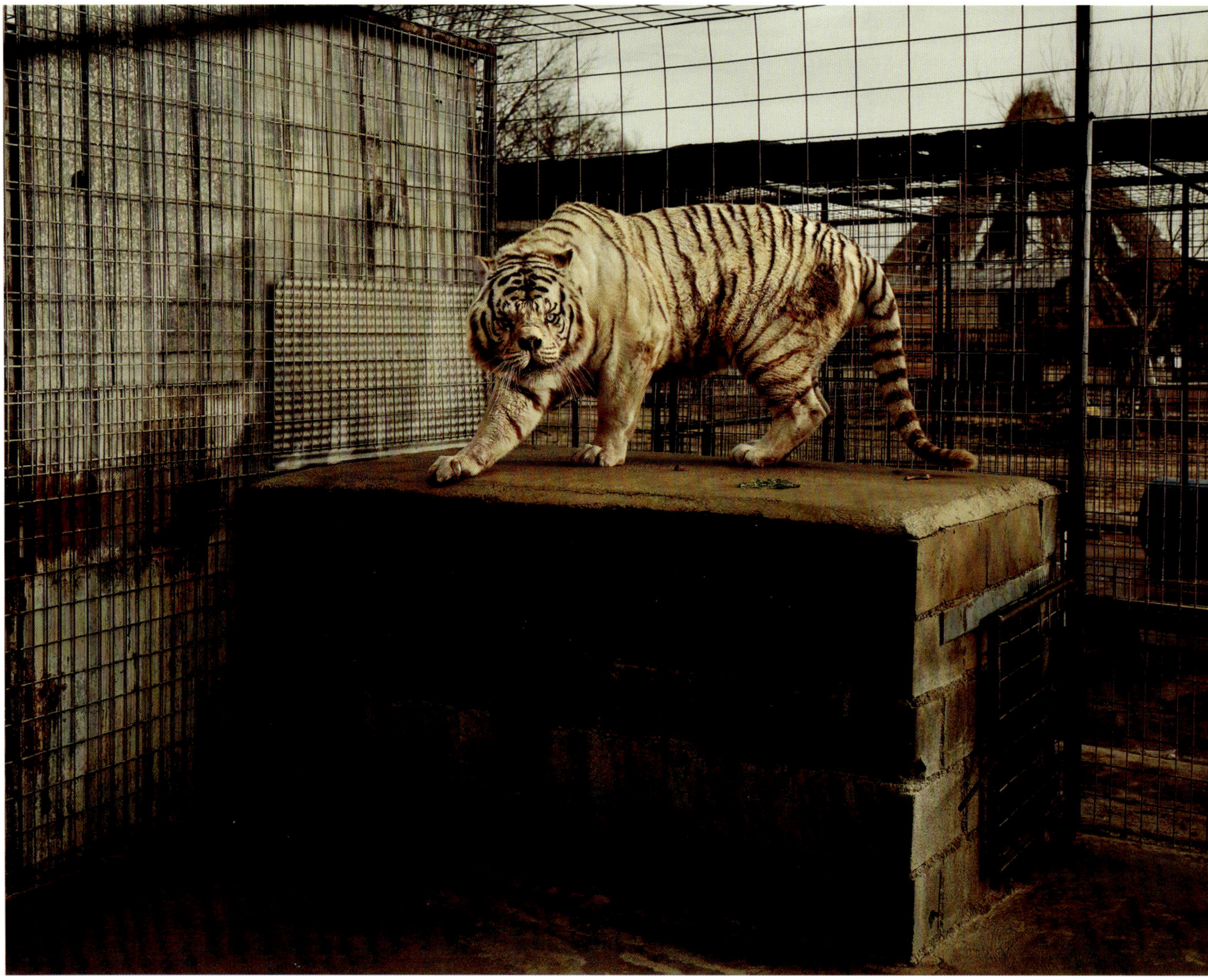

Taryn Simon

American, b. 1975

White Tiger (Kenny), Selective Inbreeding

Turpentine Creek Wildlife Refuge and Foundation

Eureka Springs, Arkansas

From the series *An American Index of the Hidden and Unfamiliar*

2007

Framed archival inkjet print

37¼ × 44¾ in. (94.62 × 113.67 cm)

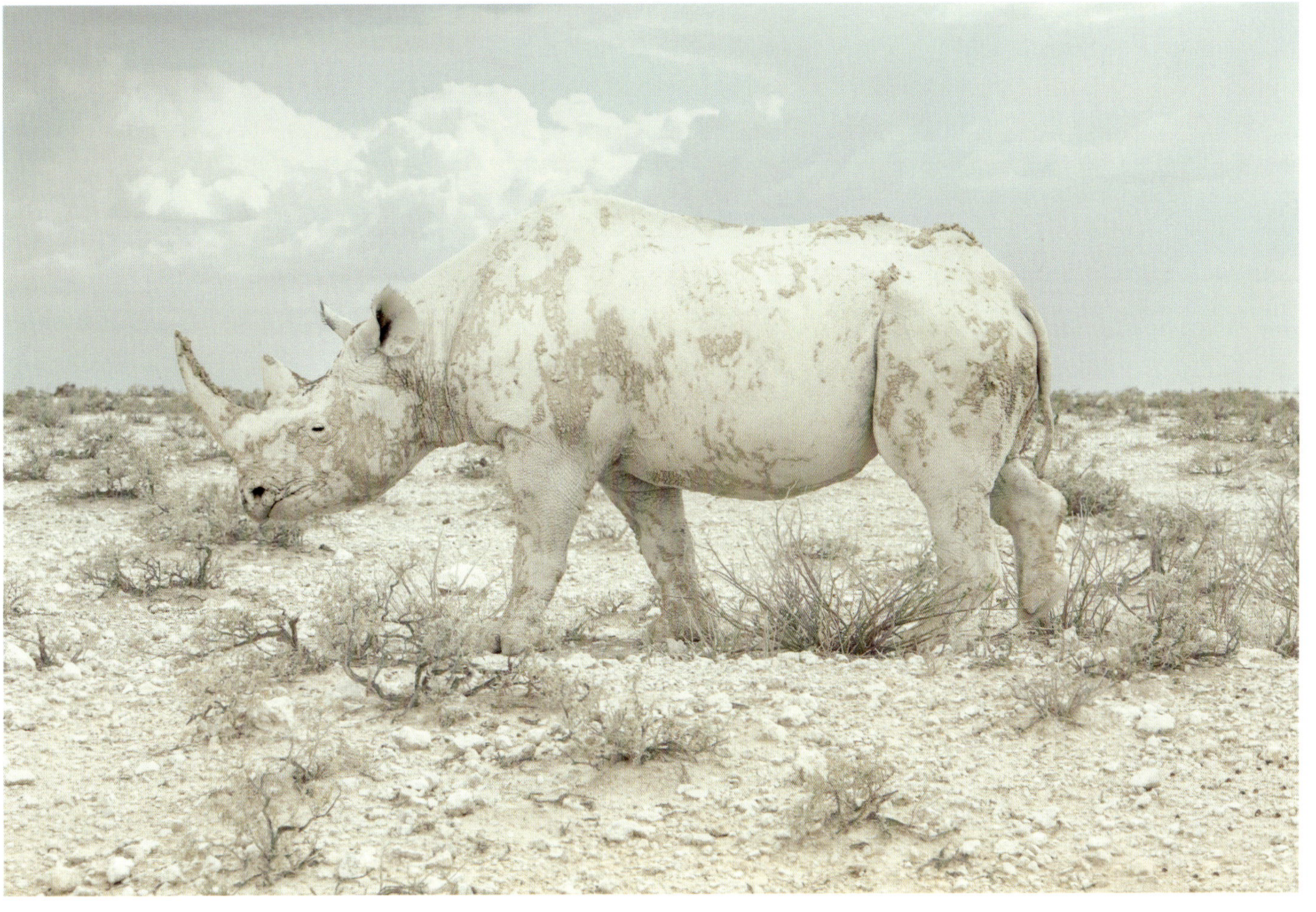

Maroesjka Lavigne

Belgian, b. 1989

White Rhino, Namibia

From the series *Land of Nothingness*

2015

Archival pigment print

29½ × 43½ in. (74.9 × 110.5 cm)

Courtesy of Robert Mann Gallery, New York

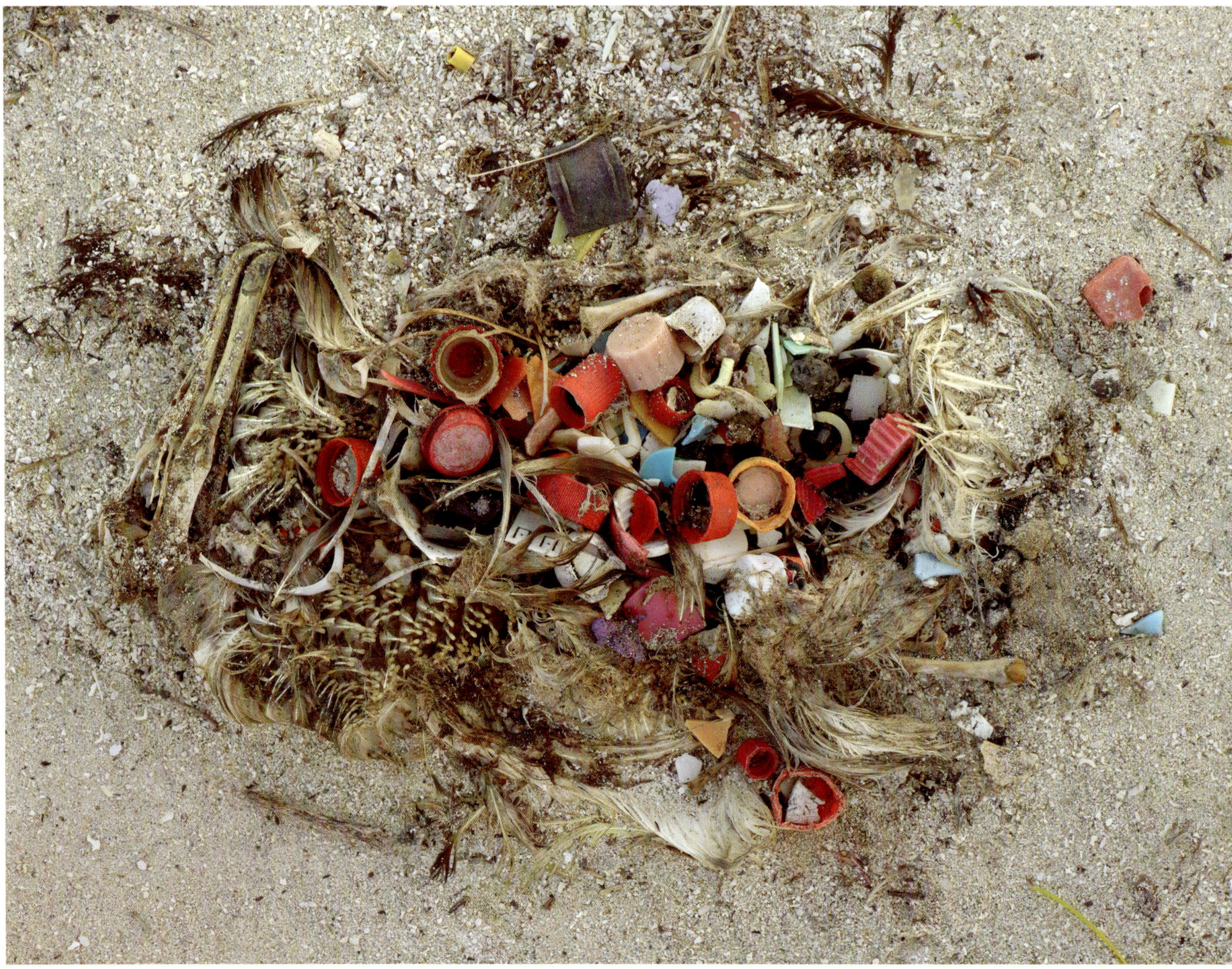

Chris Jordan

American, b. 1963

CF000668, unaltered stomach contents of juvenile Laysan albatross (2009)

From the series *Midway: Message from the Gyre*

2009

Archival pigment print

Framed: 26 × 32 in. (66 × 81.3 cm)

Courtesy of the artist

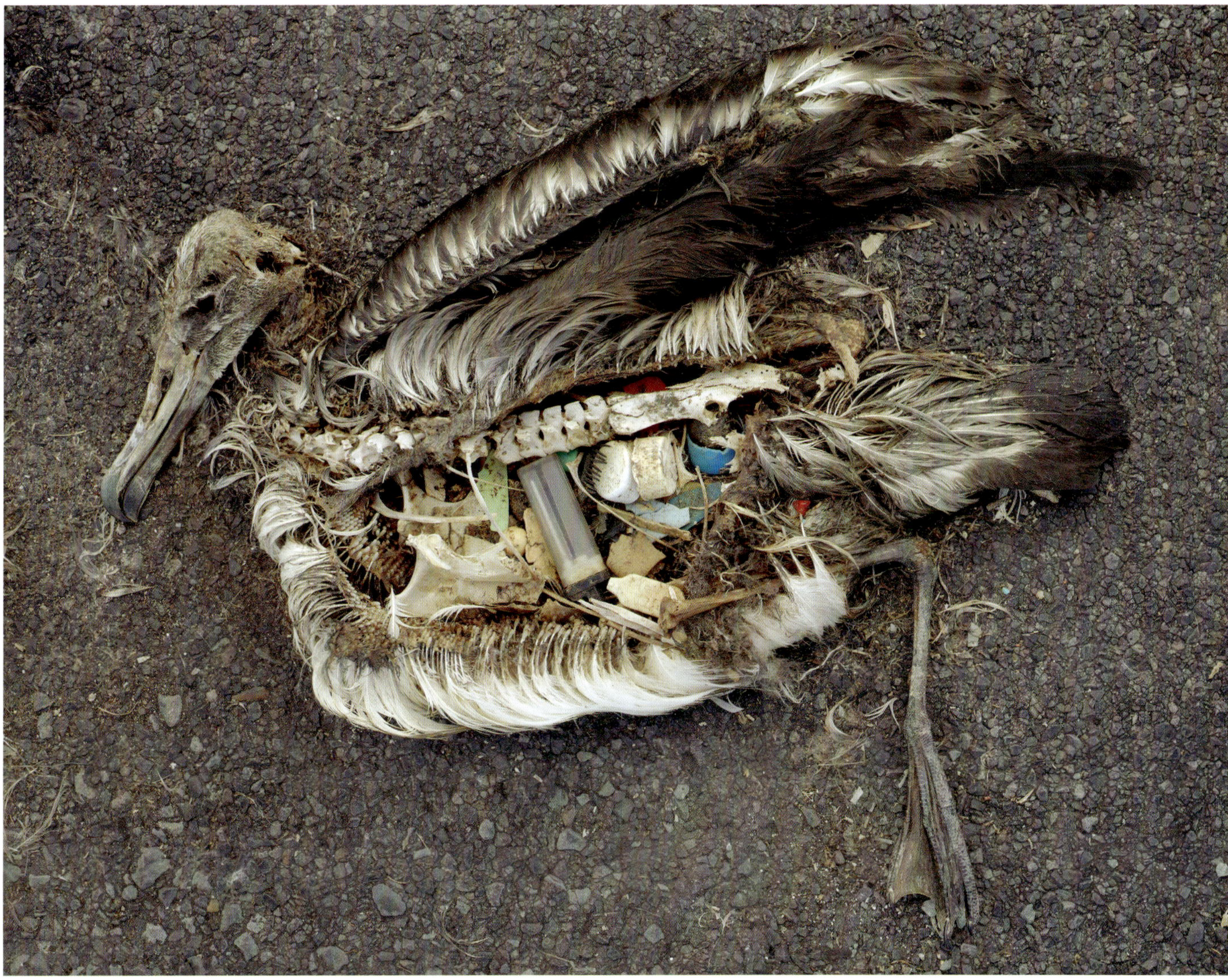

Chris Jordan

American, b. 1963

CF000313, unaltered stomach contents of juvenile Laysan albatross (2009)

From the series *Midway: Message from the Gyre*

2009

Archival pigment print

Framed: 26 × 32 in. (66 × 81.3 cm)

Courtesy of the artist

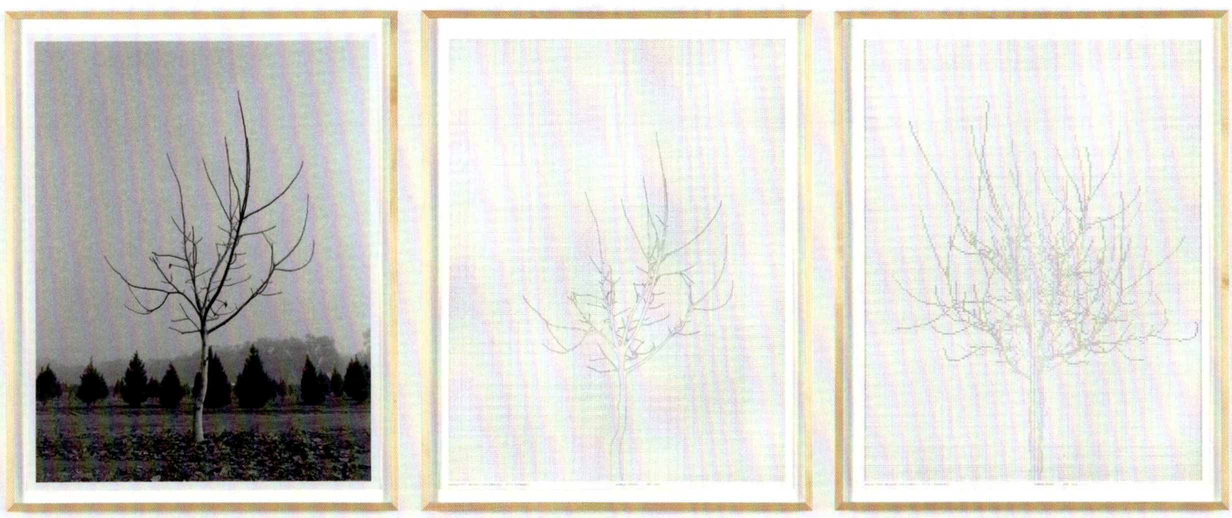

Charles Gaines

American, b. 1944

Walnut Tree Orchard, (2nd Version), Set 3

1975–2012

Photograph, ink on paper, three panels

Triptych, each framed: 31½ × 25½ × 1½ in. (80 × 64.8 × 3.8 cm)

Loan courtesy of Paula Cooper Gallery, New York

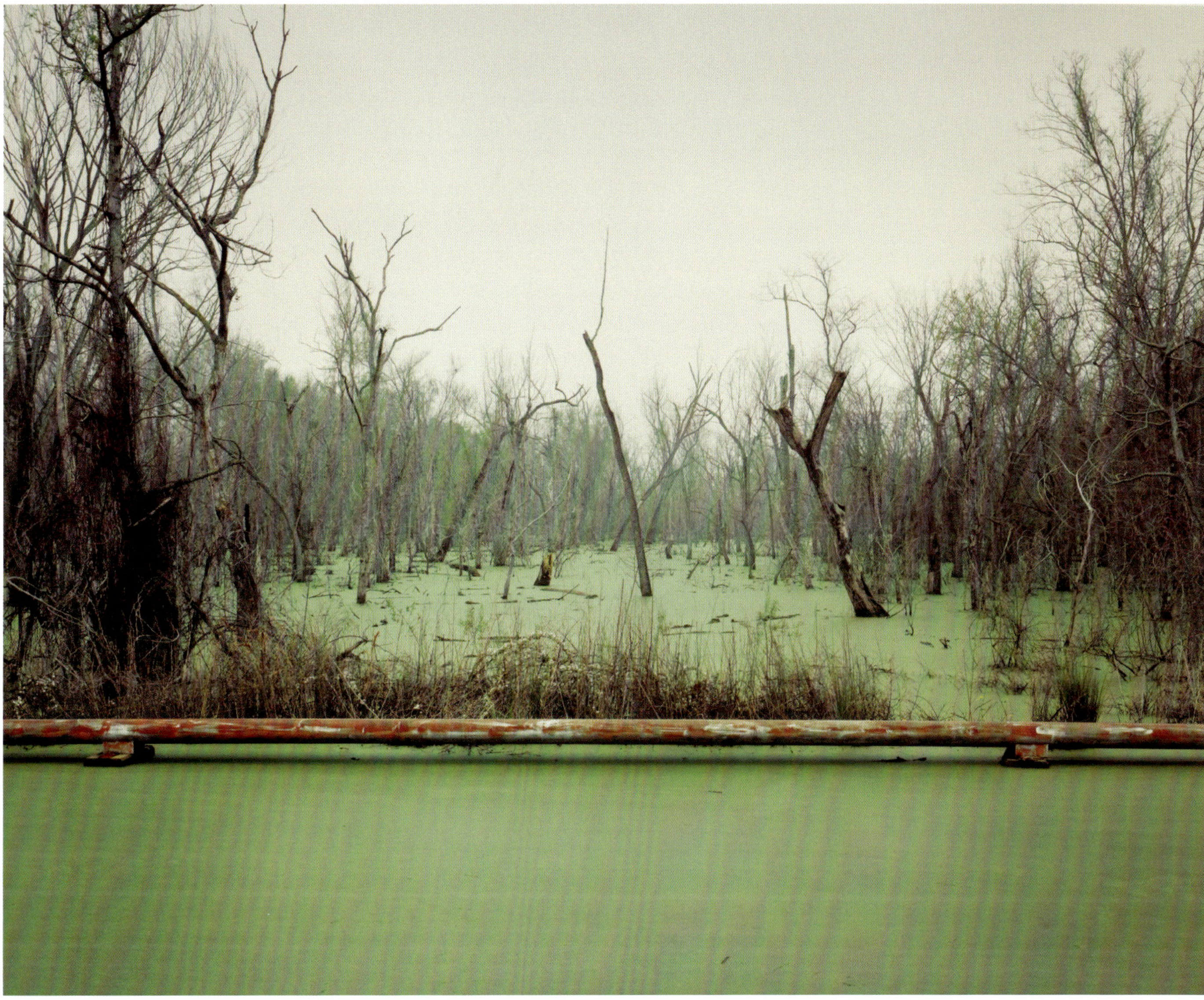

Richard Misrach

American, b. 1949

Swamp and Pipeline, Cancer Alley, Louisiana

1998

Chromogenic development print
[Fuji Crystal Archive]

38½ × 48³⁄₁₆ in. (97.8 × 122.4 cm)

Harn Museum of Art collection

Museum purchase, gift of Dr. and Mrs. David A. Cofrin

2001.2

Photography by Randy Batista

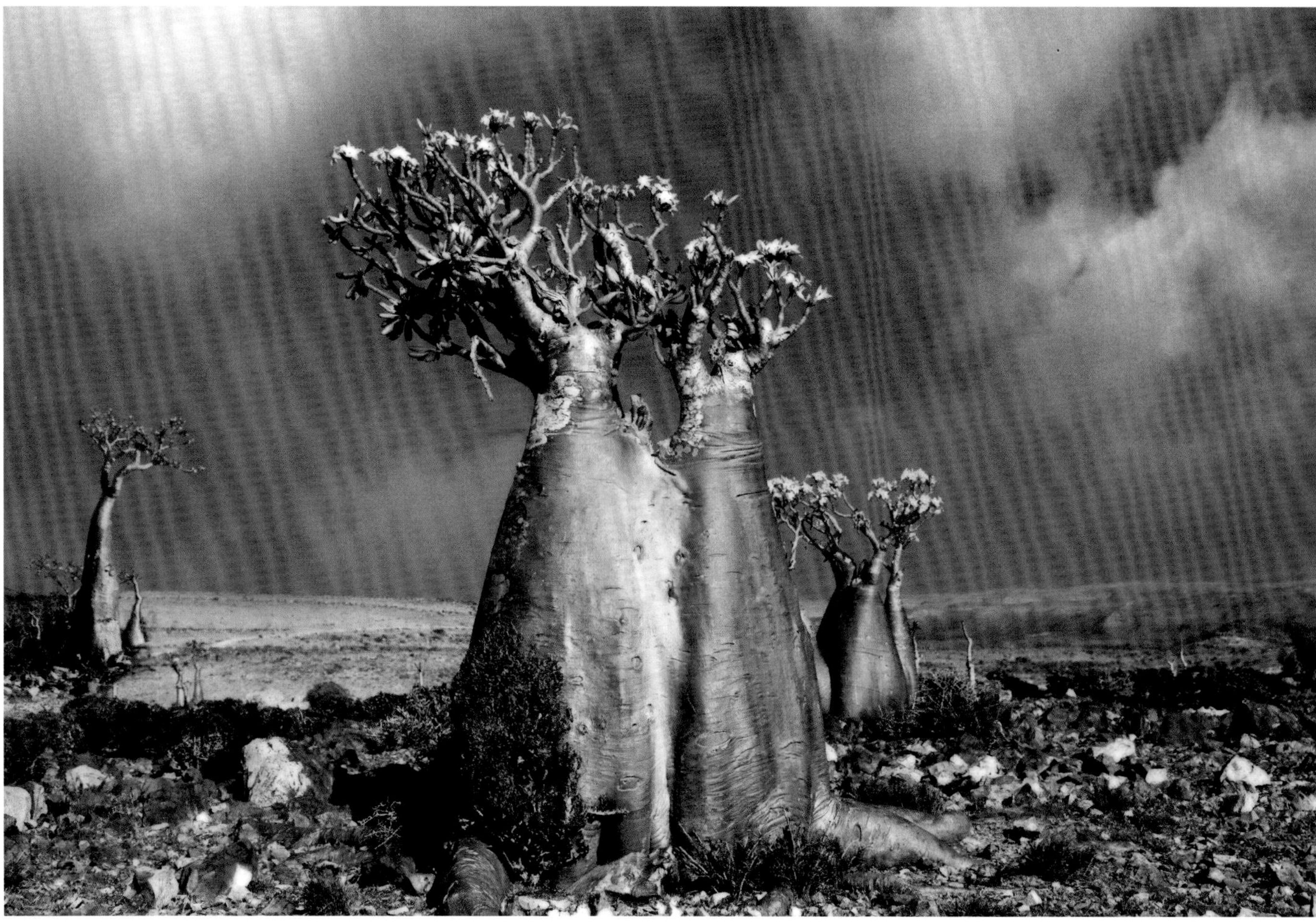

Beth Moon

American, b. 1955

Desert Rose (Wadi Fa Lang)

2010–2012

Hand-coated platinum/palladium metals on 100% cotton paper

22 × 30 in. (55.9 × 76.2 cm)

Courtesy of the artist

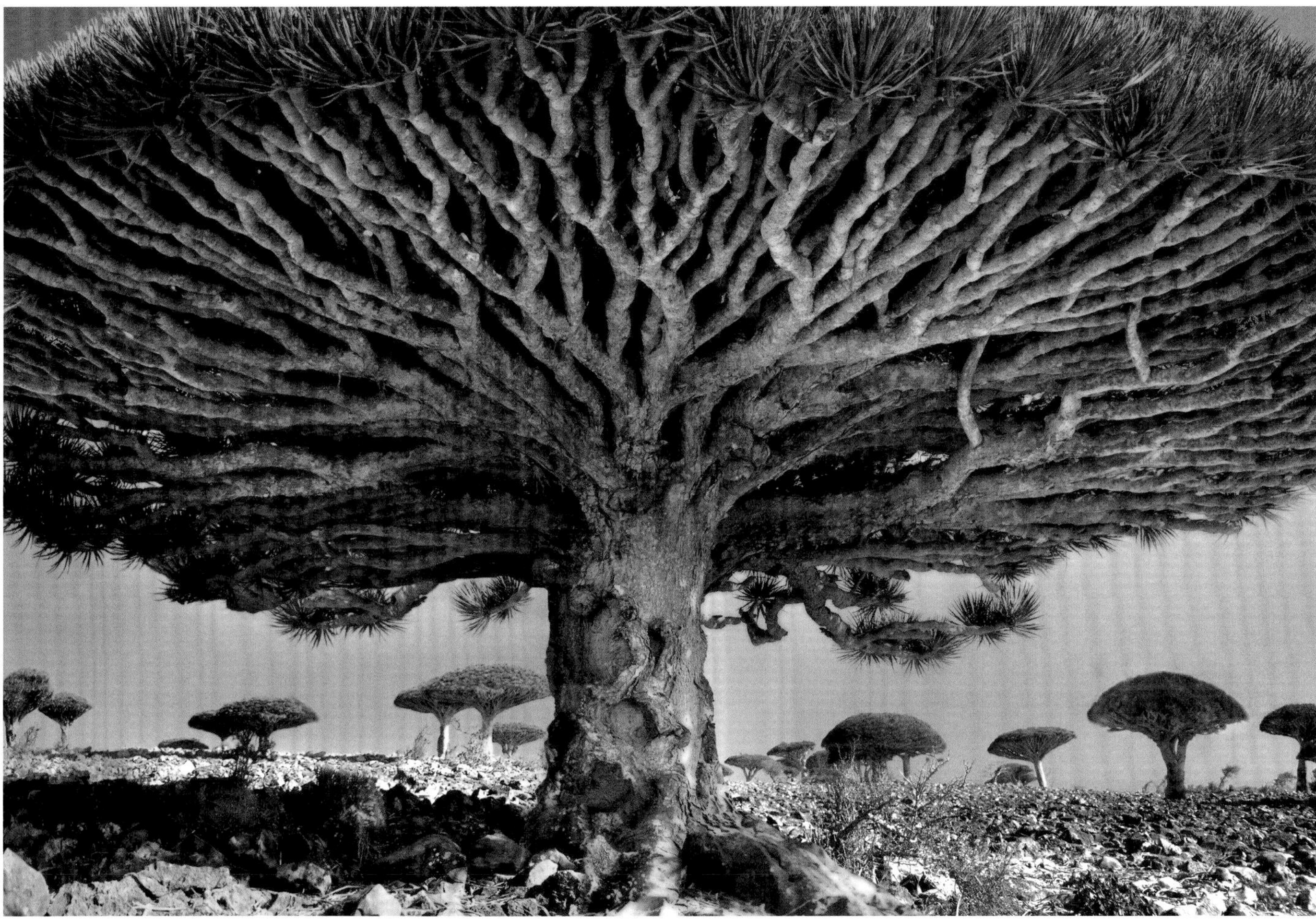

Beth Moon
American, b. 1955
Heart of the Dragon
2010
Hand-coated platinum/palladium metals on 100% cotton paper
22 × 30 in. (55.9 × 76.2 cm)
Courtesy of Corden Potts Gallery, San Francisco

PfE0482-IT-270110

Orange Grove, Rosarno, Italy 2010
In January 2010 the price obtained by Calabrian citrus growers for their Moro and Navel oranges was five euro cents per kilogram. They paid their mostly illegally employed and undocumented African and Eastern European seasonal workers between €20 and €25 for a day's work. Depending on the variety and the state of the trees a worker can pick between four and seven hundred kilograms of oranges in a day. The business was no longer profitable and many farmers left the fruit to rot.
During the 2009–2010 harvest there were between four and five thousand migrants living in and around Rosarno, most of them in abandoned buildings or plastic shelters, without running water or toilets.
On 7 January 2010 local youths fired an air-gun at African orange-pickers returning from work and injured two of them. The ensuing demonstration by migrant workers ended in severe clashes with parts of the local population, during which cars were set on fire and shop windows broken. Accommodation used by seasonal workers was burned and hundreds fled, fearing the local citizens or deportation by the authorities.
On 9 January, under police protection from jeering onlookers, about eight hundred Africans were bussed out to emergency accommodation in Crotone and Bari.
A Season in Hell: MSF Report on the Conditions of Migrants Employed in the Agricultural Sector in Southern Italy, January 2008; tagesschau.de, 10 January 2010; interviews with orange farmers and seasonal labourers, Rosarno, 27–29 January 2010

Plantage, Rosarno, Italien 2010
Für ein Kilogramm Moro- oder Navelorangen bekommen kalabrische Obstbauern im Januar 2010 von ihren Abnehmern fünf Cent. Den zumeist illegal beschäftigten afrikanischen und osteuropäischen Saisonarbeitern zahlen sie zwischen 20 und 25 Euro für einen Arbeitstag. Je nach Sorte und Baumbeschaffenheit pflückt ein Arbeiter täglich 400 bis 700 Kilogramm Orangen. Da sich für die Bauern das Geschäft nicht mehr rechnet, stellen viele die Ernte ein.
Während der Saison leben vier- bis fünftausend Immigranten in und um Rosarno, die meisten in baufälligen Gebäuden oder Plastikverschlägen ohne fließendes Wasser oder Sanitäranlagen.
Am 7. Januar 2010 schießen Jugendliche mit dem Luftgewehr auf von der Arbeit zurückkehrende schwarze Orangenpflücker und verletzen dabei zwei von ihnen. Daraufhin kommt es bei einer Demonstration von Landarbeitern zu Sachbeschädigungen und schweren Zusammenstößen mit Teilen der einheimischen Bevölkerung.
Während der folgenden zwei Tage werden mehrere Brandanschläge auf die Unterkünfte von Saisonarbeitern verübt. Hunderte fliehen vor aufgebrachten Bürgern oder fürchten eine Abschiebung durch die Behörden. Unter Polizeischutz und Zuschauerapplaus werden am 9. Januar 2010 um die 800 schwarze Migranten in Bussen aus der Stadt in Notunterkünfte nach Crotone und Bari gebracht.
A Season in Hell: MSF Report on the Conditions of Migrants Employed in the Agricultural Sector in Southern Italy, Januar 2008; tagesschau.de, 10.1.2010; Gespräche mit Orangenbauern und Saisonarbeitern, Rosarno, 27. - 9.1.2010

Eva Leitolf, Postcards from Europe, *work from the ongoing archive*

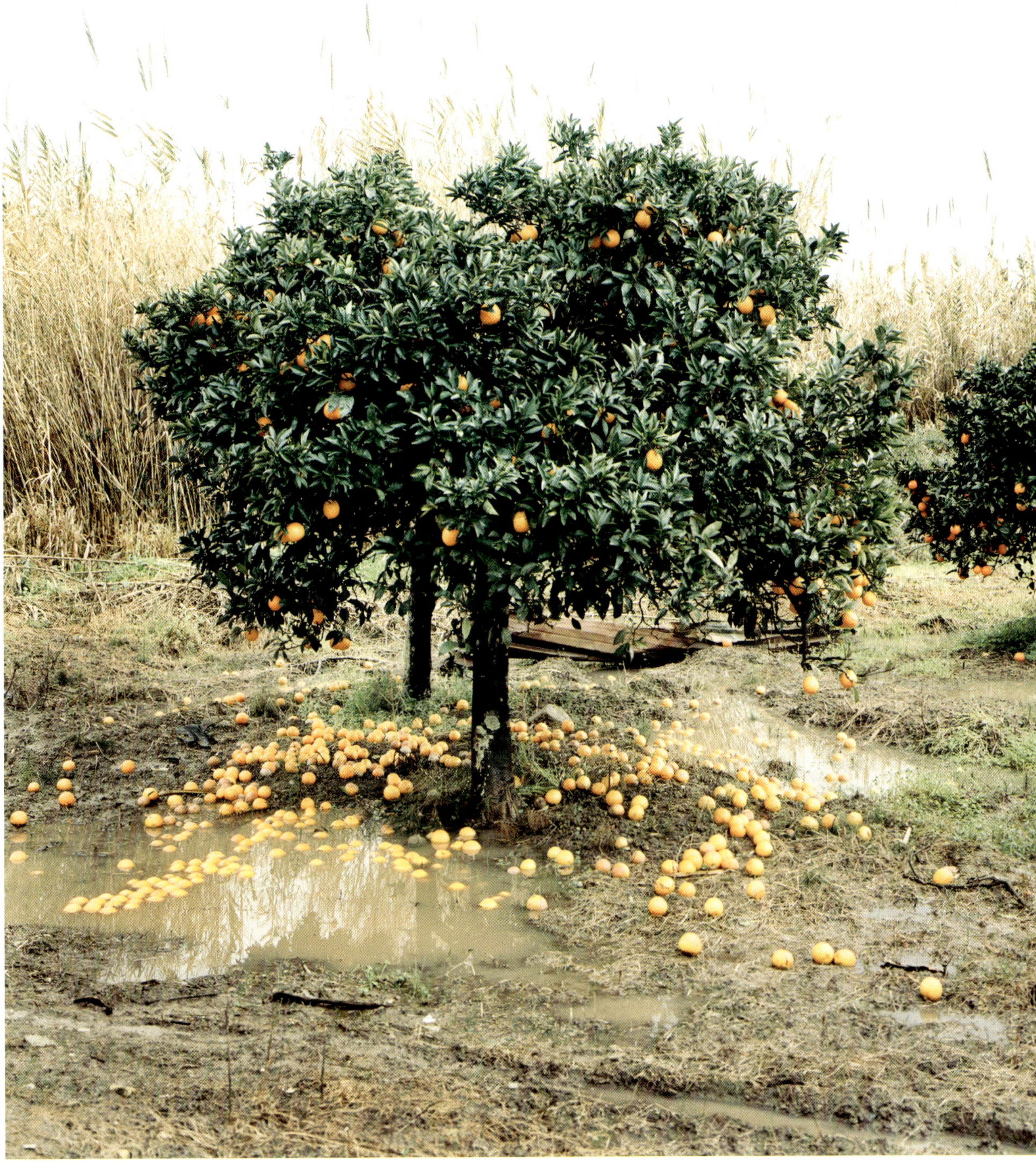

Eva Leitolf
German, b. 1966
Orange Grove, Rosarno, Italy 2010
2010
Archival pigment print on board
32⅞ × 27 in. (83.5 × 68.6 cm)
shelf, postcards
Courtesy of the artist

My art is grounded in the belief of one universal energy which runs through everything: from insect to man, from man to specter, from specter to plant, from plant to galaxy.—Ana Mendieta

SYMBIOSIS & MULTISPECIES

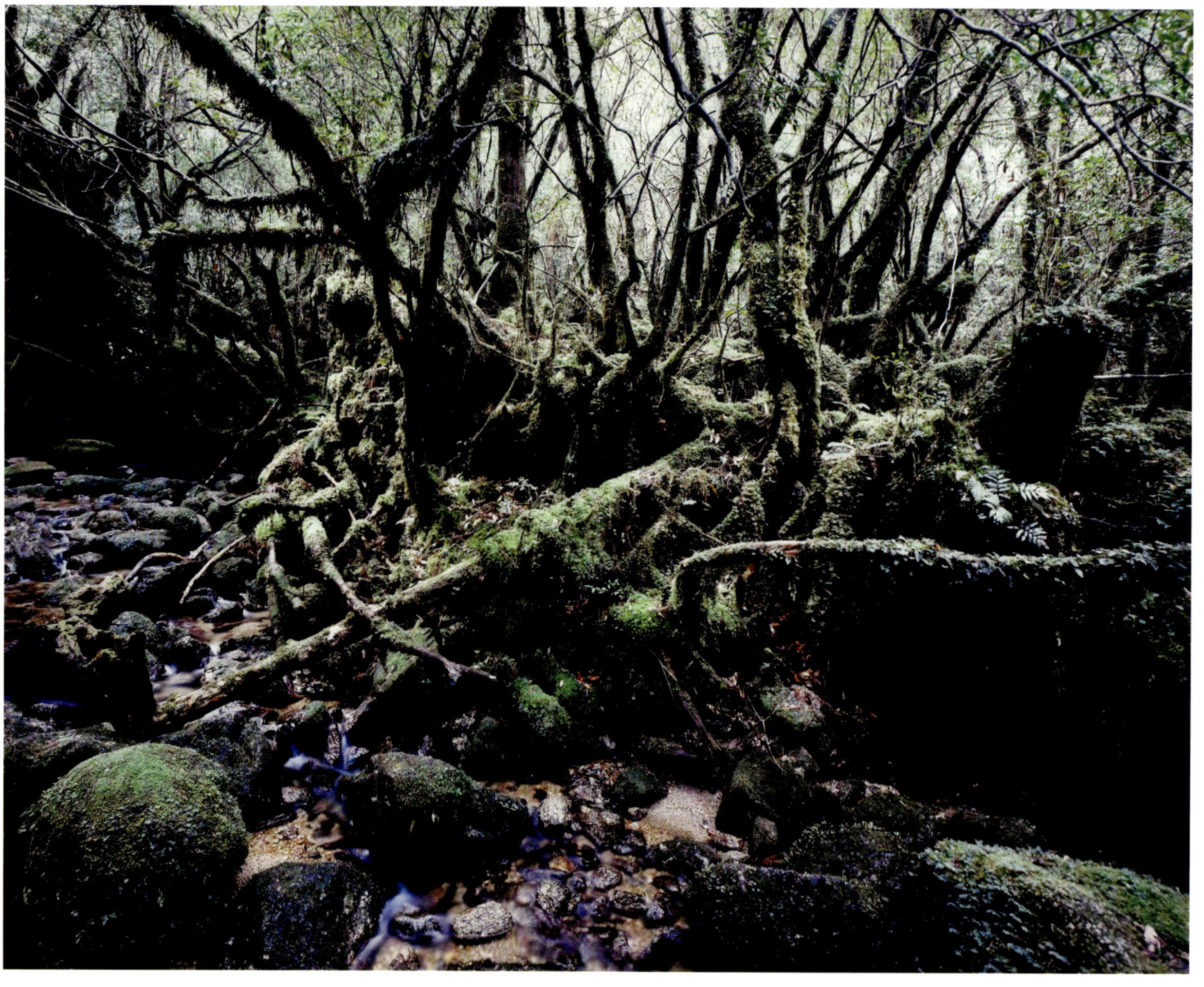

Thomas Struth
German, b. 1954
Paradise 14, Yakushima, Japan 1999
1999
Chromogenic print
55 in. × 5 ft. 9⅝ in. (139.7 × 176.8 cm)

Harn Museum of Art collection

Museum purchase, gift of Dr. and Mrs. David A. Cofrin
2001.3

Photography by Randy Batista

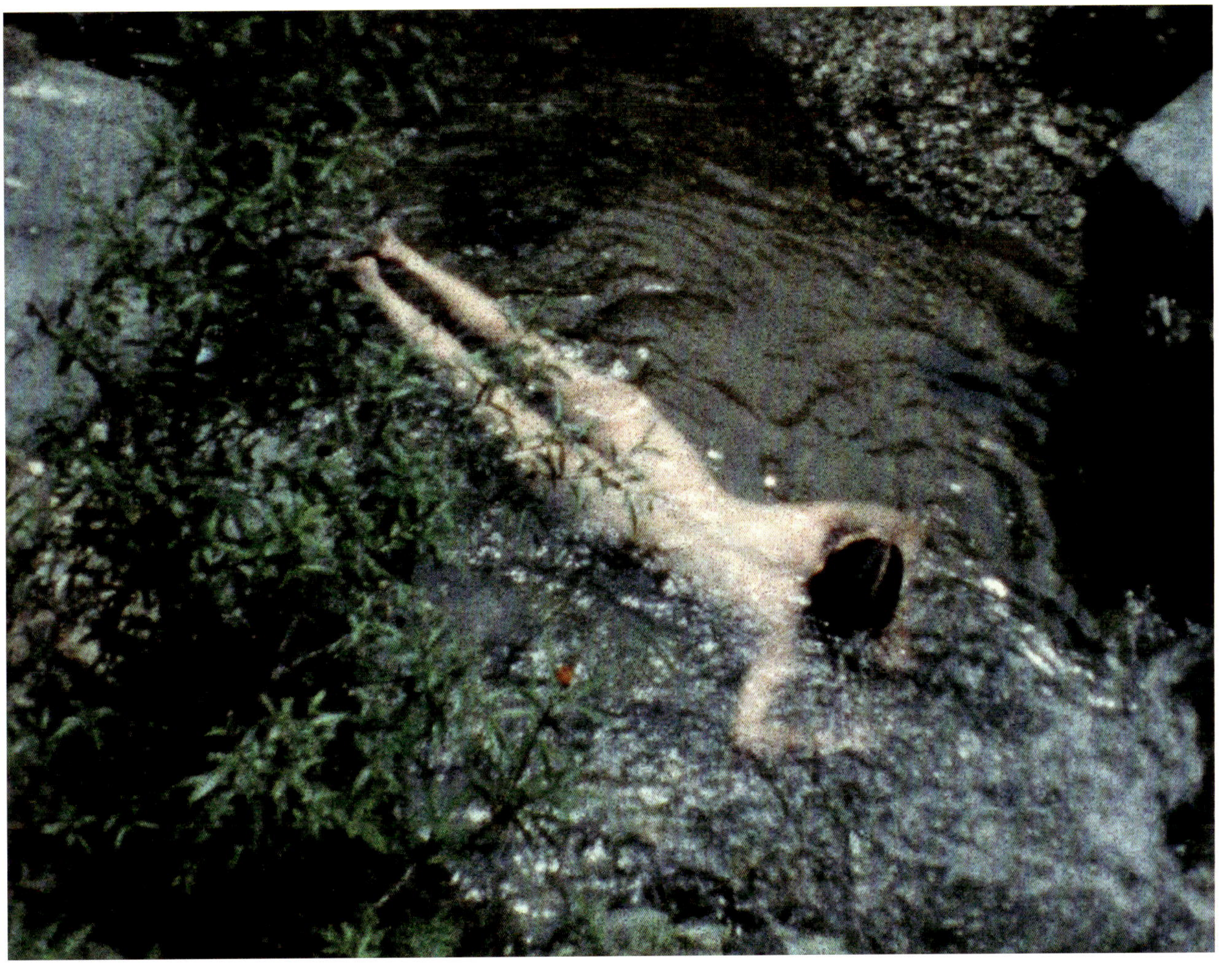

Ana Mendieta

American b. Cuba, 1948–1985

Creek

1974

Digital video transferred from Super 8 film, color, silent, 3 min., 11 sec.

Loan courtesy of The Estate of Ana Mendieta Collection, LLC., and Galerie Lelong & Co., New York

Dana Levy

Israeli

Emerging from the Swamp

2014

Single-channel film, 2 min. 30 sec.

Courtesy of the artist and Braverman Gallery

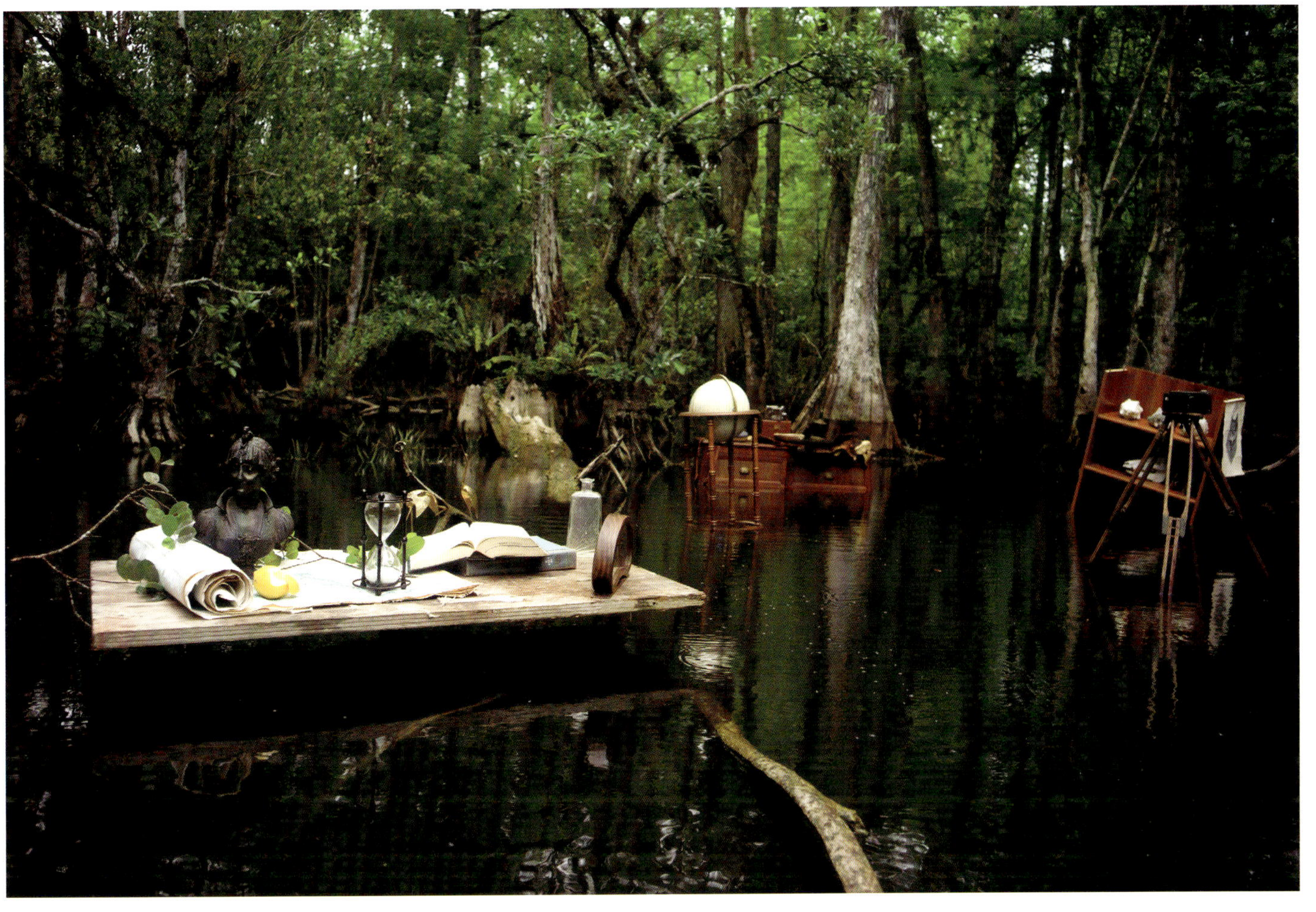

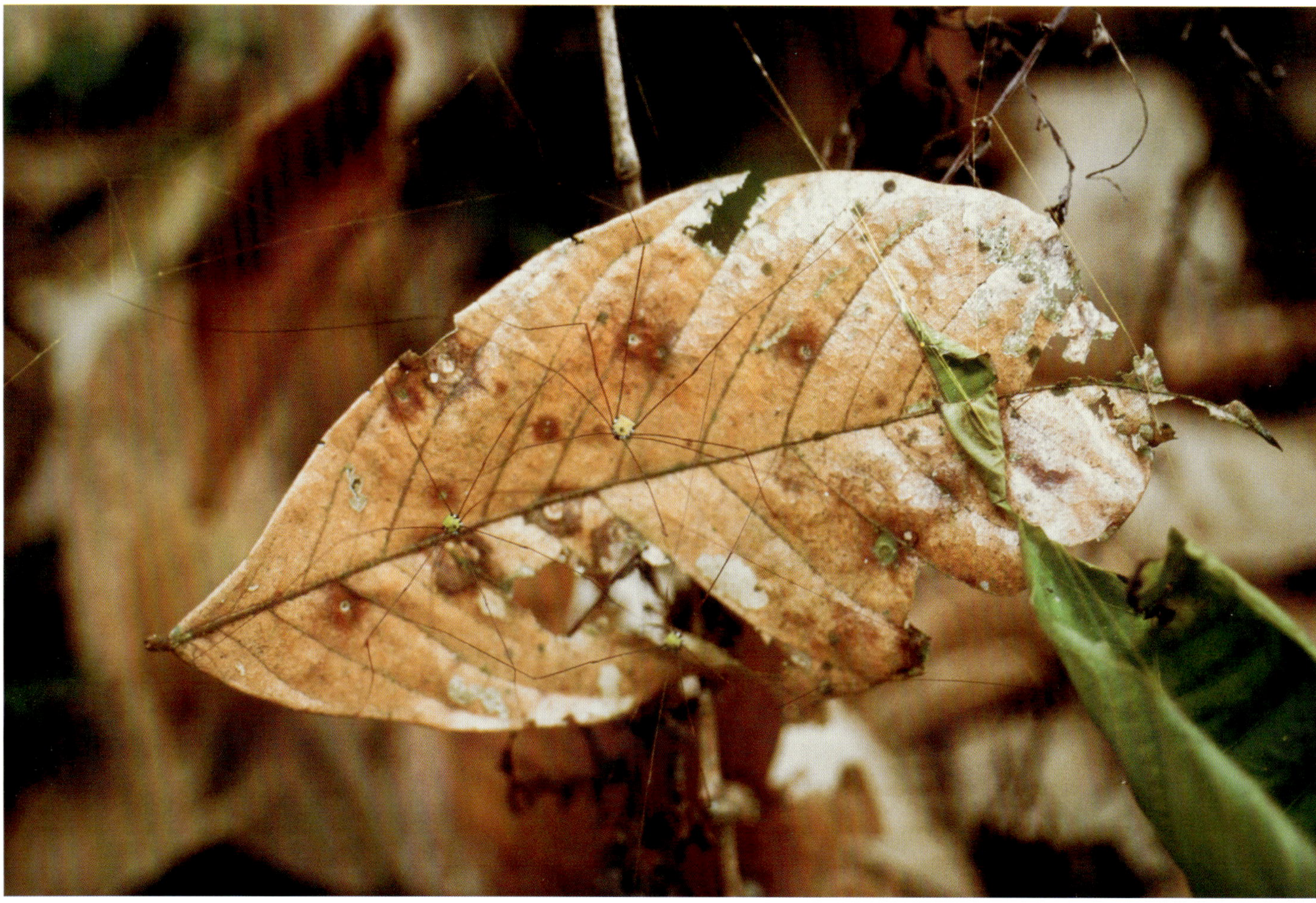

Gabriel Orozco

American b. Mexico, 1962

Spider House

2001

Cibachrome

16 × 20 in. (40.6 × 50.8 cm)

Harn Museum of Art Collection

Museum purchase, funds provided by the Caroline Julier and James G. Richardson Acquisition Fund

2002.2

Photography by Randy Batista

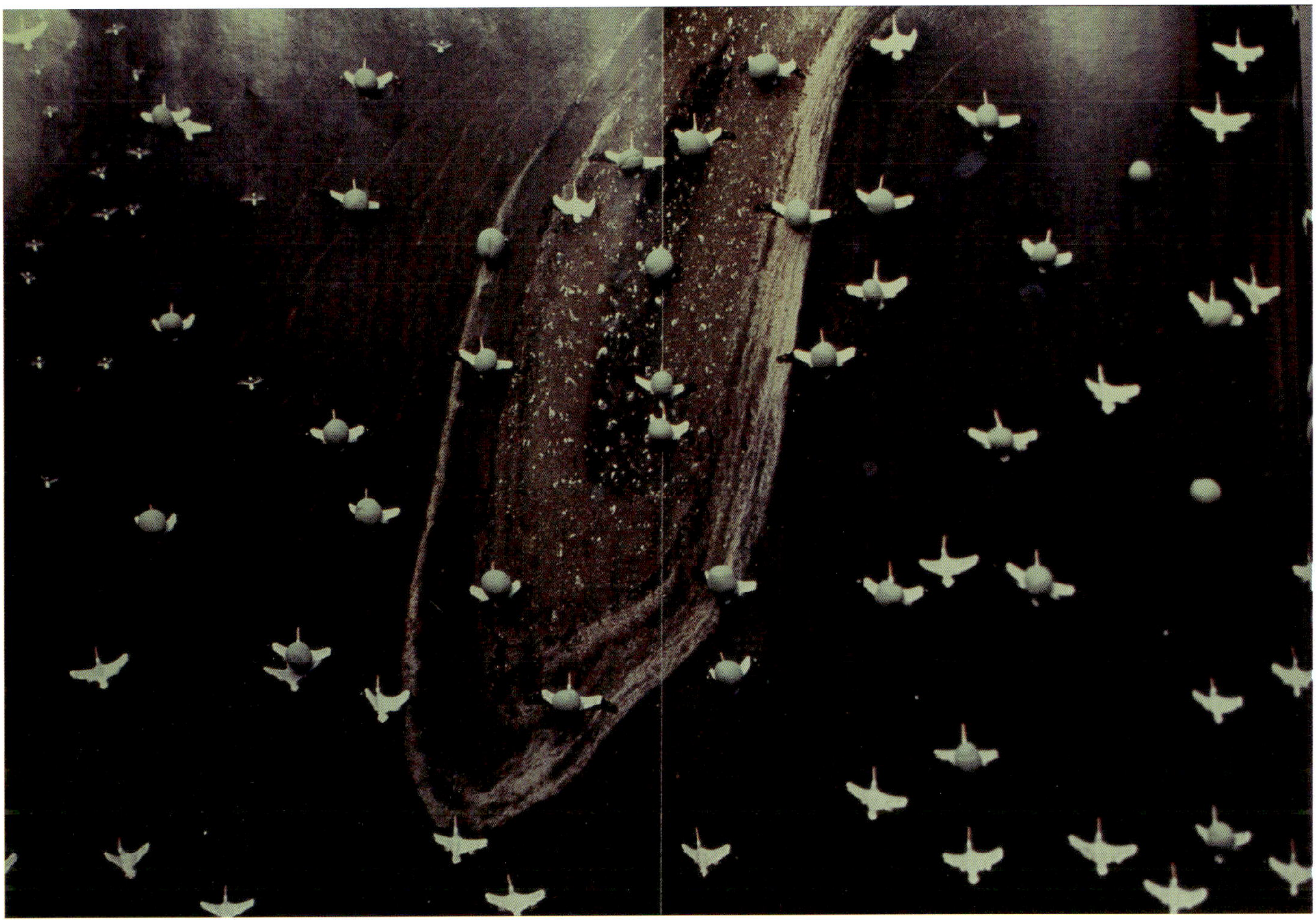

Gabriel Orozco

American b. Mexico, 1962

Migration

1993

Dye destruction print

12 7/16 × 18 5/8 in. (31.59 × 47.31 cm)

San Francisco Museum of Modern Art, Natasha and Jacques Gelman Accessions Fund purchase

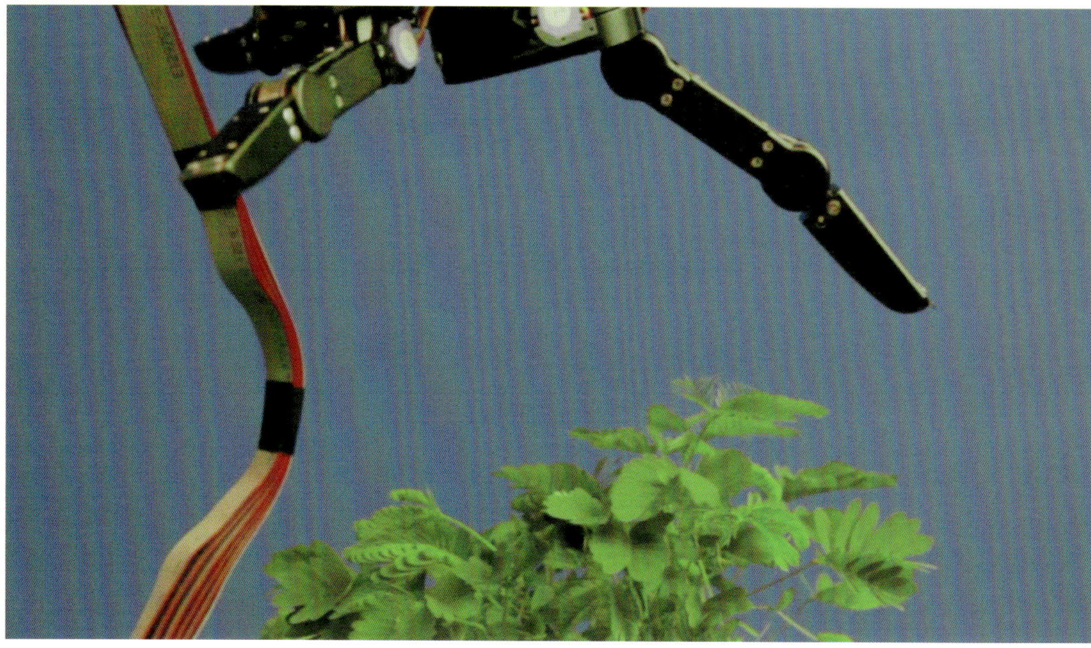

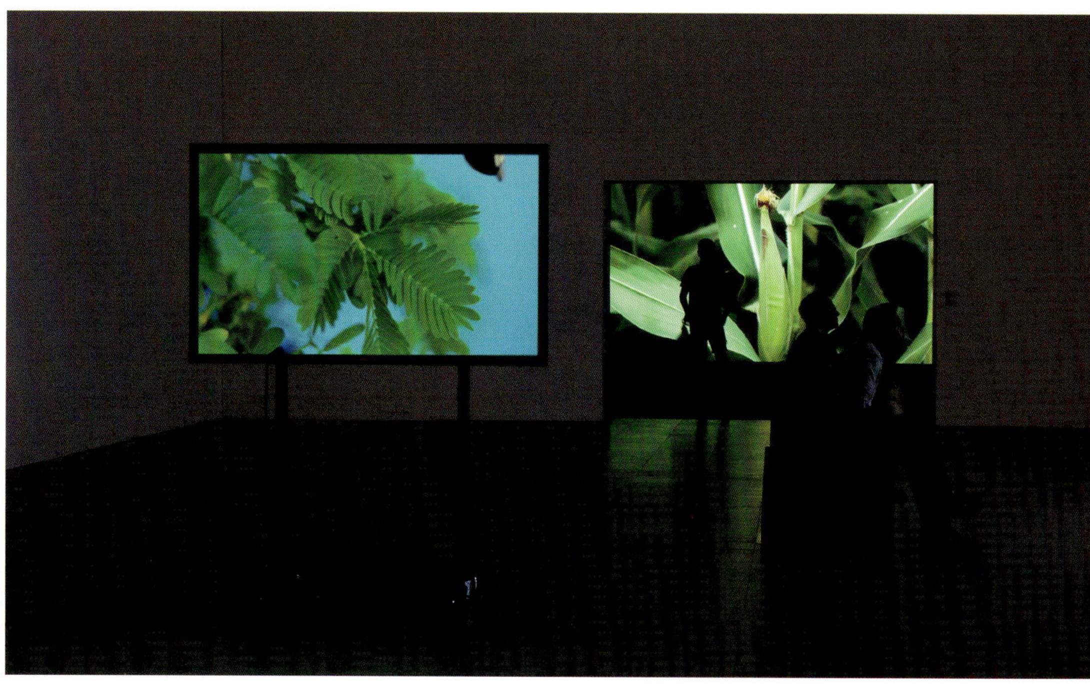

Pedro Neves Marques

Portuguese, b. 1984

The Pudic Relation Between Machine and Plant

2016

Color video, sound, 2 min. 30 sec.

Courtesy of the artist and Galleria Umberto di Marino

Installation photo by David Rato. Exhibition view of *Learning to Live with the Enemy,* including the films *The Pudic Relation Between Machine and Plant* (2016) and *YWY, The Android* (2017) at Museu Coleção Berardo, Lisbon, 2017

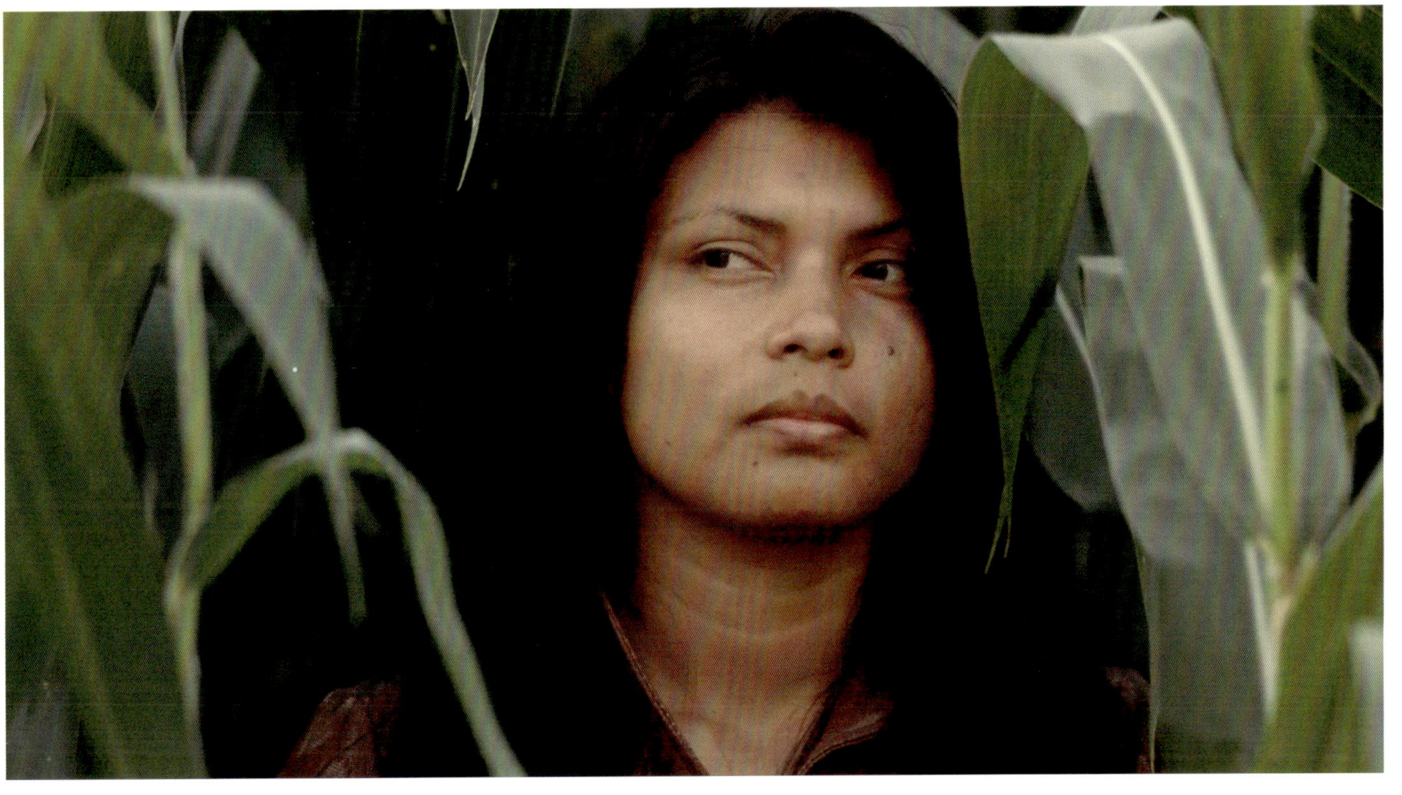

Pedro Neves Marques
Portuguese, b. 1984
YWY, The Android
2017
Color video, Portuguese with subtitles, 7 min. 27 sec.
Courtesy of the artist and Galleria Umberto di Marino

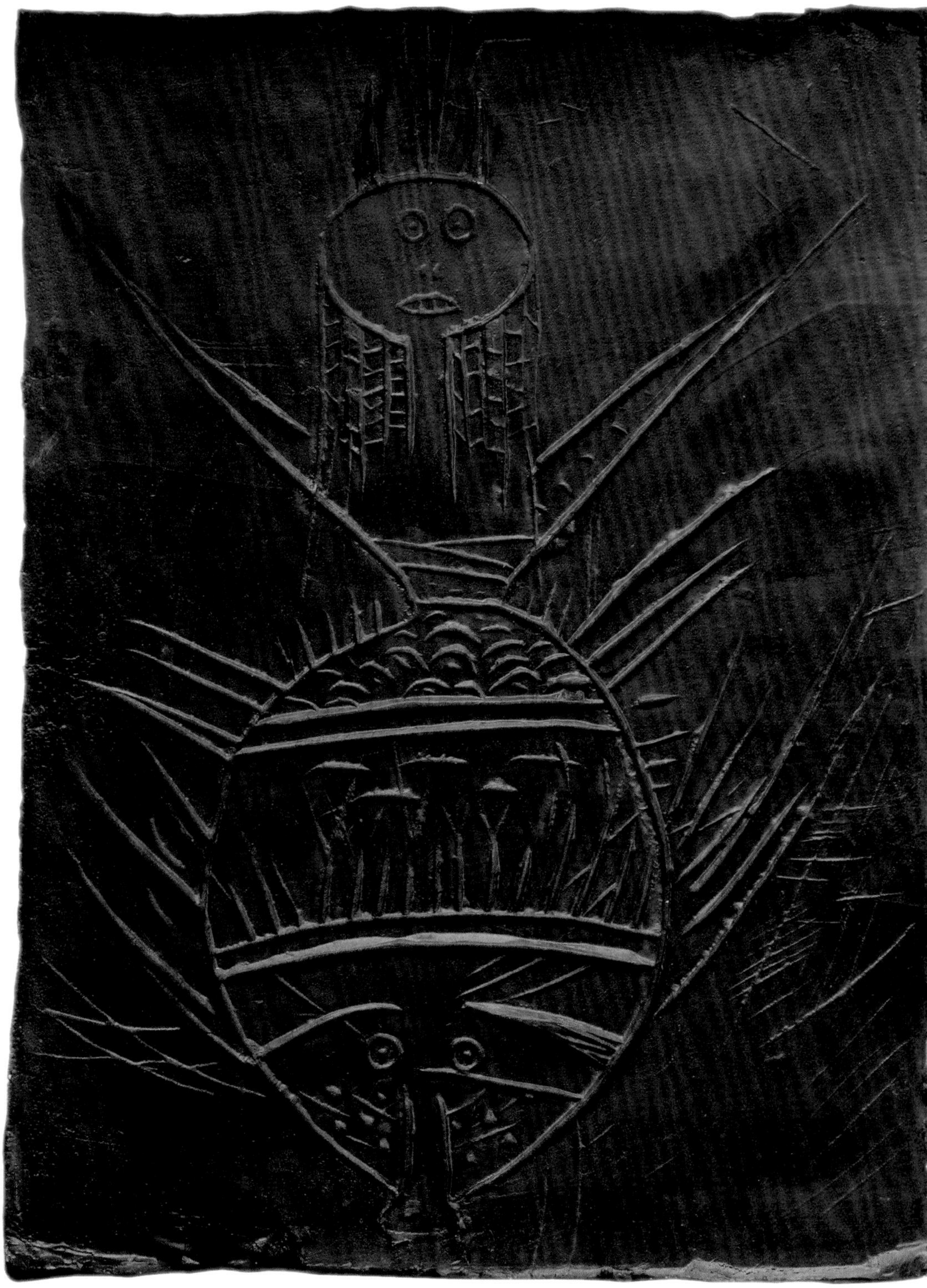

Wifredo Lam

Cuban, 1902–1982

Ídolo (Idol)

1958

Terracotta black glazed relief

15 × 11½ × 1⅝ in. (38.1 × 29.2 × 4.1 cm)

Harn Museum of Art collection

Museum purchase, funds provided by friends of the Harn Museum of Art

2008.40.1

Photography by Randy Batista

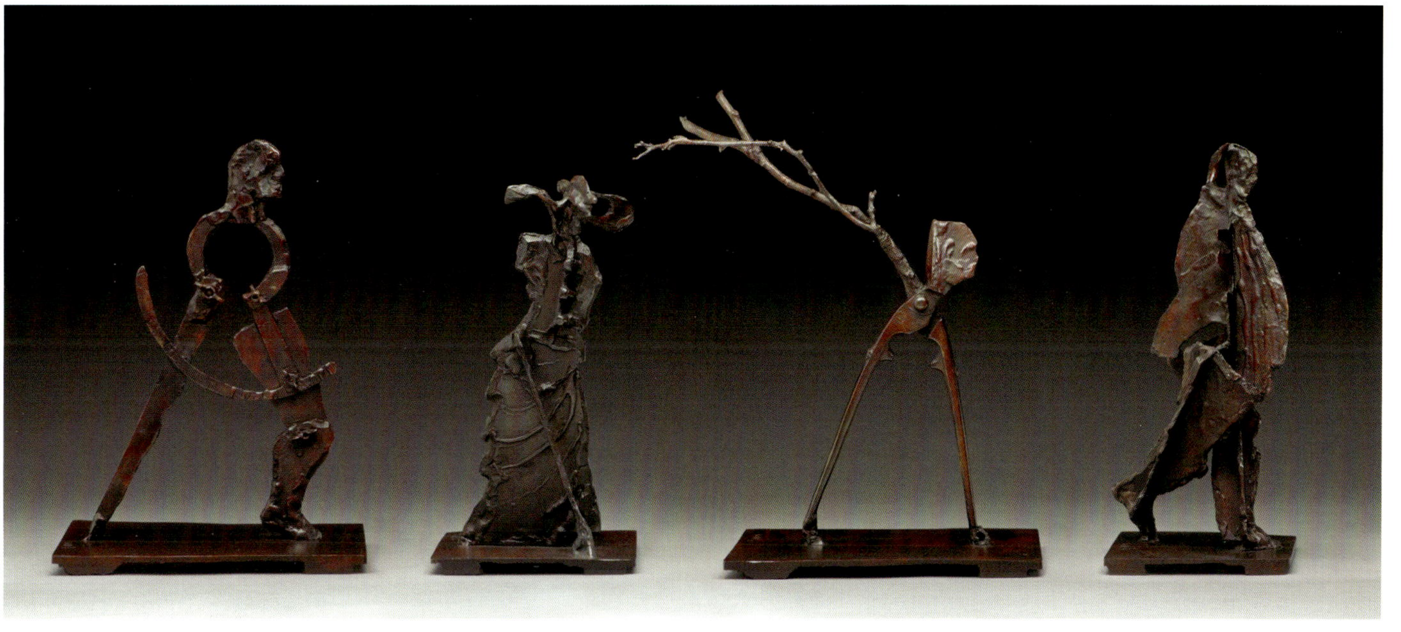

William Kentridge

South African, b. 1955

Promenade II

2002

Four bronze sculptures with dark-brown patina

Left to right: 14 × 10⅛ × 6⅝ in. (35.6 × 25.7 × 16.8 cm);
12 × 6½ × 6¼ in. (31.8 × 16.5 × 15.9 cm);
15¼ × 14 × 6¾ in. (38.7 × 35.6 × 17.1 cm);
13¾ × 6 × 7¼ in. (34.9 × 15.2 × 18.4 cm)

Harn Museum of Art collection

Museum purchase by exchange, gift of Louise H. Courtelis with additional funds provided by the Caroline Julier and James G. Richardson Acquisition Endowment

2003.13.1

Photography by Randy Batista

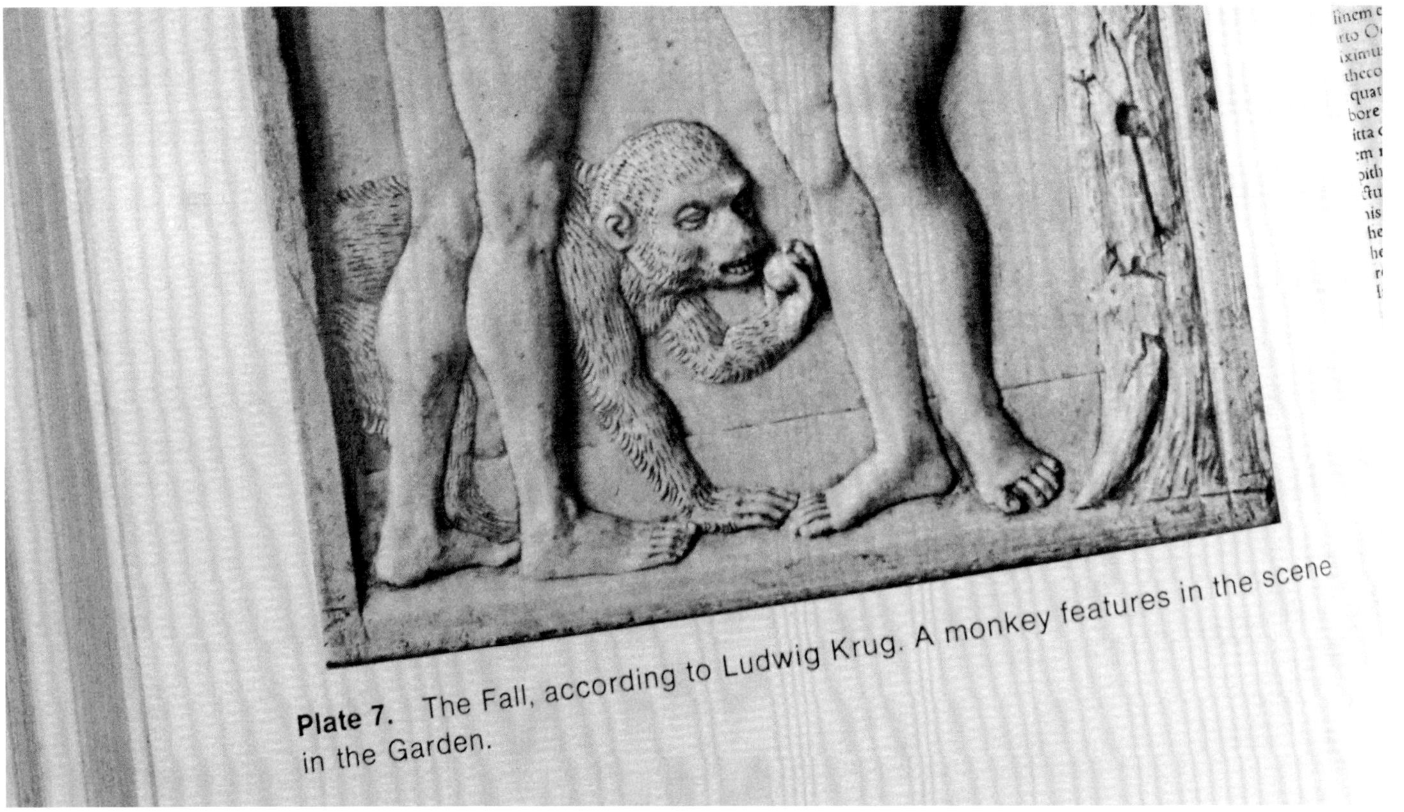

Sergio Vega

American b. Argentina, 1959

The Missing Tail

2008

HD video, 5 min., 46 sec.

Courtesy of the artist

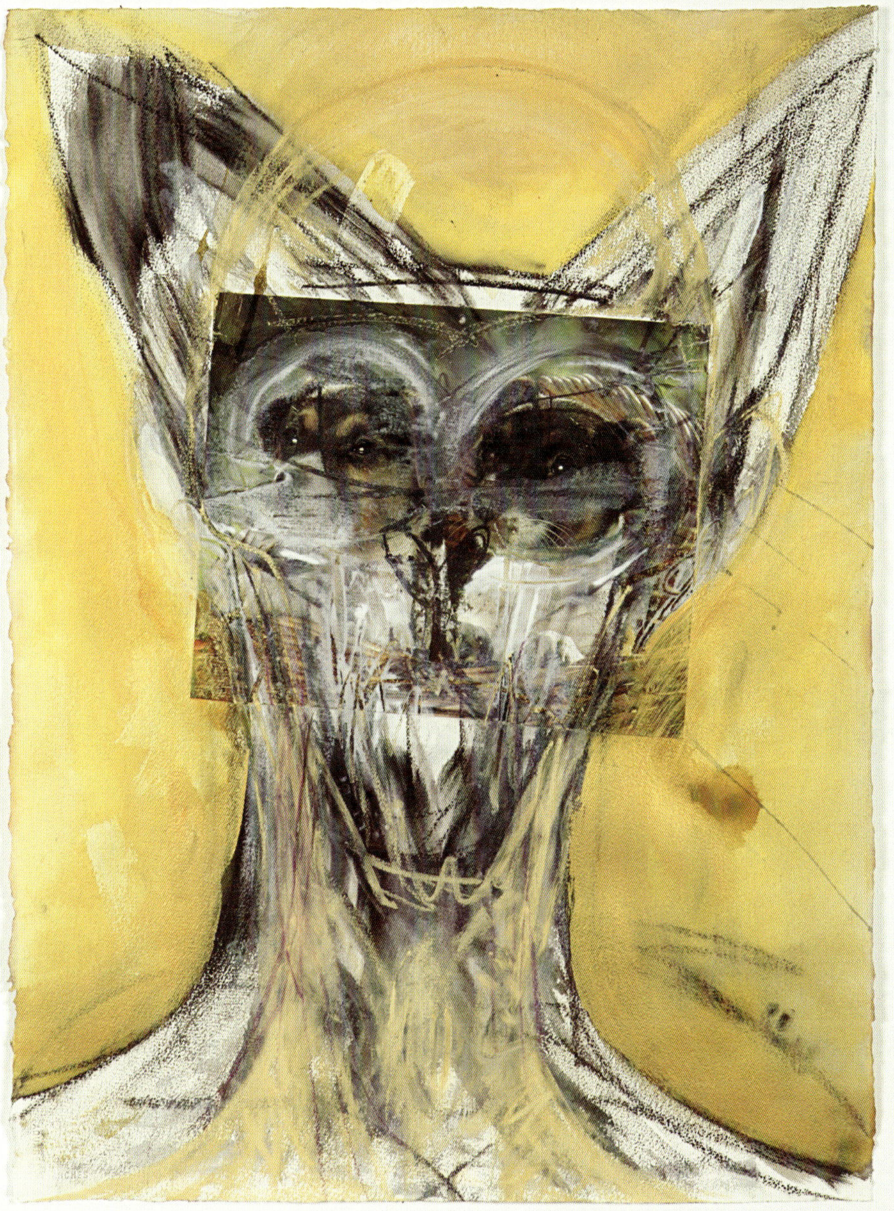

Huma Bhabha
Pakistani, b. 1962
Untitled
2014
Ink, pastel and collage on paper
29½ × 22½ in. (74.9 × 57.2 cm)
Loan courtesy of Stefanie and Ashok Chachra
Image courtesy of Salon 94

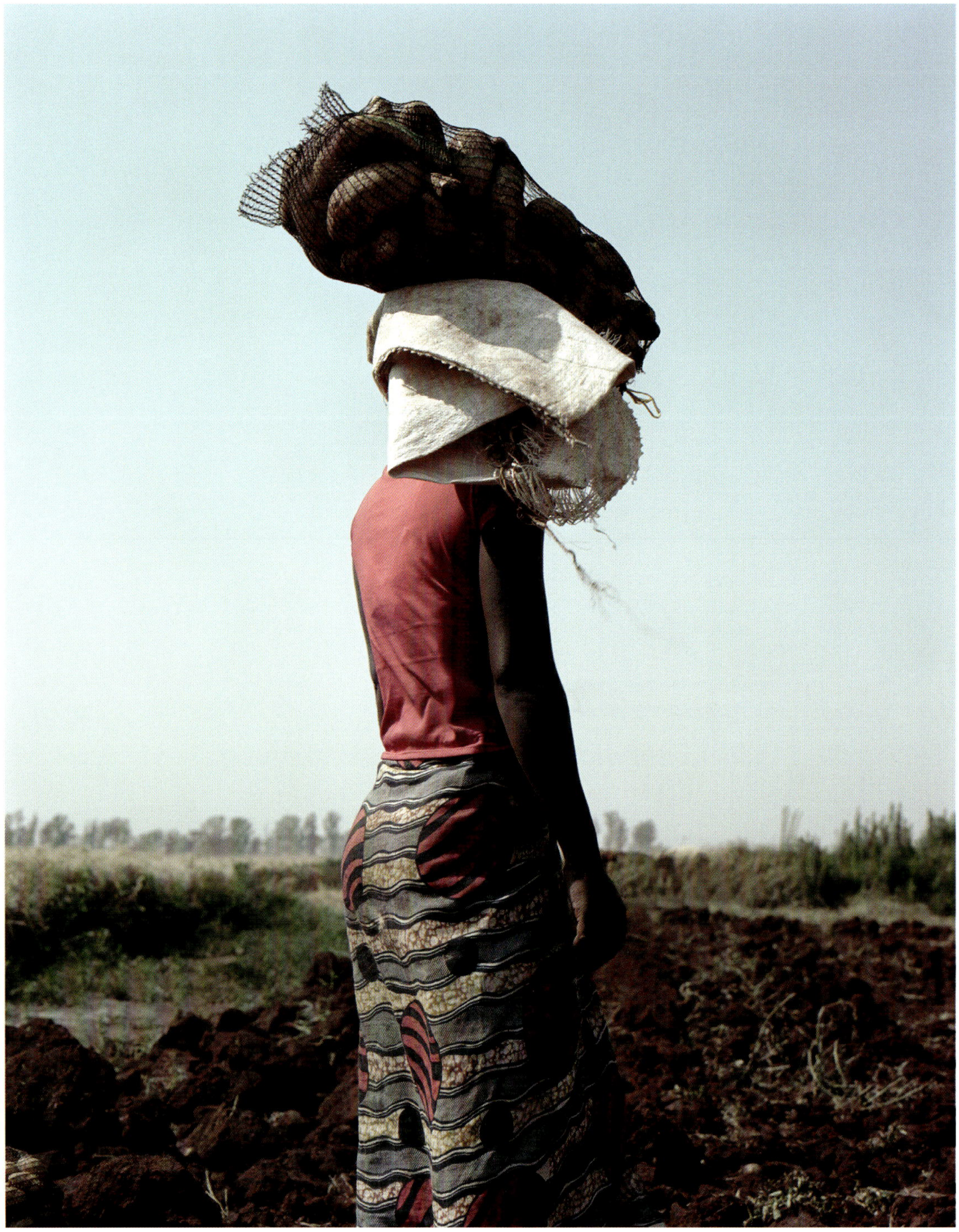

Jackie Nickerson

American, b. 1960

Ruth

From the series *Terrain*

2012

Digital chromogenic print

48 × 38½ in. (121.9 × 97.8 cm)

Courtesy of the artist and Jack Shainman Gallery, New York

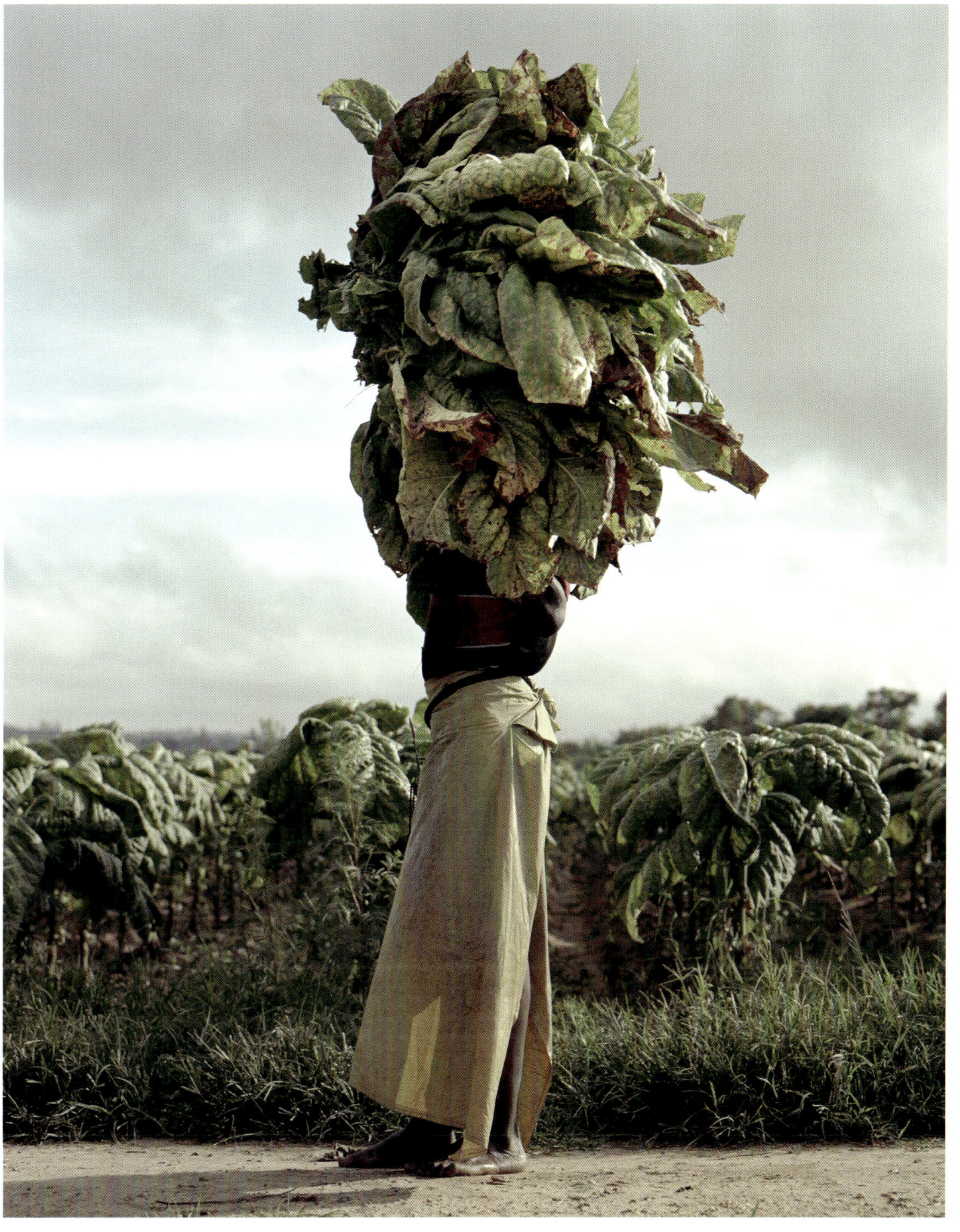

Jackie Nickerson

American, b. 1960

Oscar

From the series *Terrain*

2012

Digital chromogenic print

7 ft. 2⅝ in. × 5 ft. 10⅞ in. (220 × 180 cm)

Courtesy of the artist and Jack Shainman Gallery, New York

Grassroots resistance may prove to be the most effective and courageous way to practice stewardship of our planet.

—Kerry Oliver-Smith

JUSTICE

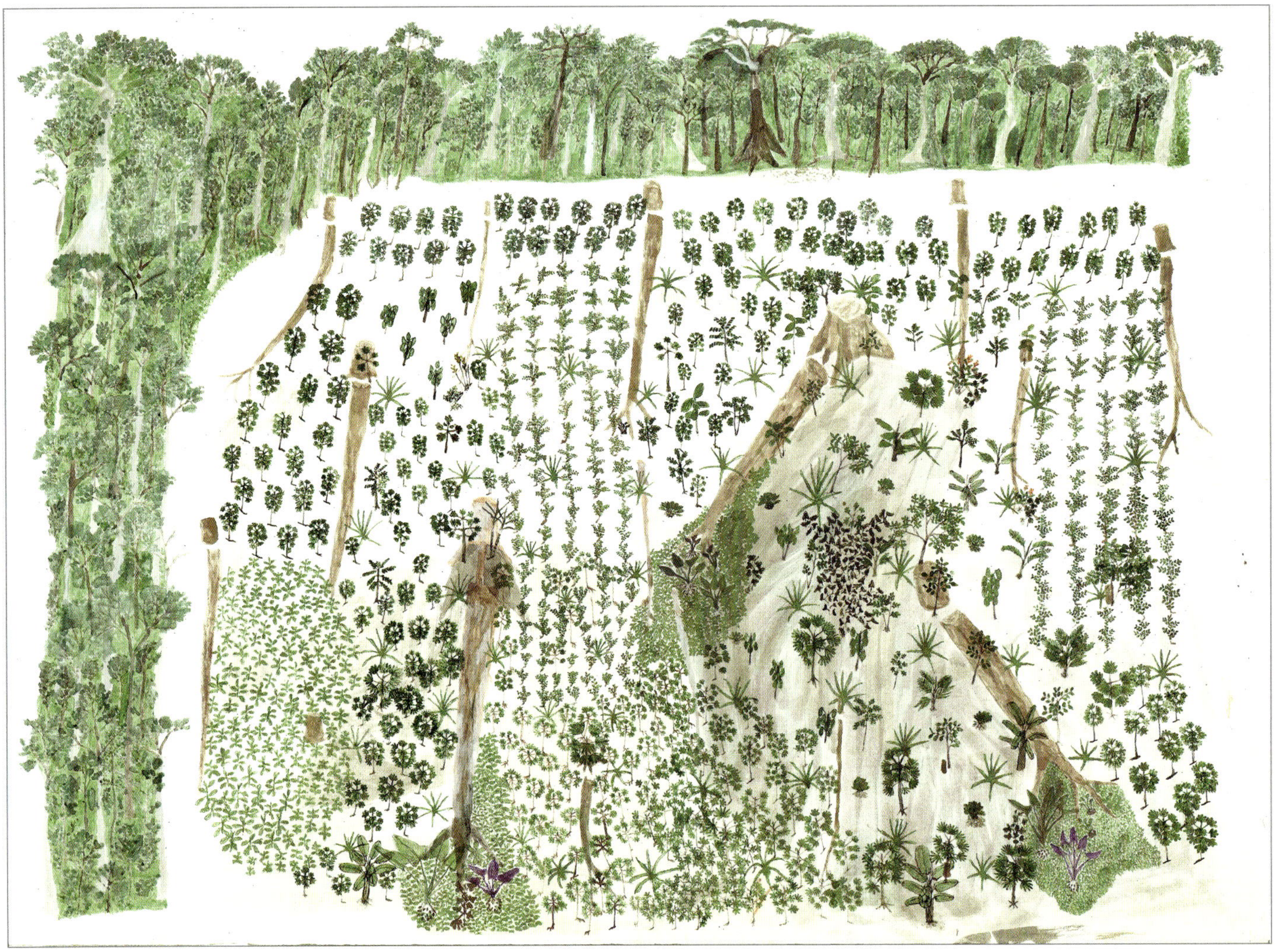

Abel Rodríguez

Colombian, b. 1944

From the series: *Annual Cycle of the Chagra*

2011

Ink on paper

19.7 × 27.6 in. (50 × 70 cm)

Courtesy of the artist and the Tropenbos International Colombia's Archive

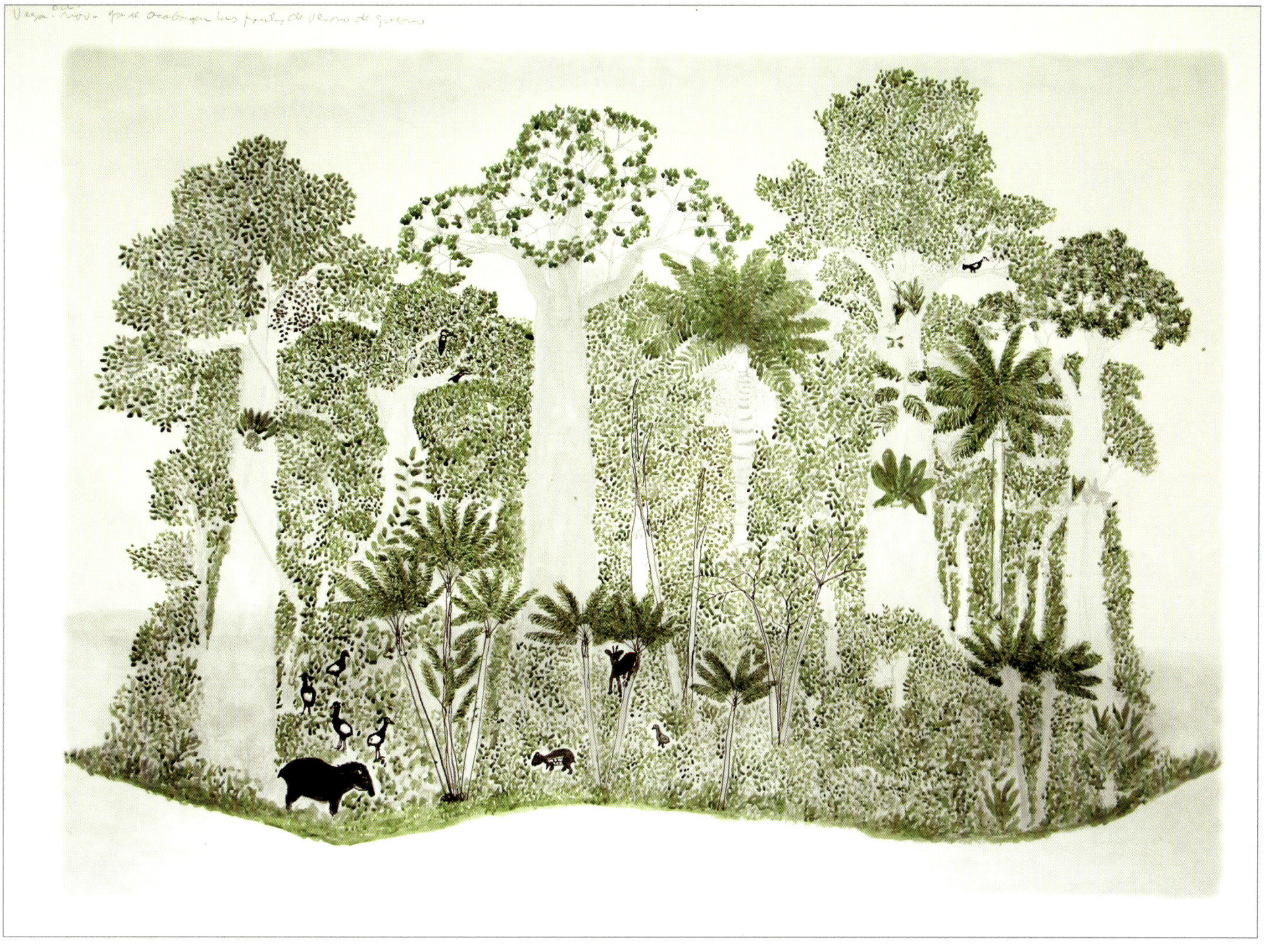

Abel Rodríguez

Colombian, b. 1944

From the series: *Annual Cycle of the Flooded Rainforest*

2009–2010

Ink on paper

19.7 × 27.6 in. (50 × 70 cm)

Courtesy of the artist and the Tropenbos International Colombia's Archive

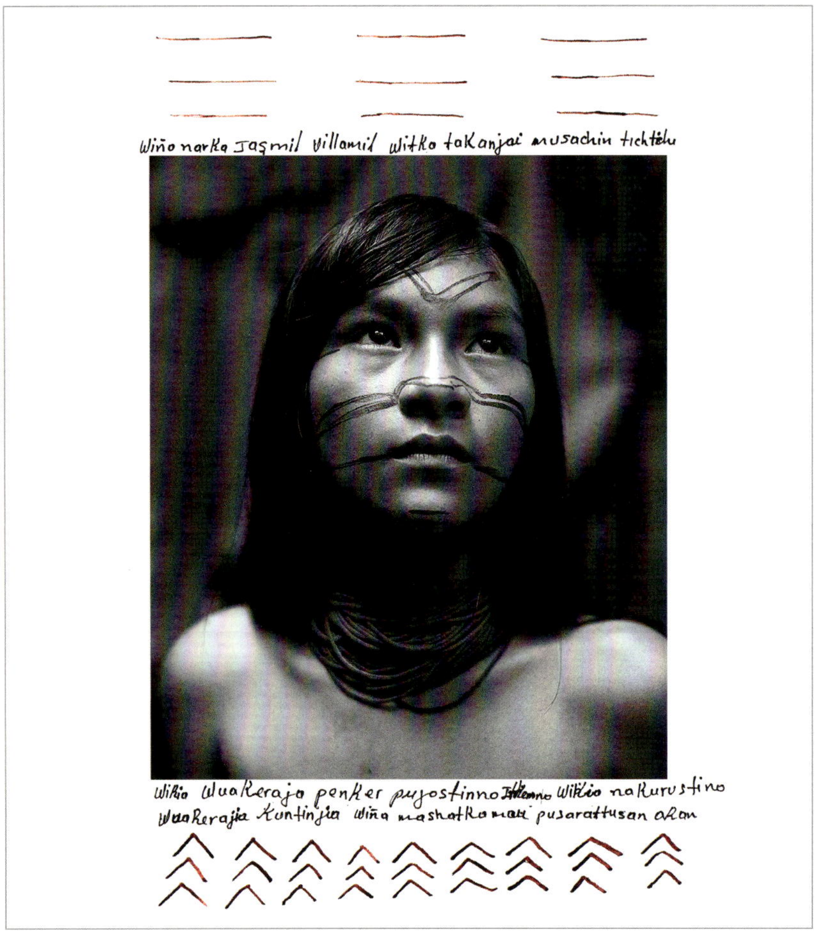

Felipe Jácome
Ecuadorian, b. 1985
Hasmil
From the series *Amazonas: Guardians of Life*
2013
Digital print
30 × 30 in. (76.2 × 76.2 cm)
Courtesy of the artist

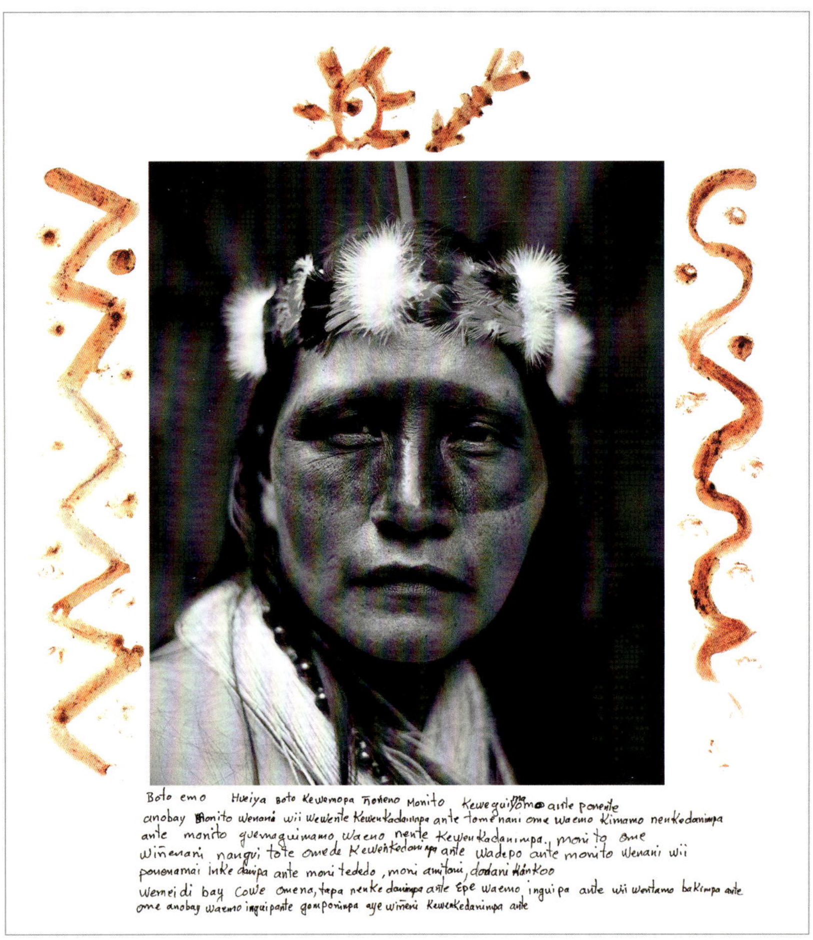

Felipe Jácome
Ecuadorian, b. 1985
Hueiya
From the series *Amazonas: Guardians of Life*
2013
Digital print
30 × 30 in. (76.2 × 76.2 cm)
Courtesy of the artist

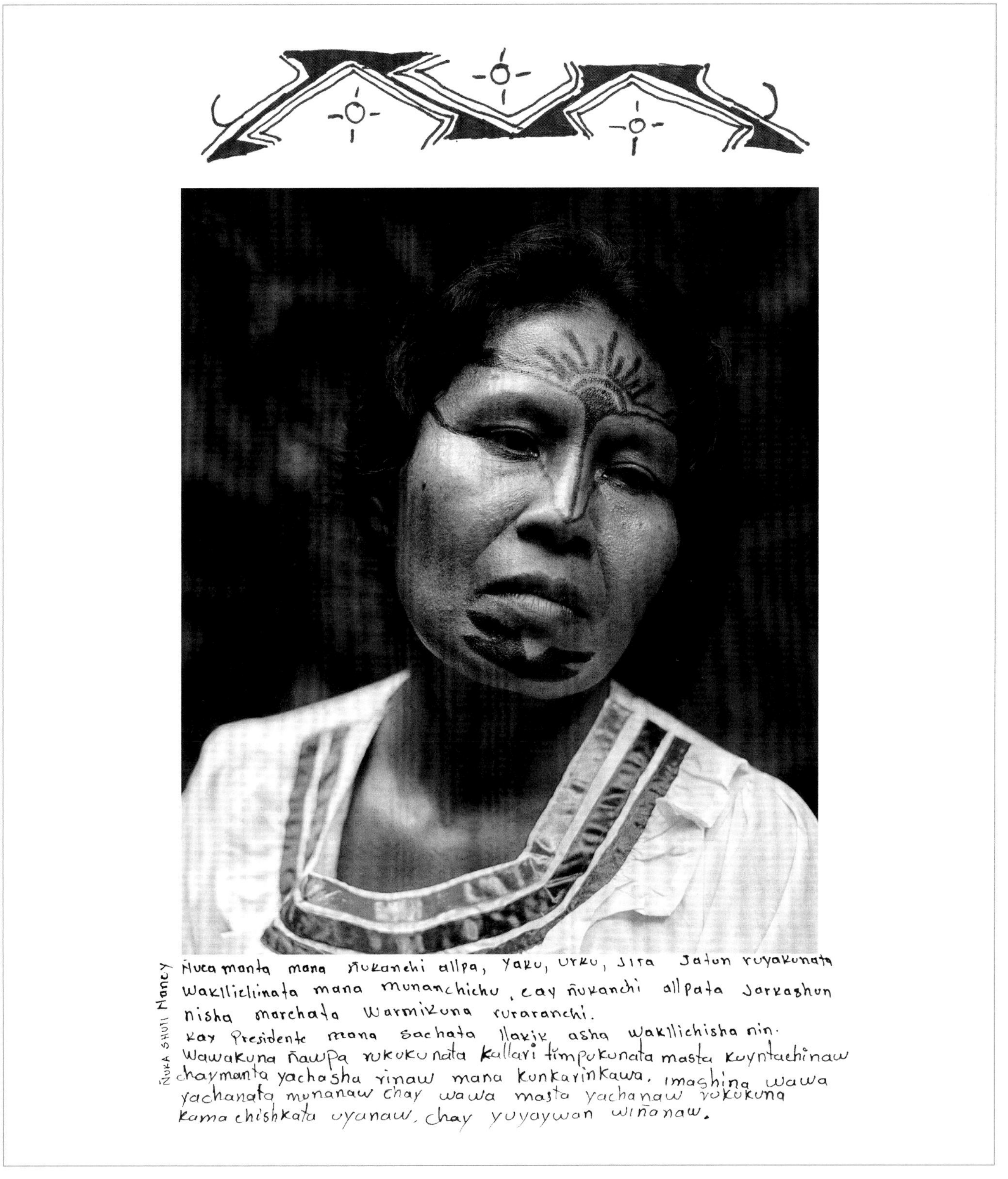

Felipe Jácome
Ecuadorian, b. 1985
Nancy
From the series *Amazonas: Guardians of Life*
2013
Digital print
30 × 30 in. (76.2 × 76.2 cm)
Courtesy of the artist

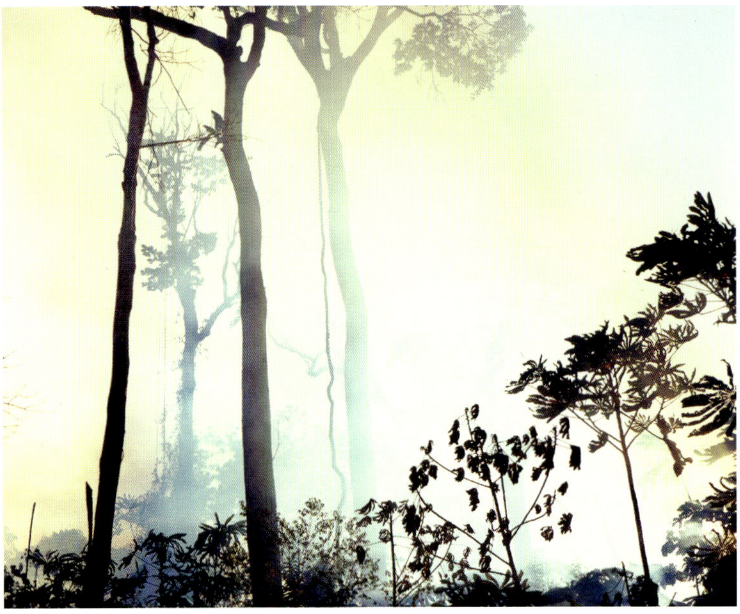

Sergio Vega
American b. Argentina, 1959
Paradise on Fire I
2007
Ultrachrome archival inkjet print
42 × 53 in. (106.7 × 134.6 cm)
Courtesy of the artist

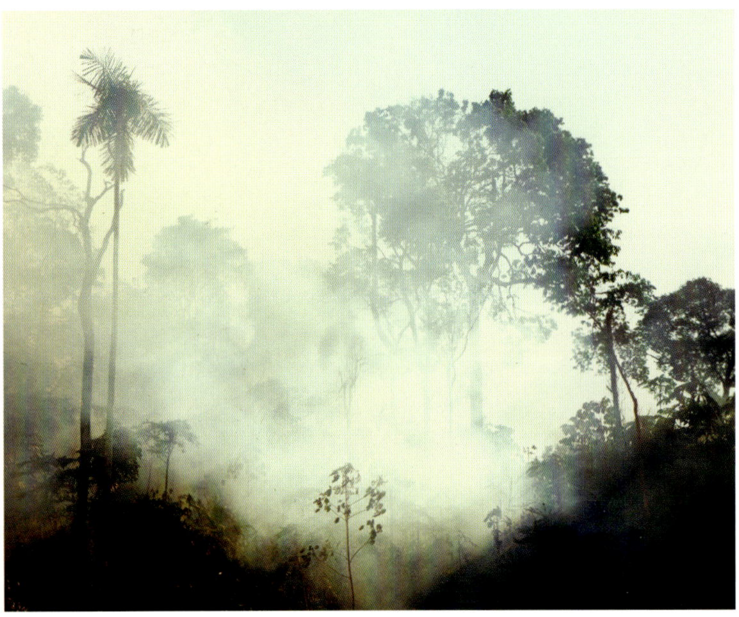

Sergio Vega
American b. Argentina, 1959
Paradise on Fire IV
2007
Ultrachrome archival inkjet print
42 × 53 in. (106.7 × 134.6 cm)
Courtesy of the artist

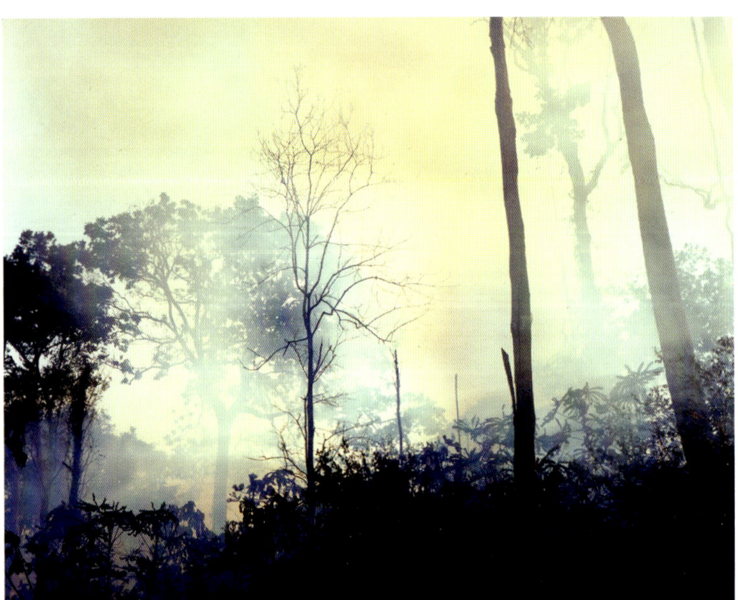

Sergio Vega
American b. Argentina, 1959
Paradise on Fire II
2007
Ultrachrome archival inkjet print
42 × 53 in. (106.7 × 134.6 cm)
Courtesy of the artist

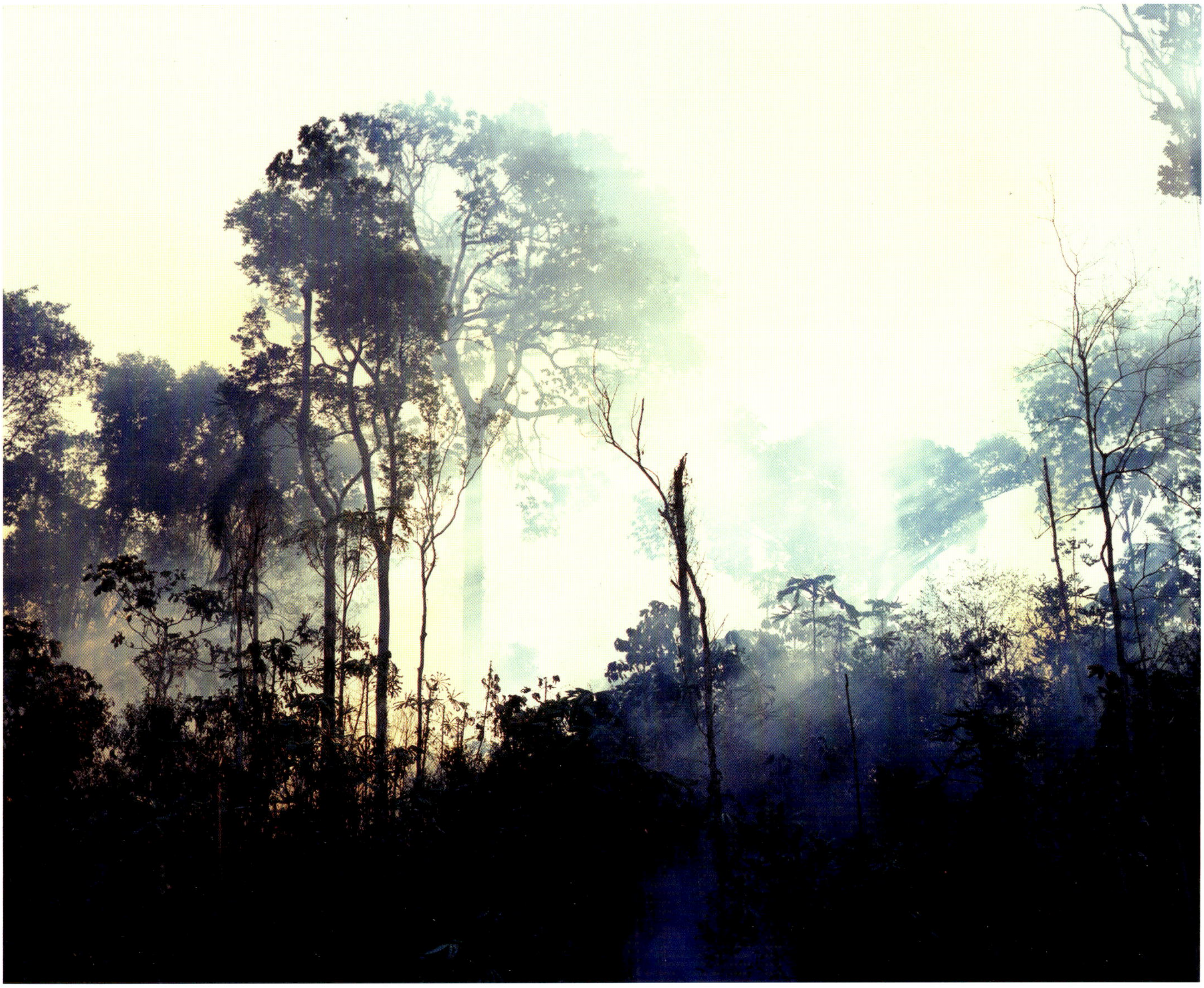

Sergio Vega
American b. Argentina, 1959
Paradise on Fire V
2007
Ultrachrome archival inkjet print
42 × 53 in. (106.7 × 134.6 cm)
Courtesy of the artist

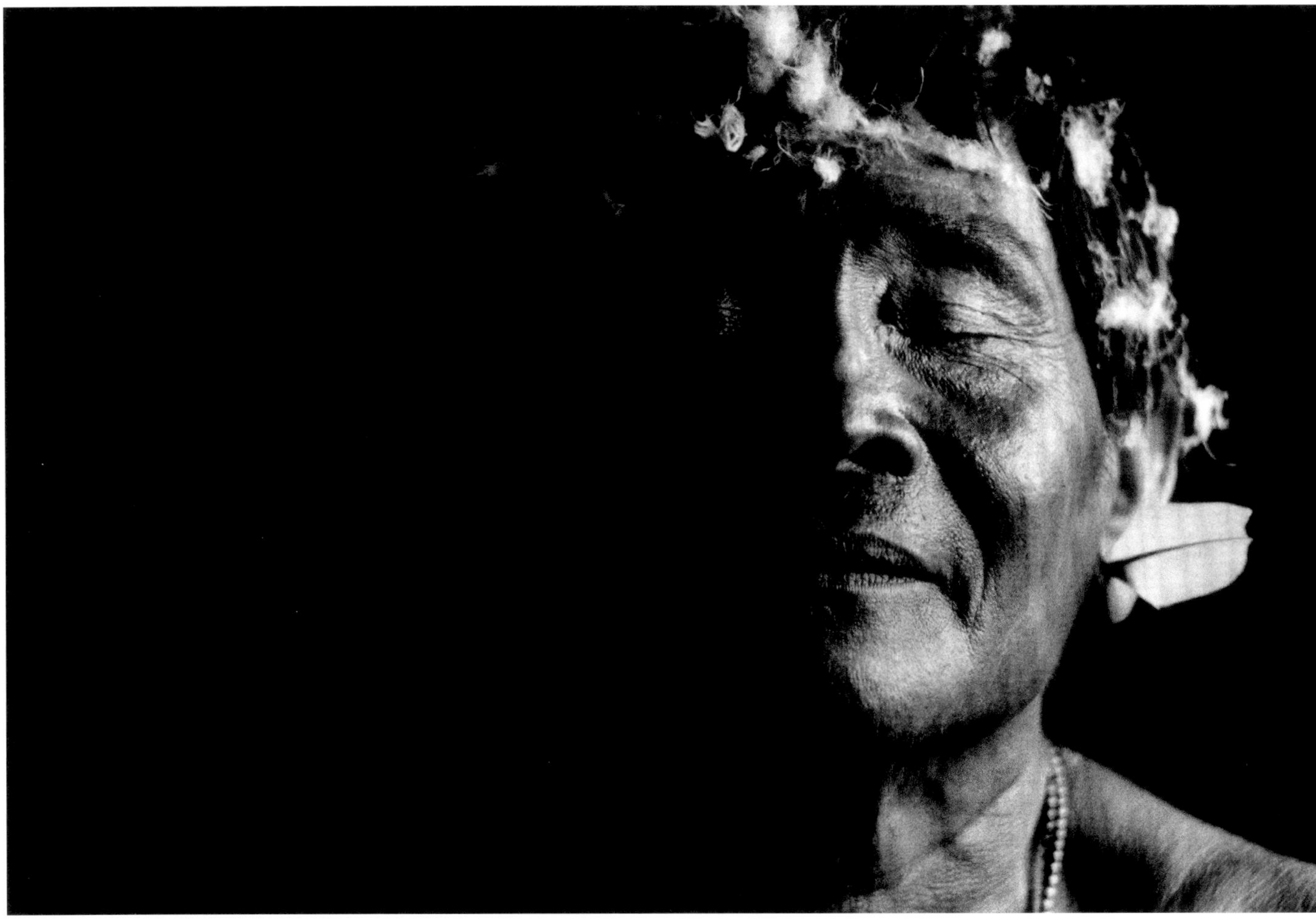

Claudia Andujar
Brazilian, b. 1931
Yanomami from *O Invisivel* series
1976
Gelatin silver on Ilford MG4FB5 K
double-weight paper
21⅞ × 32$\frac{5}{16}$ × 1⅜ in. (55.5 × 82 × 3.5 cm)
Courtesy of Galeria Vermelho, São Paulo

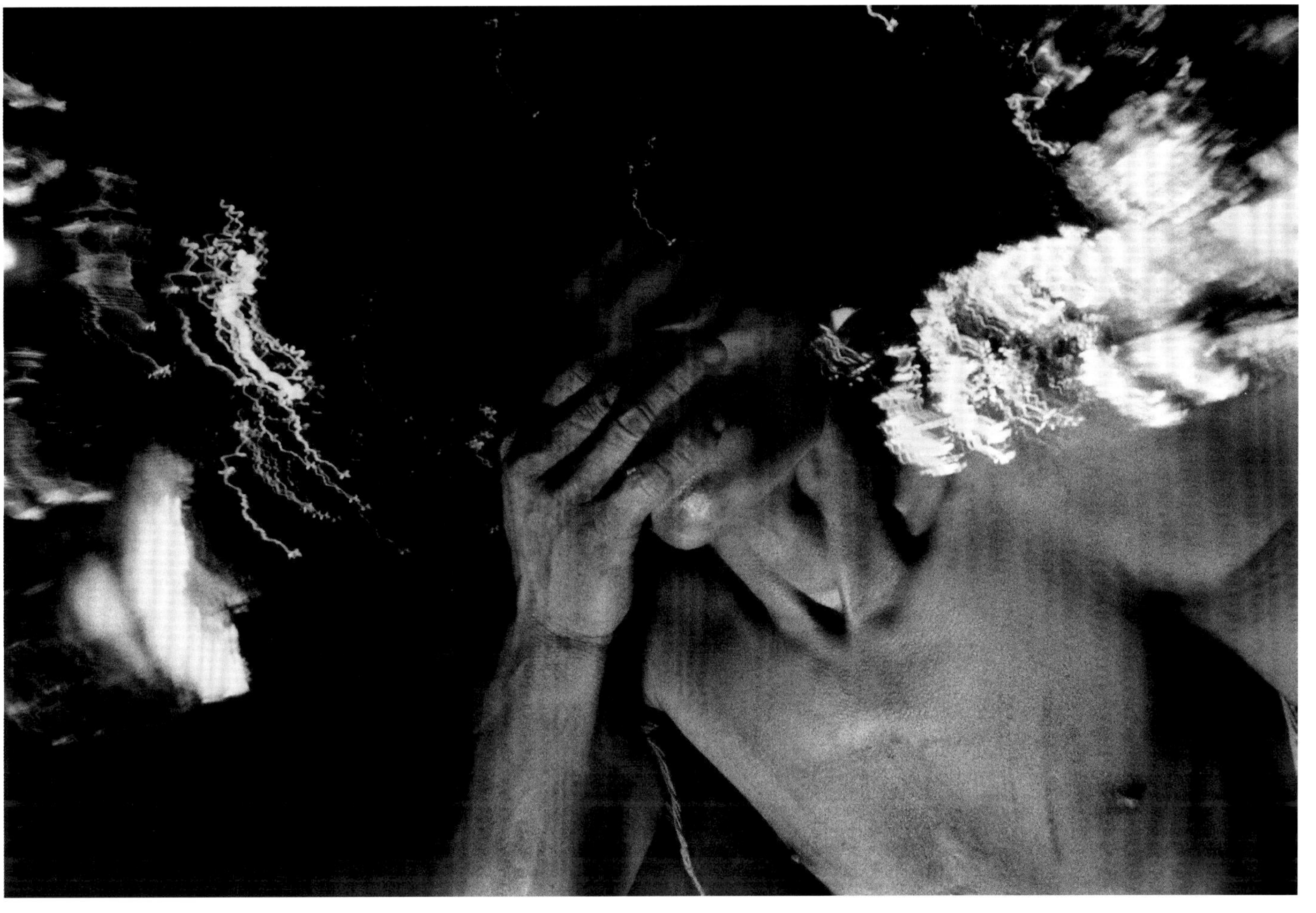

Claudia Andujar

Brazilian, b. 1931

Yanomami, 1974, Catrimani from *Reahu* series

1974

Gelatin silver on Ilford MG4FB5 K double-weight paper

28⅛ × 39¾ × 1⅜ in. (71.5 × 101 × 3.5 cm)

Courtesy of Galeria Vermelho, São Paulo

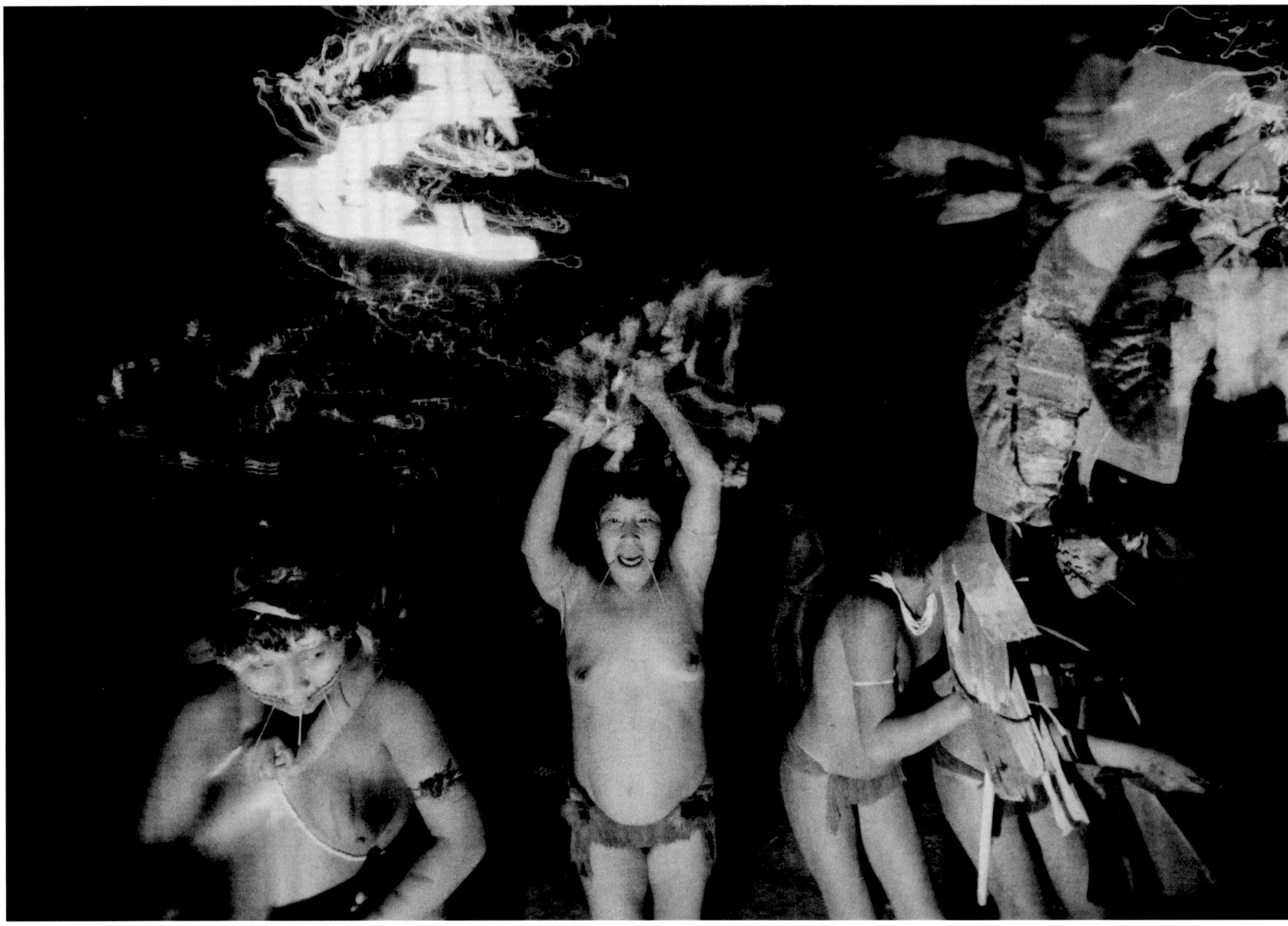

Claudia Andujar

Brazilian, b. 1931

Untitled from *Reahu* series

1976

Gelatin silver on Ilford MG4FB5 K double-weight paper

27⁹⁄₁₆ × 38⁹⁄₁₆ × 1⅜ in. (70 × 98 × 3.5 cm)

Courtesy of Galeria Vermelho, São Paulo

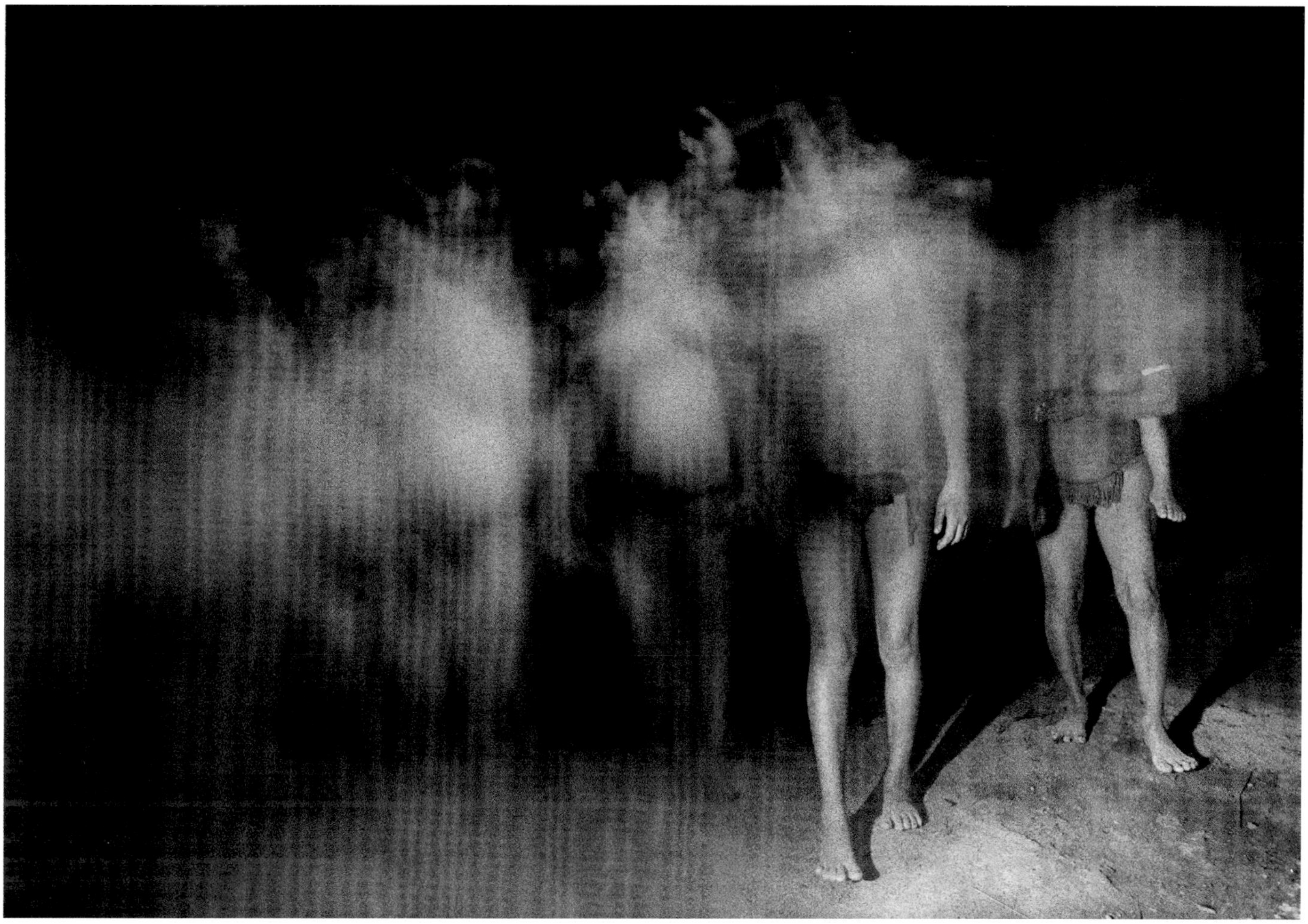

Claudia Andujar

Brazilian, b. 1931

Untitled from *Reahu* series

1974

Gelatin silver on Ilford MG4FB5 K double-weight paper

28¾ × 39⅜ × 1⅜ in. (73 × 100 × 3.5 cm)

Courtesy of Galeria Vermelho, São Paulo

Jennifer Allora and Guillermo Calzadilla

The bird of Hermes is my name, eating my wings to make me tame

2010

Painted bronze sculpture

23⅝ × 19⅝ × 15⅝ in. (60 × 49.8 × 39.7 cm)

Loan courtesy of the artists and Lisson Gallery, New York

Photography: Dave Morgan

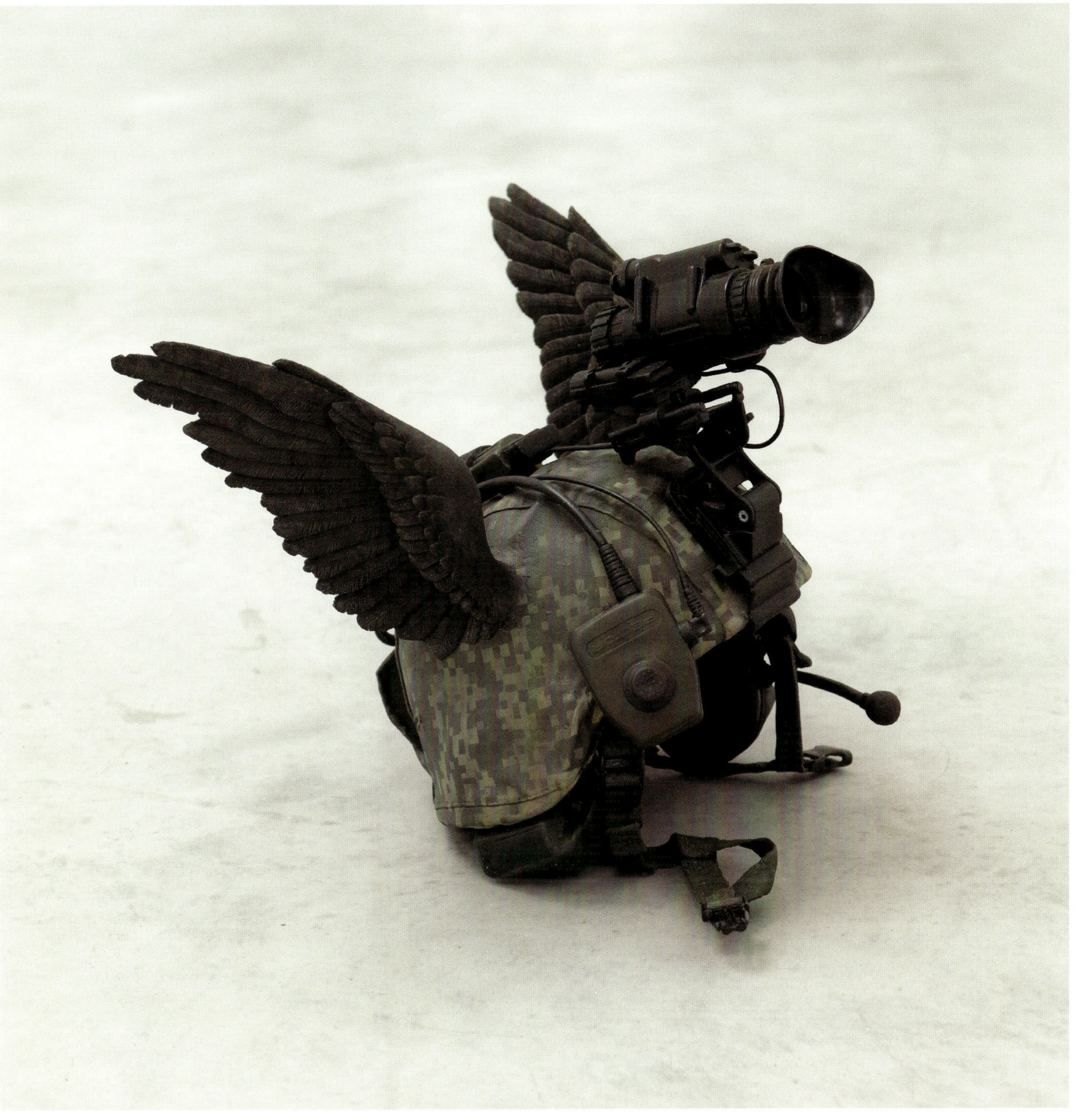

Without a commitment to the enduring possibility of a better world, we simply resign ourselves, and the planet, to extinction as usual.—Rory Rowan

IMAGINARY FUTURES

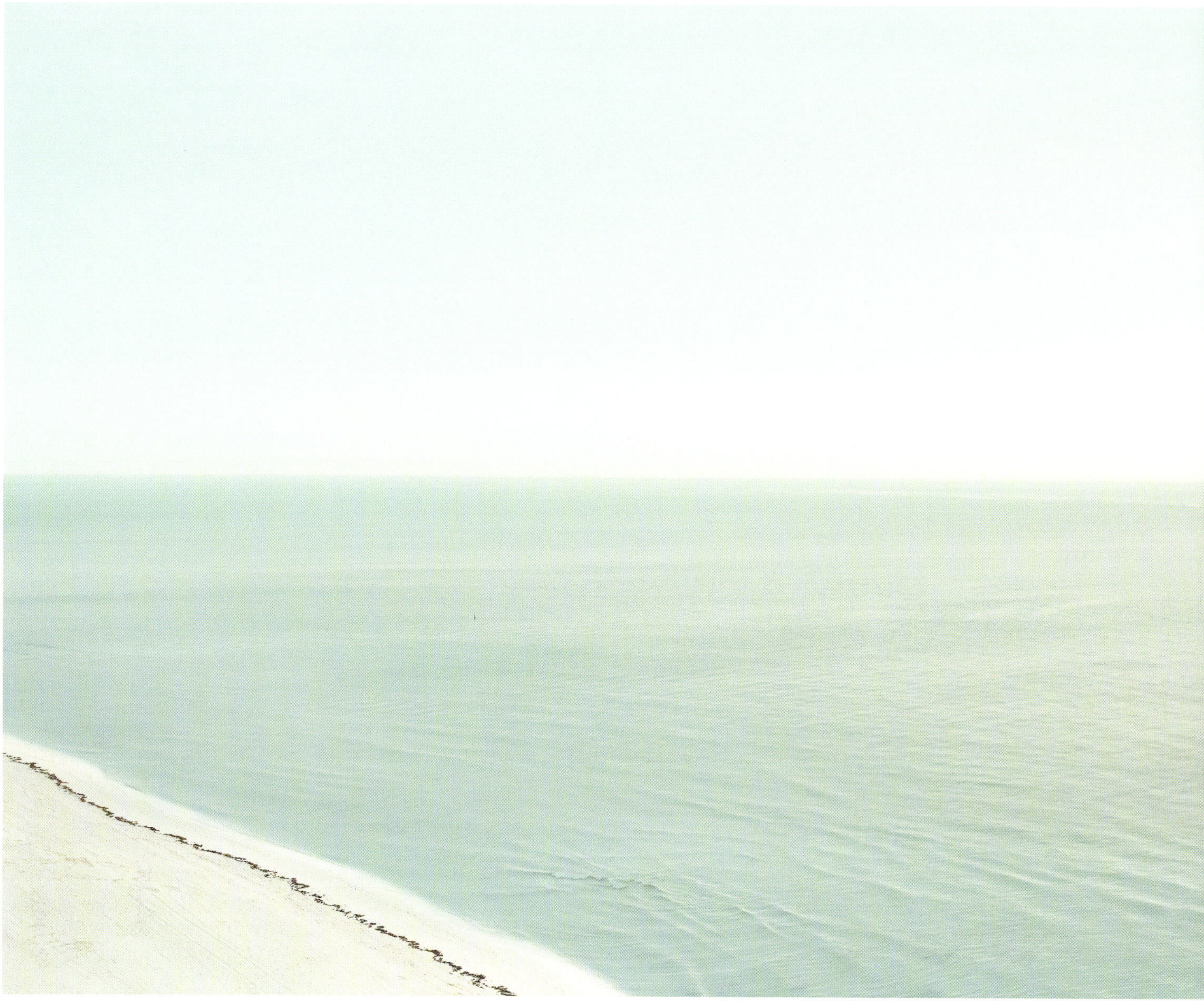

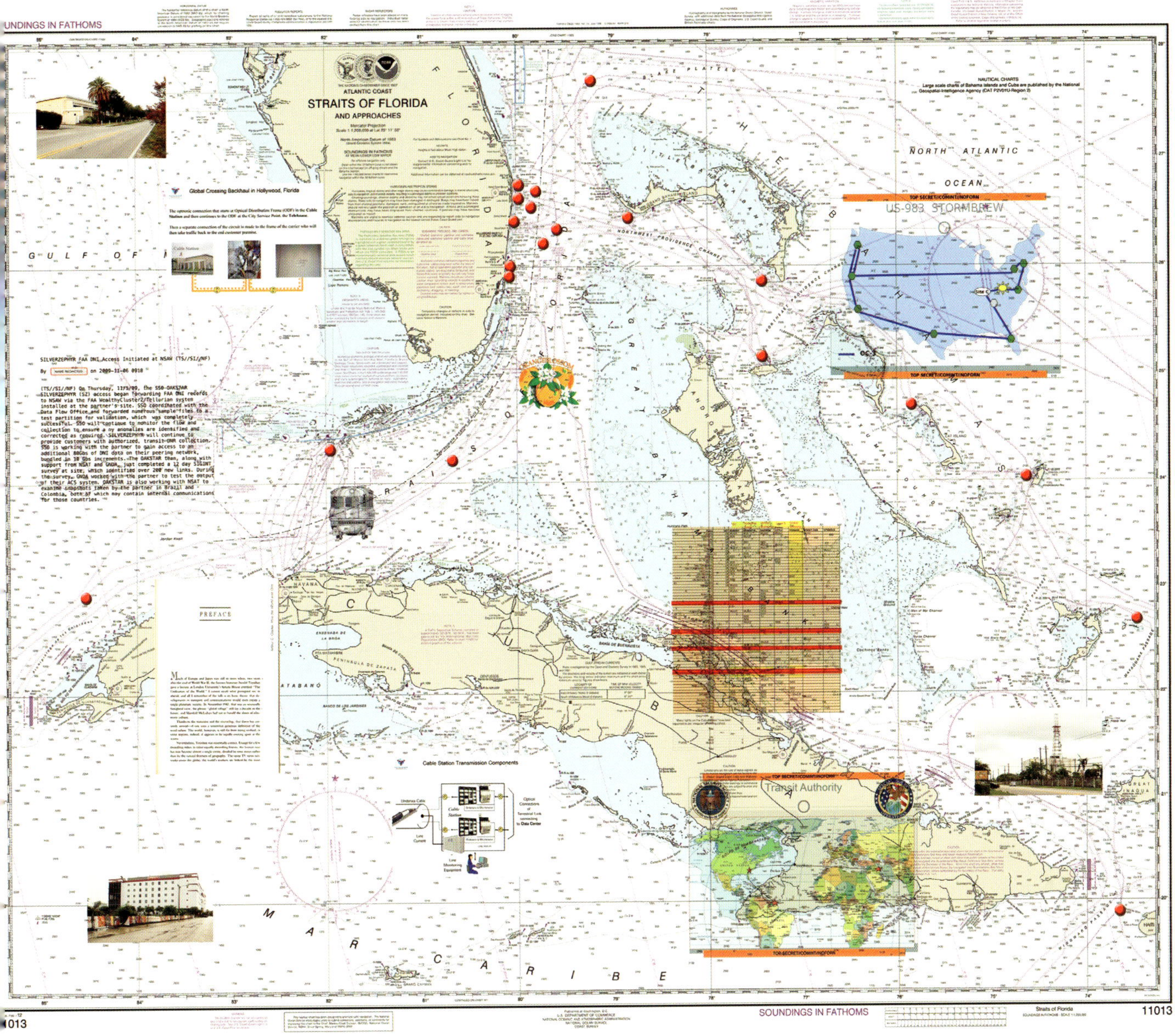

Trevor Paglen

American, b. 1974

NSA-Tapped Fiber Optic Cable Landing Site, Miami Beach, Florida, United States

2015

Chromogenic print and mixed media on navigational chart

Print: 48 in. × 5 ft. 1¹³⁄₁₆ in. (121.9 × 157 cm)

Map: 48 × 58⅛ in. (121.9 × 147.6 cm)

Harn Museum of Art collection

Museum purchase, the Caroline Julier and James G. Richardson Acquisition Fund and the Fogler Family Endowment

2015.52

Allan Sekula

American, 1951–2013

CIA black site seen from across the lake just before the wrong film was confiscated, Kiejkuty, Poland, July 2009

From the series *Polonia and Other Fables*

2009

Chromogenic print

30 × 30 in. (76.2 × 76.2 cm)

Courtesy of Christopher Grimes Gallery, Santa Monica

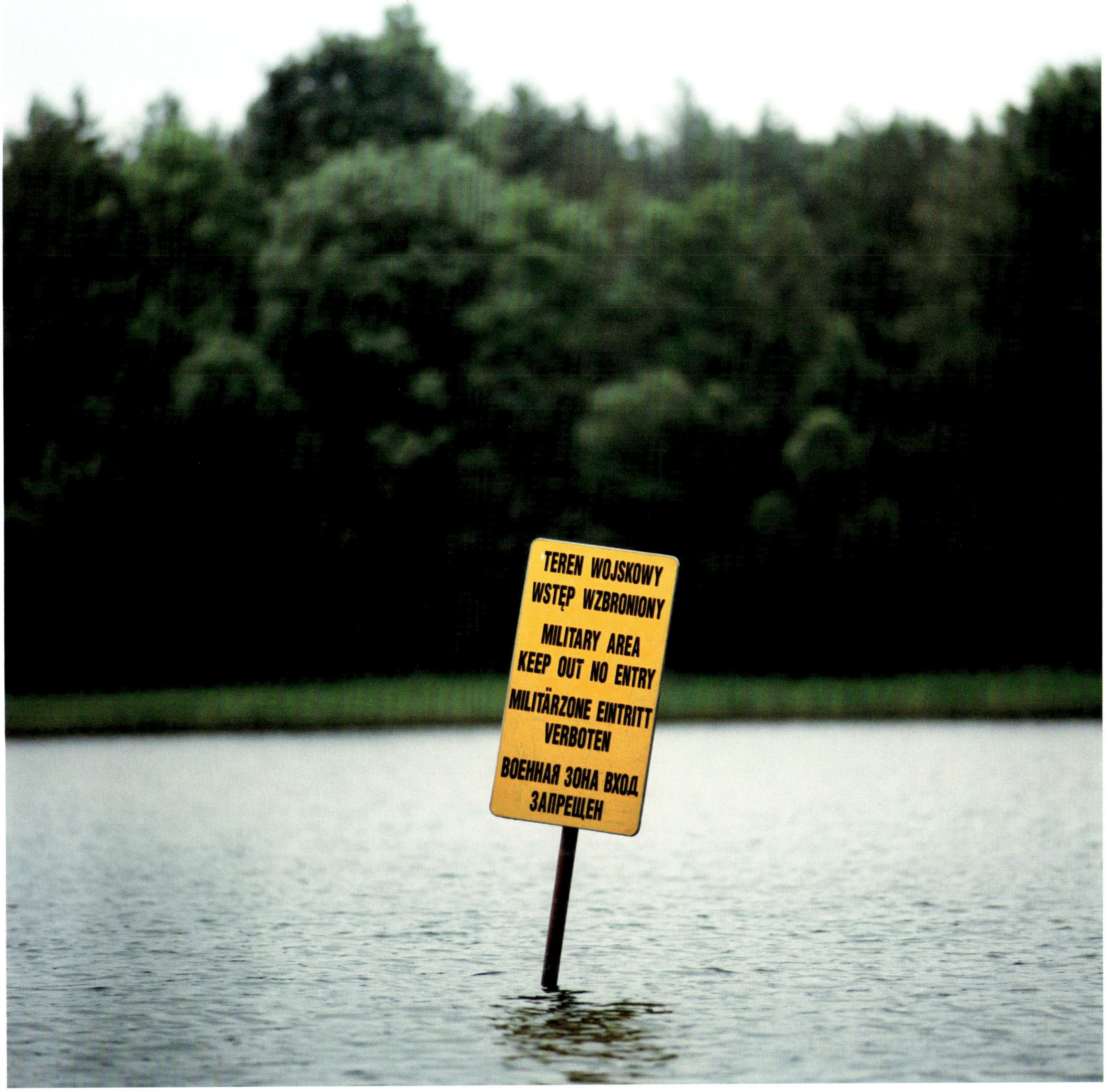
TEREN WOJSKOWY
WSTĘP WZBRONIONY
MILITARY AREA
KEEP OUT NO ENTRY
MILITÄRZONE EINTRITT
VERBOTEN
ВОЕННАЯ ЗОНА ВХОД
ЗАПРЕЩЕН

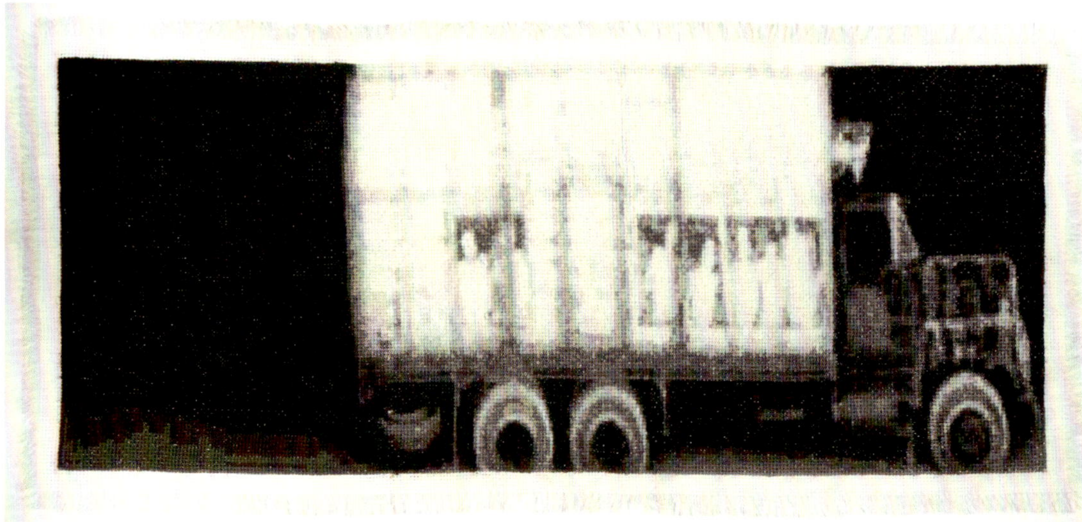

Noelle Mason
American, b. 1988
Coyotaje (La Mula)
From the series *X-Ray Vision vs. Invisibility*
2011
Hand-embroidered 14-count cross-stitch on cotton
12½ × 24½ in. (31.8 × 62.2 cm)
Courtesy of the artist

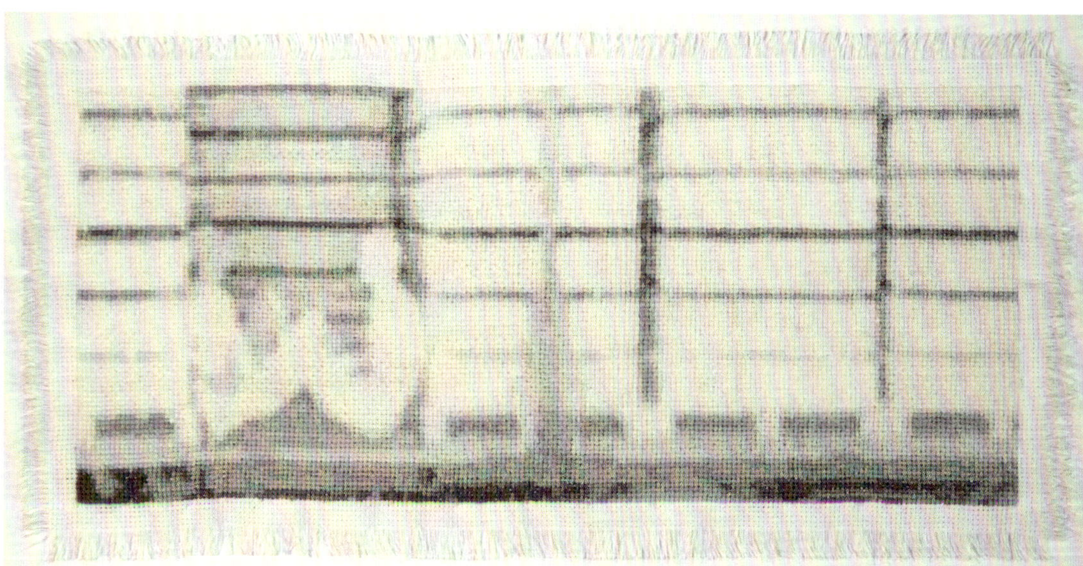

Noelle Mason
American, b. 1988
Coyotaje (Los Amantes)
From the series *X-Ray Vision vs. Invisibility*
2012
Hand-embroidered 14-count cross-stitch on cotton
10½ × 18 in. (26.7 × 45.7 cm)
Courtesy of the artist

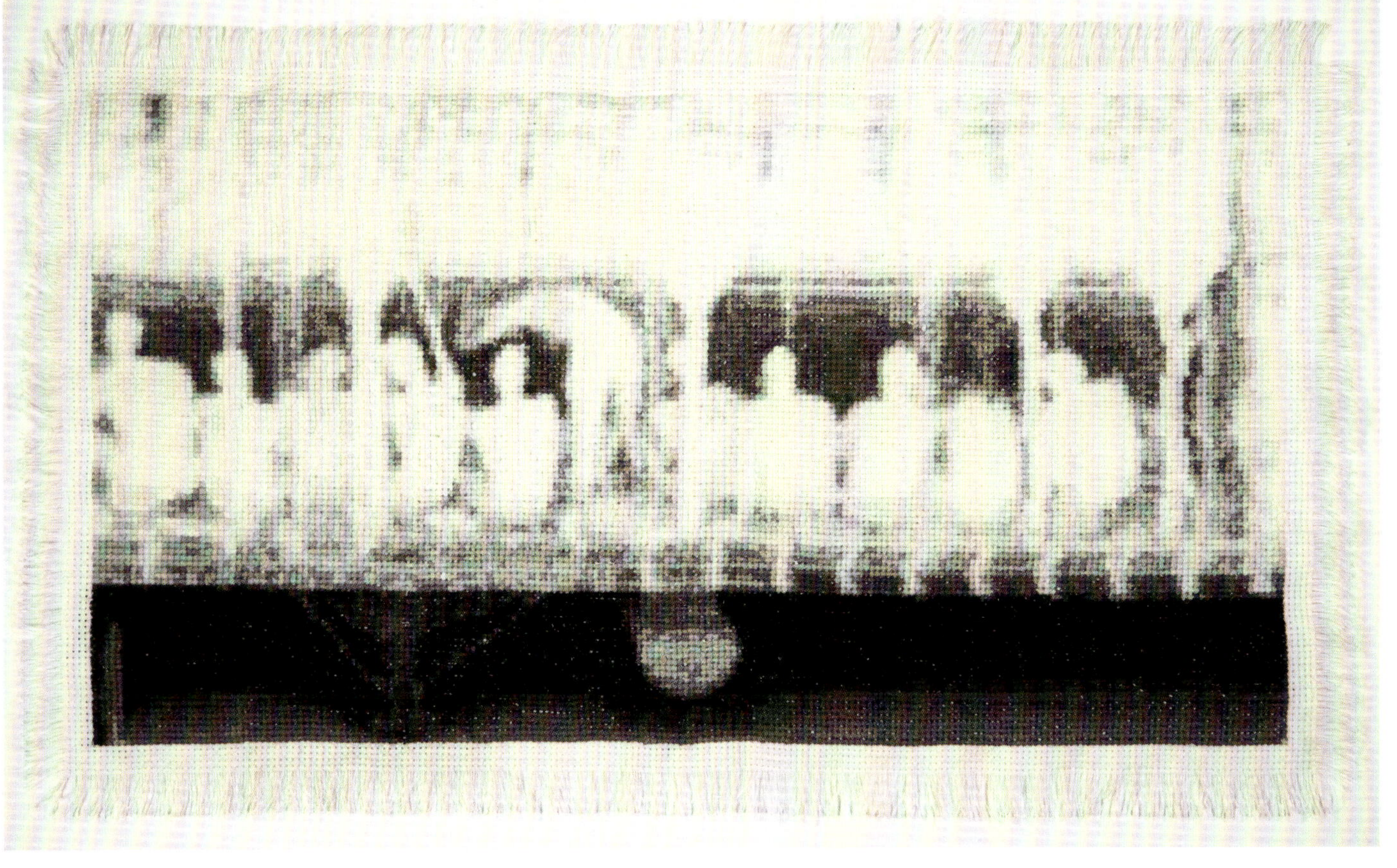

Noelle Mason

American, b. 1988

Coyotaje (Ultima Cena)

From the series *X-Ray Vision vs. Invisibility*

2012

Hand-embroidered 14-count cross-stitch on cotton

12 × 18 in. (30.5 × 45.7 cm)

Courtesy of the artist

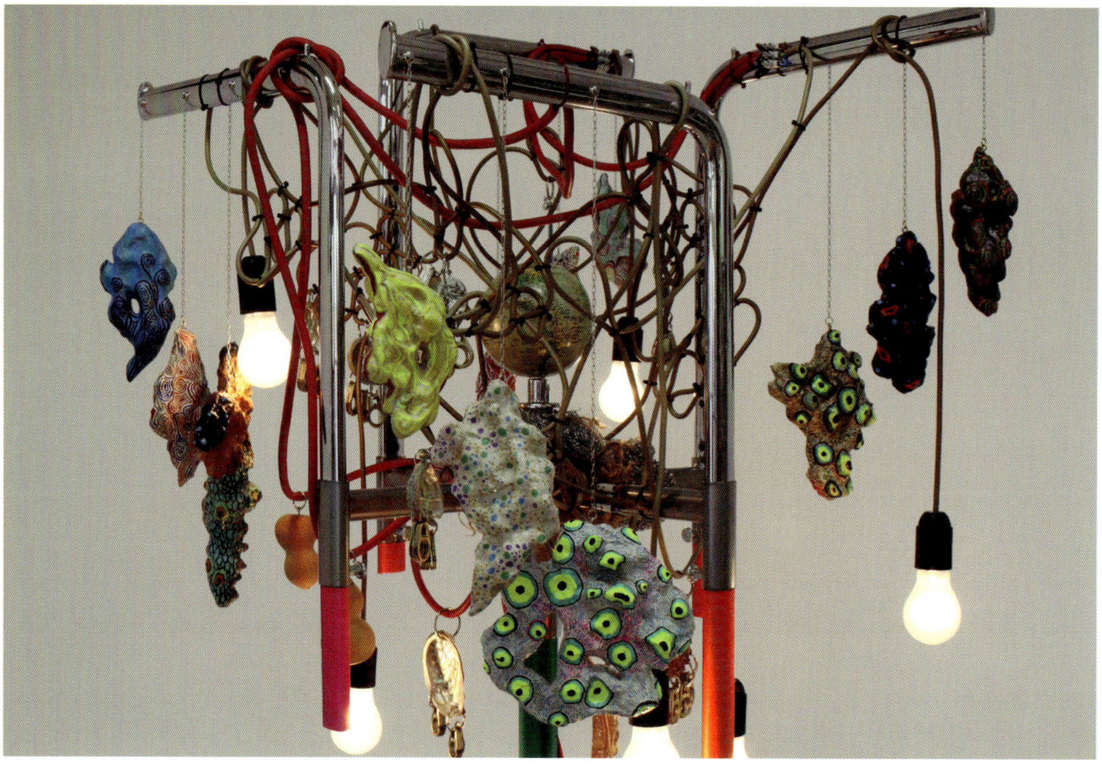

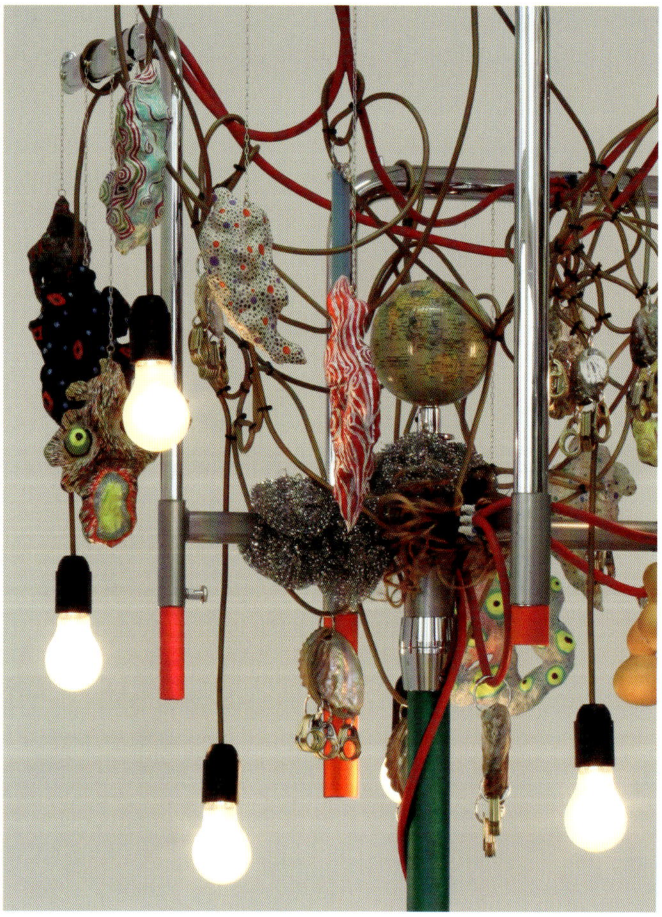

Haegue Yang

South Korean, b. 1971

Ornamental Mountains and Seas—Monster and Cloud

2011

Mixed media, single-shaft clothing rack on casters with four arms, frosted light bulbs, cable, cord, wigs, bells, papier-mâché, watercolor, lacquer, can tab, metal, abalone shells, gourd, zip ties, metal sponge, globe, metal chain

5 ft. 10¾ in. × 29⅞ in. (179.7 × 75.9 cm)

Harn Museum of Art collection

Museum purchase, funds provided by the Caroline Julier and James G. Richardson Acquisition Fund and the David A. Cofrin Fund for Asian Art

2013.12

Images courtesy of Galerie Chantal Crousel

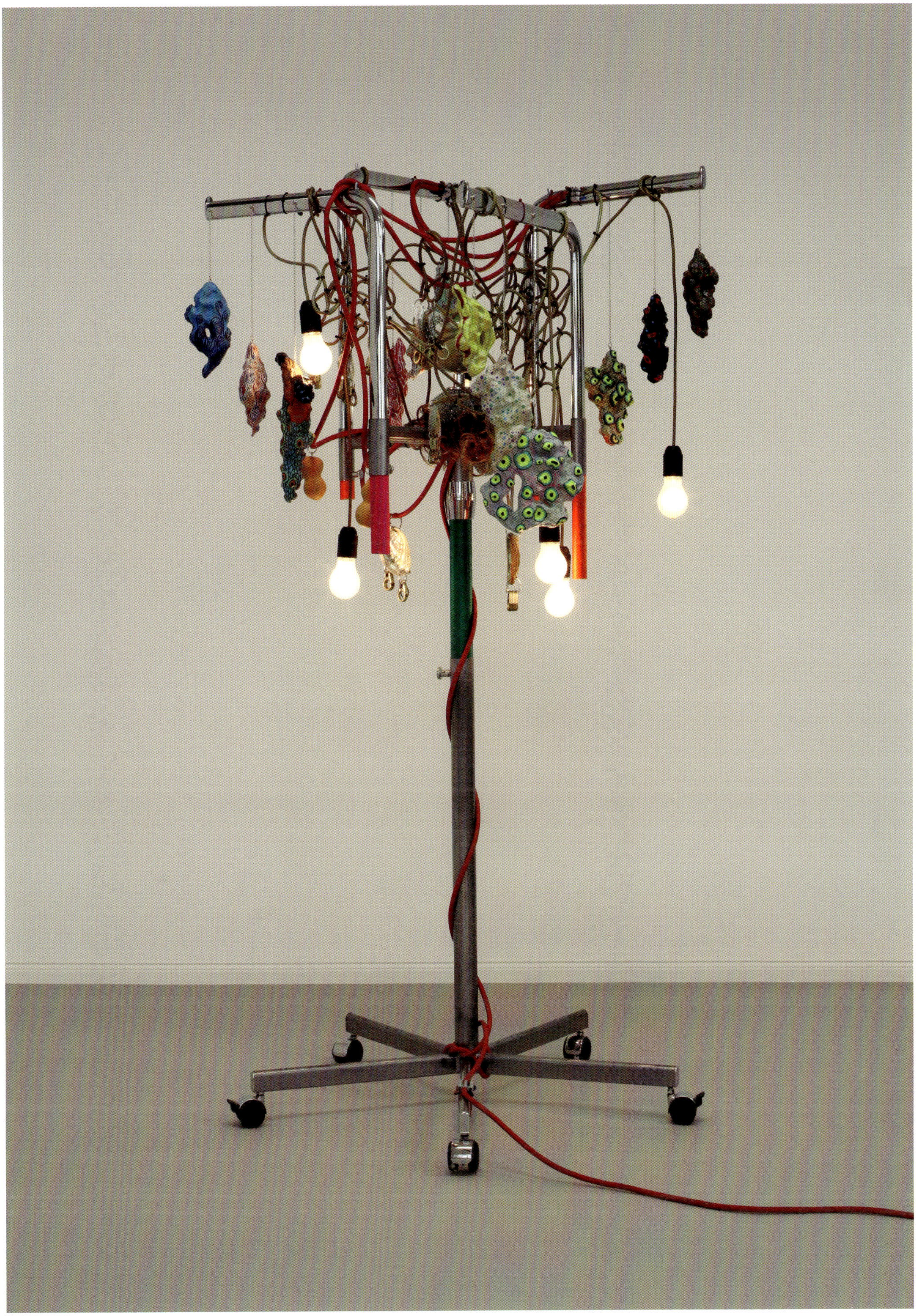

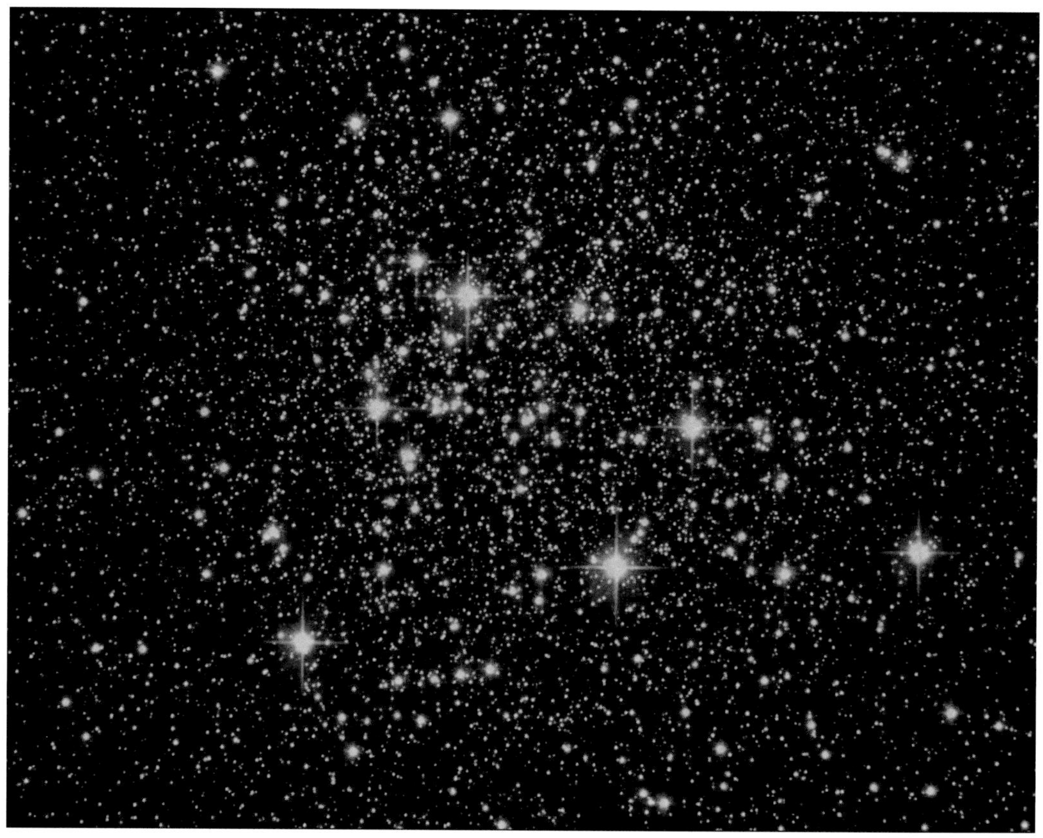

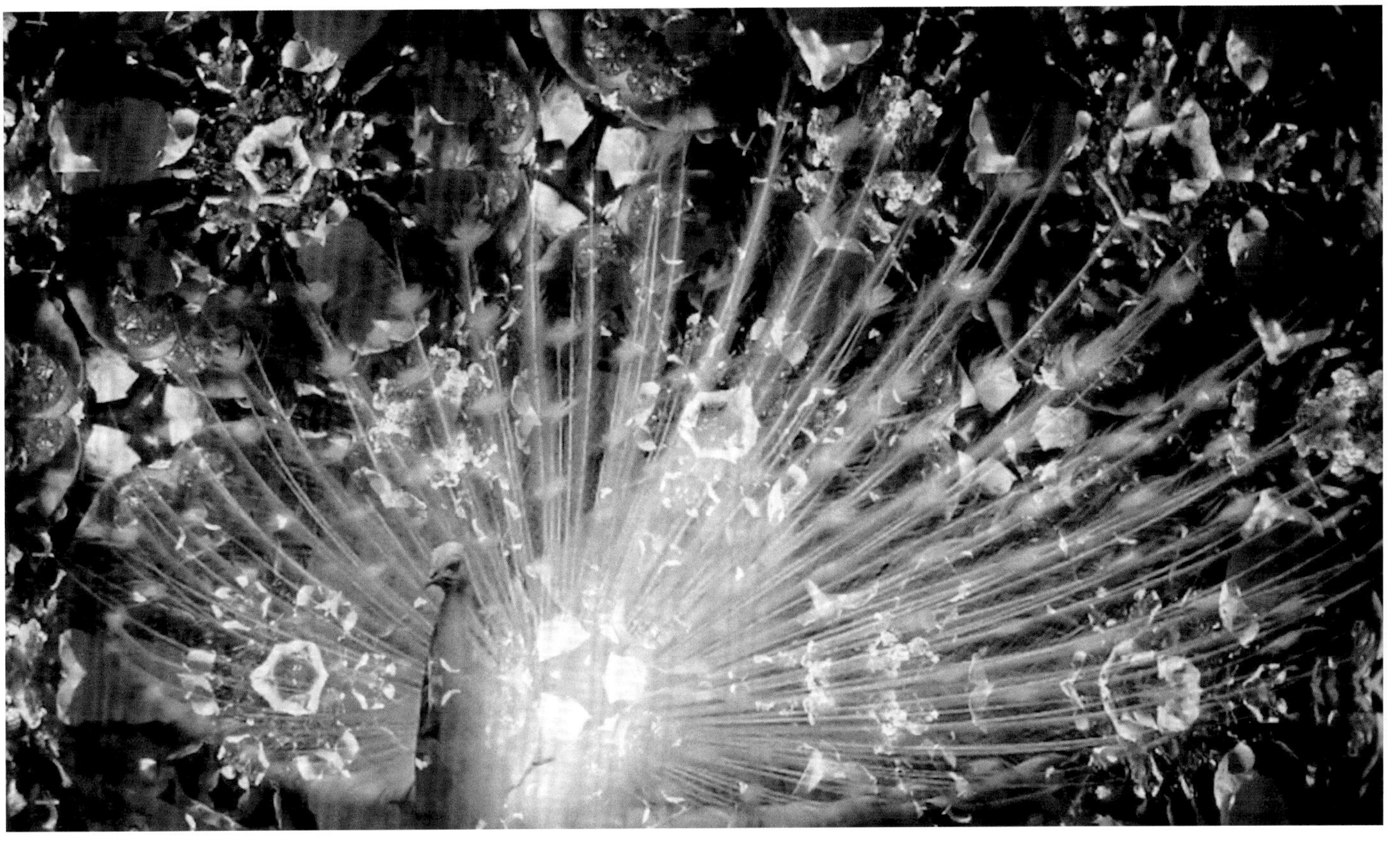

Andrew Yang

American, b. 1973

Interviews with the Milky Way

2016

Two-channel video

Courtesy of the artist

Dornith Doherty

American, b. 1957

Millennium Seed Bank Research Seedlings and Lochner-Stuppy Test Garden No. 4

2011

Digital chromogenic lenticular photograph, edition of 3

76¾ × 35½ in. (194.9 × 90.2 cm)

Courtesy of Moody Gallery, Houston, Texas, and Holly Johnson Gallery, Dallas, Texas

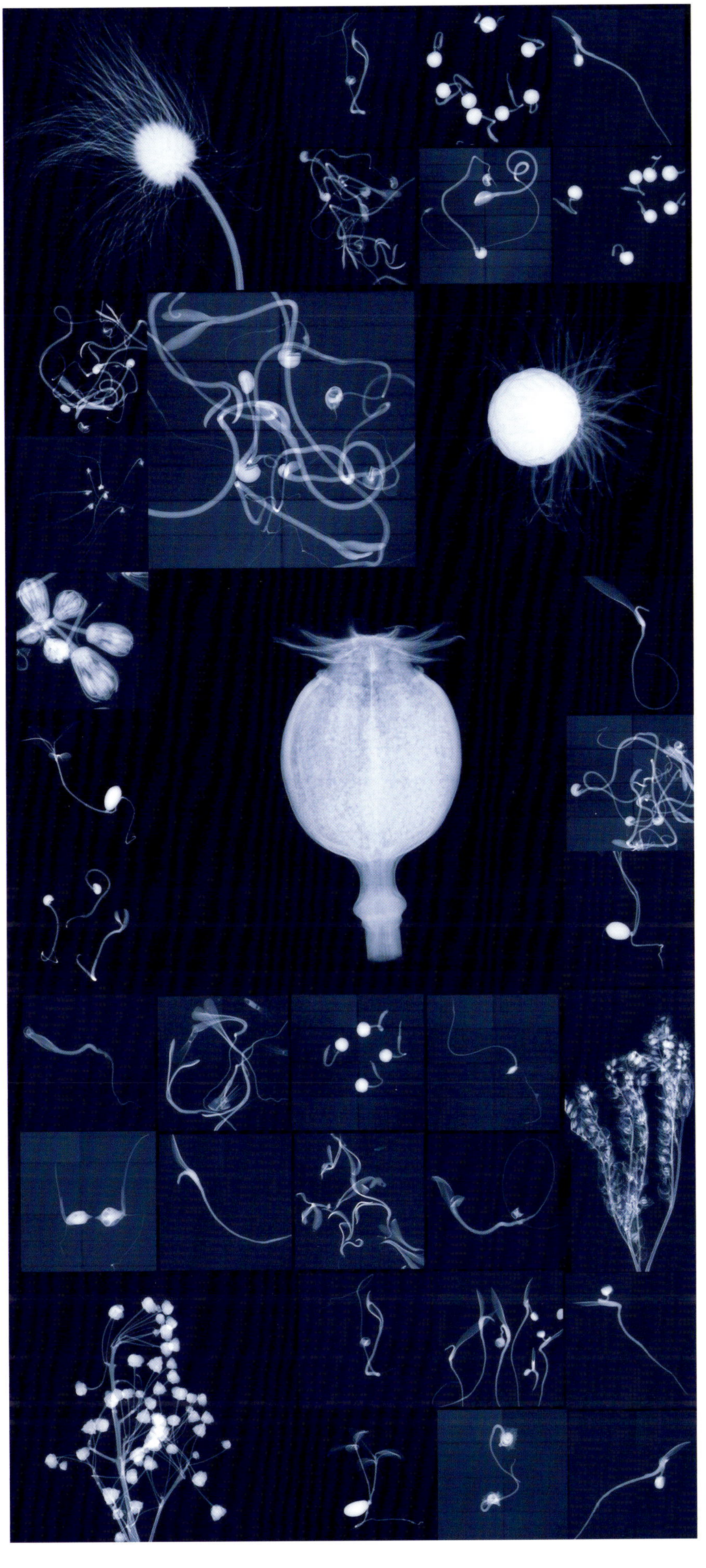

CONTRIBUTORS

Marisol de la Cadena is professor of anthropology at the University of California, Davis. Her work includes the study of politics (including ontological politics), multispecies, indigeneity, history and the ahistorical world, world anthropologies and the anthropologies of worlds. De la Cadena is interested in the perspectives and interface of science and the humanities, encompassing humans, animals, and "things." She also focuses on life-and-death conditions of ecological and political change in a time of extreme droughts, floods, and war. Her books include *Earth Beings: Ecologies of Practice across Andean Worlds* (2015); *Cultures of Race and Hybridity in Latin America* (2011); *Formaciones de indianidad: Articulaciones raciales, mestizaje, y nacion en America Latina* (2008); and *Indigenous Mestizos: The Politics of Race and Culture in Cuzco, Peru (1910–1991)* (2000). De la Cadena was a recipient of the John E. Sawyer Mellon-Sawyer Seminar on the Comparative Study of Cultures (2012–16), and she received the John Simon Guggenheim Memorial Foundation Research Fellowship (2008).

T. J. Demos is professor in the Department of the History of Art and Visual Culture, University of California, Santa Cruz, and founder and director of its Center for Creative Ecologies. He writes widely on the intersection of contemporary art, global politics, and ecology and is the author of numerous books, including *Against the Anthropocene: Visual Culture and Environment Today* (2017); *Decolonizing Nature: Contemporary Art and the Politics of Ecology* (2016); *The Migrant Image: The Art and Politics of Documentary During Global Crisis* (2013)—winner of the College Art Association's 2014 Frank Jewett Mather Award—and *Return to the Postcolony: Spectres of Colonialism in Contemporary Art* (2013). Demos cocurated *Rights of Nature: Art and Ecology in the Americas* at Nottingham Contemporary in January 2015, and organized *Specters: A Ciné-Politics of Haunting*, at the Reina Sofia Museum in Madrid in 2014.

Natasha Myers is an anthropologist of art, science, and ecology based at York University, where she directs the Plant Studies Collaboratory, convenes the Politics of Evidence Working Group, and co-organizes the Toronto Technoscience Salon. Her first book, *Rendering Life Molecular* (2015), is an ethnography of an interdisciplinary group of scientists who make living substance come to matter at the molecular scale. The book received the 2016 Robert K. Merton Award from the Science, Knowledge, and Technology Section of the American Sociological Association. Her current projects span investigations of the arts and sciences of vegetal sensing and sentience, the politics and aesthetics of garden enclosures in a time of climate change, and, most recently, she has launched a long-term ethnography experimenting with the arts of ecological attention in an ancient oak savannah in a large urban park in Toronto. "Becoming Sensor," her research-collaboration with award-winning dancer and filmmaker Ayelen Liberona can be viewed at http://becomingsensor.com. Links to her various projects, publications, actions, and events can be found at http://natashamyers.org.

Kerry Oliver-Smith is curator of contemporary art at the Harn Museum of Art at the University of Florida. She oversees the museum's contemporary collection in all media from 1945 to the present and has curated and coordinated more than sixty exhibitions. Her research interests focus on the juncture of art and politics, with an emphasis on photography and film/video practice.

Oliver-Smith's many publications include *The Swamp: On the Edge of Eden; Project Europa: Imagining the (Im)Possible;* and *Cuba Avant-Garde.* She has received several grants, including two from the National Endowment for the Arts, two from the Andy Warhol Foundation, and research grants from the University of Florida. Select exhibitions include *The Architecture of Time in Video Installation; Terry Adkins: Deeper Still;* and *Art, Media and Material Witness.* Her exhibitions have traveled nationally and internationally. For over a decade, she curated *RISK* Cinema, an experimental and art film series. Prior to her position as the curator of contemporary art at the Harn, she served as the museum's curator of education.

Oliver-Smith was born in Argentina and brought up in Latin America. A founder and artistic codirector of Florida's Hippodrome State Theatre, she has a degree in film and media studies and has worked extensively in theater and film including projects in the United States, England, Scotland, and Spain.

Trevor Paglen is an artist and writer. His art spans multiple media including sculpture, image-making, engineering, investigative journalism, and writing that addresses issues of mass surveillance and data collection. He is the author of *Invisible: Covert Operations and Classified Landscapes* (2010); *Blank Spots on the Map: The Dark Geography of the Pentagon's Secret World (2009); I Could Tell You But Then You Would Have to Be Destroyed by Me* (2007), as well as numerous articles. In his most recent work, *The Last Pictures* (2012), Paglen helped MIT scientists design a spacecraft intended to last billions of years and to be used as a vehicle to house an archival disc upon which the artist inscribed one hundred photographs that represented the historic and cultural moment. Paglen's work has been featured in one-person shows at Vienna Secession, Van Abbemuseum, Frankfurter Kunstverein, Eli & Edythe Broad Art Museum, and Protocinema Istanbul. He has been included in group exhibitions at the San Francisco Museum of Modern Art, the Tate Modern, and the Metropolitan Museum of Art, among other venues.

Joanna Zylinska is professor of new media and communications at Goldsmiths, University of London; and an author, curator, and fine-art photographer. She specializes in new media, ethics, photography, and art. Her books include *Nonhuman Photography* (2017); *Minimal Ethics for the Anthropocene* (2014); and *Bioethics in the Age of New Media* (2009). Her writing has been translated into French, German, Norwegian, Russian, Polish, Turkish, and Chinese. Zylinska is a coeditor of the JISC-funded platform Living Books about Life, which hosts a series of electronic open-access books that provide a bridge between the humanities and the sciences. In 2013 she was artistic director of Transitio_MX05 Biomediations: Festival of New Media Art and Video in Mexico City. Her current projects involve photographing media entanglements, exploring "the end of man" in all its tragicomical aspects, and starting a new work on hydromedia.

ARTISTS

Jennifer Allora and Guillermo Calzadilla critically address the intersections and complicities between the cultural, the historical, and the geopolitical through a complex, research-oriented practice. The Puerto Rico–based artists have studied the ephemeral nature of collective drawing with monumental sticks of chalk at the Biennial de Lima, Peru (*Chalk [Lima]* [1998–2002]); the imprints of colonial, nationalist, and military violence on the diverse populations and landscapes of Vieques, Puerto Rico (*Land Mark [Foot Prints]* [2001–2002]; *Land Mark* [2003]; *Returning a Sound* [2004]; *Under Discussion* [2006]; *Half Mast/Full Mast* [2011]); and the resonance of playing, warping, and combining music from various moments in history (*Clamor* [2006]; *Wake Up* [2007]; *Sediments Sentiments—Figures of Speech* [2008]; *Stop, Repair, Prepare: Variations on Ode to Joy for a Prepared Piano* [2008]; *Raptor's Rapture* [2012]; *Apotomē* [2013]; *3* [2013]); as well as the entanglement between biophysics, semiotics, and actuality (*Growth* [2004]; *Puerto Rican Light: Cueva Vientos* [2015]).

Collaborating since 1995, Allora and Calzadilla represented the United States in the 54th Venice Biennale (2011). Solo exhibitions include Art Gallery of Alberta, Canada (2016); Dia Art Foundation, Guayanilla-Peñuelas, Puerto Rico (2015); Philadelphia Museum of Art (2014); Indianapolis Museum of Art (2012); Haus der Kunst München, Germany (2008); Stedelijk Museum Amsterdam (2008); Kunsthalle Zürich (2007); and Walker Art Center, Minneapolis (2004). Among numerous group exhibitions, they participated in the 10th Gwangju Biennale, South Korea (2014); *Documenta 13,* Kassel, Germany (2012); *Performance 9,* Museum of Modern Art, New York (2011); and the 29th São Paulo Biennial, Brazil (2010).

Claudia Andujar was born in Switzerland in 1931 but grew up in Transylvania close to the border between Hungary and Romania, where as a child she witnessed the horrors of the Nazi occupation. Andujar received grants from the John Simon Guggenheim Foundation and the São Paulo State Research Support Foundation (FAPESP) to photograph and investigate the Yanomami culture. From 1978 to 2000, Andujar worked for the NGO Commission Pro-Yanomami and coordinated the campaign for the demarcation of the Yanomami Indian Territory in the Brazilian Amazon. In 1993, the Brazilian government recognized the Yanomami lands as a Yanomami Territory. In 2000, the Lannan Foundation of New Mexico awarded her the Annual Cultural Freedom Prize as Photographer and Human Rights Advocate. In 2003, she received the 5th Prize Severo Gomes from the Teotônio Vilela Human Rights Commission, São Paulo, Brazil. In 2005, her individual show *Vulnerabilidade do Ser,* held at the Pinacoteca do Estado, São Paulo, won the APCA prize for best photography exhibition. In 2008, she was honored by the Ministry of Culture of Brazil for her artistic and cultural achievements.

Her work has been shown internationally, in both solo and group exhibitions. Her photographs are in the collections of the Museum of Modern Art, New York; Eastman House, Rochester, New York; Amsterdam Art Museum; and other museums around the world. She has contributed to numerous book projects, documentaries, and photographic exhibitions on the Amazon and its indigenous populations.

Sammy Baloji frequently highlights cultural and historical tensions by juxtaposing past and present, the real and the ideal. Much of his work explores architecture and the human body as sites of social history and memory, and witnesses to operations of power. His *Mémoire* series contrasts the colonial history and the postcolonial decline of Lubumbashi copper mining.

Baloji's solo exhibition venues include Musée du quai Branly, Paris; Mu.Zee, Oostend, Belgium; Royal Museum for Central Africa, Tervuren; Museum for African Art, New York; WIELS, Brussels; Power Plant, Toronto; Galerias Municipais/EGEAC, Lisbon; Open Society Foundations, New York; and Autograph ABP, London. Group exhibitions include *Documenta 14,* Kassel, Germany, and Athens (2017); 11th Shanghai Biennale (2016); 13th Biennale de Lyon; 2015 Venice Biennale; *Senses of Time: Video and Film-Based Works of Africa* (2015–2017), Smithsonian NMAfA, Washington, DC; LACMA, and other venues; and *Africa,* Louisiana Museum of Modern Art, Humlebæk, Denmark.

His awards include the Robert Gardner Fellow in Photography, Peabody Museum of Archeology, Harvard University (2017); Chevalier des Arts et des Lettres (2016); Prix OIF, Dak'Art Biennale (2016); Smithsonian Artist Research Fellowship (2015); Rolex Mentor and Protégé Arts Initiative Award, with mentor Olafur Eliasson (2014); Spiegel Prize, Patrick De Spiegelaere Fund (2012); and Prince Claus Award (2008).

Subhankar Banerjee is a self-taught artist, writer, scholar, and an accidental activist. He is Lannan Foundation Endowed Chair and Professor of Art and Ecology at the University of New Mexico. His work is exhibited widely, including at the 12th Shanghai Biennale (2018); 18th Sydney Biennale (2012); *Nature's Nation: American Art and Environment,* Princeton University Art Museum (2018); *Rights of Nature: Art & Ecology in the Americas,* Nottingham Contemporary, United Kingdom (2015); and *Long Environmentalism: Activism | Photographs | Writing,* University of New Mexico Art Museum (2017–2018).

Banerjee is editor of *Arctic Voices: Resistance at the Tipping Point*; coeditor, with T. J. Demos and Emily Eliza Scott, of a forthcoming volume provisionally titled "Routledge Companion to Art, Visual Culture, and Climate Change"; and editor of another forthcoming Routledge volume provisionally titled "Multispecies Justice." Banerjee has convened two recent environmental justice public forums: the last oil (thelastoil.unm.edu, 2018); and Decolonizing Nature (decolonizingnature.unm.edu, 2017). He received a Cultural Freedom Award from the Lannan Foundation and a Green Leaf Artist Award from the United Nations Environment Programme.

Huma Bhabha's work addresses themes of colonialism, war, displacement, and memories of place. Her work has been the subject of numerous national and international exhibitions, including *Unnatural Histories,* MoMA PS1, New York; *All the World's Futures,* 56th International Art Exhibition La Biennale di Venezia, Italy; *Players,* Collezione Maramotti, Reggio Emilia, Italy; *Huma Bhabha,* Aspen Art Museum, Colorado; *Stranger,* Museum of Contemporary Art, Cleveland; A Different Kind of Order: The ICP Triennial, International Center of Photography, New York; *Land Marks,* Metropolitan Museum of Art, New York; *Intense Proximity,* La Triennale, Palais de Tokyo, Paris; 2010 Whitney Biennial, Whitney Museum of American Art, New York;

and the 7th Gwangju Biennale, South Korea. In 2008, she received the Aldrich Contemporary Art Museum Emerging Artist Award; and in 2013 she was awarded the Berlin Prize, Guna S. Mundheim Fellowship, American Academy in Berlin.

Bhabha's works are in numerous collections, such as the Bronx Museum of Art, New York; Museum of Fine Arts, Houston; Museum of Modern Art, New York; Metropolitan Museum of Art, New York; Nerman Museum, Overland Park, Kansas; Centre Georges Pompidou, Paris; Saatchi Gallery, London; Whitney Museum of American Art, New York; and Yale University Art Gallery, New Haven.

Liu Bolin discusses the social concerns of his home country, China, through his artistic practice, most prominently through his "camouflage" installations. His *Hiding in the City* series has been displayed in numerous museums and institutions across the globe. Inspired by his powerful visual messages, artists, institutions, and organizations such the Louvre, *Harper's Bazaar* magazine, JR, Carlos Cruz-Diez, Jon Bon Jovi, and Kenny Scharf have invited Liu Bolin to collaborate on creative projects.

Liu's work has been exhibited worldwide in solo shows, including the exhibitions *Ghost Stories*, Maison Européenne de la Photographie, Paris (2017); *Liu Bolin: Hiding in the City*, Boise Art Museum, Idaho (2015); *Disappearing*, Museo de Contemporáneo de Buenos Aires, Argentina (2015); *Liu Bolin*, Dennos Museum, Traverse City, Michigan (2015); *Liu Bolin*, Kunstverein Ludwigsburg, Germany (2013); *Liu Bolin: The Invisible Man*, Brattleboro Museum and Art Center, Vermont (2013); *Liu Bolin*, the Longyear Museum of Anthropology, Colgate University, Hamilton, New York (2012–2013); *Liu Bolin: A Secret Tour*, Museo H. C. Andersen, Galleria Nazionale d'Arte Moderna, Rome (2012); *The Invisible Man*, Ekaterina Cultural Foundation, Moscow (2012); *The Invisible Man*, Fotografiska Museet, Stockholm (2011); *Hiding in Italy*, Fondazione Forma per la Fotografia, Milan (2010); and *Hiding in the City*, El Museo de Bellas Artes de Caracas, Venezuela (2010).

Edward Burtynsky depicts global industrial landscapes in works that are represented in the collections of more than sixty major museums, including the National Gallery of Canada, Ottawa; Museum of Modern Art, New York; Guggenheim Museum, New York; Reina Sofia Museum, Madrid; Tate Modern, London; and the Los Angeles County Museum of Art.

Exhibitions include *Water* (international touring exhibition), New Orleans Museum of Art & Contemporary Art Center, New Orleans (2013); *Oil* (five-year international touring show), Corcoran Gallery of Art, Washington, DC (2009); China (touring 2005–2008); *Manufactured Landscapes*, National Gallery of Canada (touring 2003–2005); and *Breaking Ground* (touring 1988–1992), produced by the Canadian Museum of Contemporary Photography, Ottawa. Burtynsky's visually compelling works are currently being exhibited in solo and group exhibitions across Canada, the United States, Europe, and Asia.

Edward Burtynsky's distinctions include the TED Prize; Governor General's Awards in Visual and Media Arts; Outreach Award at the Rencontres d'Arles; Roloff Beny Book Award; and the Rogers Best Canadian Film Award.

Sandra Cinto has developed, throughout her career, a rich vocabulary of symbols and lines to create lyrical landscapes and narratives that hover between fantasy and reality. Since the early 1990s, Cinto has presented her work at museums and institutions worldwide, including important solo exhibitions at the CAAM Centro Atlántico de Arte Moderno, Madrid (2014); Museu Oscar Niemeyer, Curitiba, Brazil (2014); Instituto Tomie Ohtake, São Paulo, Brazil (2010); MACUF Museum of Contemporary Art Union Fenosa, La Coruña, Spain (2007); Wall Project at São Paulo Museum of Modern Art (2003); and Museu de Arte da Pampulha, Belo Horizonte, Brazil (2003).

Among her many public projects and commissions, her most notable include *One Day, After the Rain*, commissioned by the Phillips Collection in Washington, DC (2012–2013); *Encounter of Waters,* Seattle Art Museum's Olympic Park Pavilion (2012–2014); *A Casa das Fontes (The House of Fountains)*, an installation conceived for Casa do Sertanista in São Paulo, Brazil (2013); *When the Night Comes into My Room*, an outdoor public commission for Obra Viva/Esculturas Públicas (Living Work/Public Sculptures), Parque Ecológico Municipal Estoril–Virgilio Simionatto in São Bernardo do Campo, Brazil (2012); and *Japonism,* a public commission for the SESC swimming pool in Santo André, Brazil (2011).

Elena Damiani studied architecture at the Universidad Peruana de Ciencias Aplicadas in Lima, Perú, and subsequently transferred to the Escuela Superior de Bellas Artes Corriente Alterna, graduating in Fine Arts. She received her master's degree in Fine Arts at Goldsmiths College, University of London.

Damiani's work has been exhibited at the Gwangju Biennale, South Korea (2016); Bienal de Cuenca, Ecuador (2016); 4th Poly/Graphic Triennial San Juan (2015); Vienna Biennale (2015); Venice Biennale (2015); MUAC Museo Universitario Arte Contemporaneo, Mexico City (2015); Garage Museum of Contemporary Art, Moscow (2015); MOCAD Museum of Contemporary Art Detroit (2015); Americas Society, New York (2014); BIM Bienal de la Imagen y Movimiento, Buenos Aires (2014); Mercosul Biennial, Porto Alegre, Brazil (2013); Museo Tamayo, Mexico City (2013); and MAC Museo de Arte Contemporaneo, Lima (2013); and elsewhere.

She was awarded the Grants & Commissions Program Cisneros Fontanals Art Foundation CIFO (2016), the commission for a permanent site-specific installation at the Americas Society's David Rockefeller Atrium in New York (2014). She currently lives and works in Lima.

Dornith Doherty explores the relationship between humans, science, and nature. Her images investigate the contemporary landscape while also commenting on critical issues affecting it. Doherty's extensive body of work explores the subtle yet complex encounters between the natural environment and human interference by focusing her work on specific aspects of landscape and resource preservation. Most recently, her archival pigment prints and lenticular photographs include seed and plant X-rays that evoke tensions between storage and dispersal, and reproduction and extinction. Her work questions the complicated philosophical, anthropological, and ecological issues surrounding the role of science, technology, and human agency in the context of seed banks.

Doherty is a 2012 Guggenheim Foundation Fellow and has also received grants from the Fulbright Foundation, Japan Foundation, Society for

Contemporary Photography, Indiana Arts Commission, and United States Department of the Interior. She was one of two named 2016 Texas State Artist by the Texas state legislature. In 2017–2018, her work was featured in a solo exhibition, *Archiving Eden*, at the Amon Carter Museum of American Art, Fort Worth, Texas. Her work has been exhibited and collected extensively, both nationally and internationally. She is currently a Distinguished Research Professor at the University of North Texas and lives in Southlake, Texas.

Charles Gaines has been an influential practitioner of conceptualism since the 1970s. His first museum survey was held in 2014 at the Studio Museum in Harlem, New York. Titled *Charles Gaines: Gridwork 1974–1989*, it traveled to the Hammer Museum, Los Angeles. He participated in the 2007 and 2015 Venice Biennales and was the subject of a prominent 2014 exhibition, *Notes on Social Justice,* and a celebrated 2016 exhibition, *Charles Gaines: Numbers and Trees: Central Park Series I,* Paula Cooper Gallery, New York. The Institute of Contemporary Art, Miami, presented *Charles Gaines: Numbers and Trees: Central Park Series IV* in 2017–2018. Gaines has received a National Endowment for the Arts Fellowship (1977), a California Community Foundation Grant (2011), and a Guggenheim Fellowship (2013).

Among the many permanent collections holding his work are the Museum of Modern Art, New York; Whitney Museum of American Art, New York; Los Angeles County Museum of Art; and Lentos Museum, Linz, Austria. Gaines lives and works in Los Angeles and has been a full-time faculty member at the California Institute of the Arts since 1989.

Mishka Henner is a key practitioner among the generation of artists redefining the role of photography in the Internet age. In 2013, Henner was awarded the Infinity Award for Art by the International Center of Photography. He was short-listed for the Deutsche Börse Photography Prize in the same year and, in 2014, was on the short list for the Prix Pictet for his large-scale works focusing on landscapes carved by the beef and oil industries of America. Henner was showcased as part of the group show *New Photography* at the Museum of Modern Art, New York, in 2015. A major solo show, *Counter Intelligence,* at Orebro Konsthall, Sweden, featured works across several series in the spring of 2017.

His works have featured in large historical surveys at the Centre Pompidou–Metz; Metropolitan Museum of Art, New York; and Fotomuseum Winterthur, Switzerland. He has also participated in contemporary surveys at the McCord Museum, Montreal; Les Rencontres d'Arles; and International Center of Photography, New York.

Henner's works are in numerous public collections, including the Centre Pompidou; Metropolitan Museum of Art, New York; New York Public Library; Victoria and Albert Museum, London; Nelson-Atkins Museum of Art, Kansas City; and Tate Collection of Artists' Books, London.

Felipe Jácome is a documentary photographer born in Ecuador who studied at Johns Hopkins University and the London School of Economics. His work has focused on issues of human mobility and human rights. In 2010, he won the Young Reporter Competition of the International Committee of the Red Cross. Jácome's photos have appeared in media such as the *National Geographic,*

Washington Post, Foreign Policy, Guardian, Vice, and on CNN. In recent years Jácome's work has taken refuge from the omnipresence and banalization of photographs in the truthful and necessary nature of documentation. He has begun to collaborate with his subjects in the creation of "visual testimonies" that combine portraiture, writing, and artistic expressions, in order to explore issues such as gender, youth, resilience, displacement, and resistance. Jácome's work has been exhibited in London, Geneva, Amsterdam, Quito, and Washington, DC.

Chris Jordan is a multimedia artist based in Seattle. His work explores contemporary mass culture from a variety of photographic and conceptual perspectives, connecting the viewer viscerally to the enormity and power of humanity's collective unconscious. Jordan's work reaches an increasingly broad international audience through his exhibitions, books, website, interviews on radio and television, and speaking engagements and school visits all over the world. He is currently involved in an international tour of his first feature film, *ALBATROSS,* bringing to the world the awareness and message of plastic pollution's devastating effect on the albatrosses of Midway Island.

Recent solo exhibitions of his work have been held at Appleton Museum of Art, Ocala, Florida (2016); Ryerson Image Centre, Ryerson University, Toronto (2016); Horace Mann School, Bronx, New York (2016); Amarillo Museum of Art, Texas (2015); and Sophie Gannon Gallery, Melbourne, Australia (2015).

His works are included in the permanent collections of the Getty Museum; Los Angeles County Museum of Art (LACMA); Museum of Fine Arts, Houston; Santa Barbara Museum of Art; San Jose Museum of Art; Birmingham Museum of Art; Austin Museum of Art; Boise Art Museum; Nevada Museum of Art, Reno; North Carolina Museum of Art, Raleigh; and Jordan Schnitzer Museum of Art, Eugene, Oregon.

William Kentridge uses film, drawing, sculpture, animation, and performance to transmute sobering political events into powerful poetic allegories. Kentridge has had major exhibitions at San Francisco Museum of Modern Art (2009); Philadelphia Museum of Art (2008); Moderna Museet, Stockholm (2007); and the Metropolitan Museum of Art, New York (2004); among other venues. He has also participated in *Prospect.1 New Orleans* (2008); the Sydney Biennale (1996, 2008); and *Documenta 10* and *11* (1997, 2002). His opera and theater works, often produced in collaboration with Handspring Puppet Company, have appeared at Brooklyn Academy of Music (2007); Standard Bank National Arts Festival, Grahamstown, South Africa (1992, 1996, 1998); and Festival d'Avignon, France (1995, 1996).

His production of Dmitri Shostakovich's opera *The Nose* premiered in 2010 at the Metropolitan Opera, New York, in conjunction with a retrospective organized by San Francisco Museum of Modern Art and the Museum of Modern Art, New York.

A selection of Kentridge's awards include Penagos Prize, MAPFRE Foundation (2014); Humanitas Visiting Professor in Contemporary Art at Oxford University (2013); Kyoto Prize (2010); Kaiserring Prize, Mönchehaus-Museum für Moderne Kunst, Goslar, Germany (2003); Sharjah Biennial 6 Prize, United Arab Emirates (2003); and Carnegie Prize, Carnegie International, Carnegie Museum of Art, Pittsburgh (2000).

Wifredo Lam was a Cuban-born artist best known for his large-scale paintings that reference modernist aesthetics and Afro-Cuban imagery to explore themes of social injustice, spirituality, and rebirth. During the early 1920s, Wifredo Lam exhibited at the Salón de la Asociación de Pintores y Escultore, Havana. In 1923, Lam moved to Madrid, where he studied at the studio of Fernando Alvarez de Sotomayor, the director of the Museo del Prado (and a teacher of Salvador Dalí). He had his first solo show at the Galerie Pierre Loeb in Paris in 1939, and his work was exhibited with Picasso's at the Perls Galleries, New York. Between 1942 and 1950, the artist exhibited there regularly. In 1960, Lam established a studio in Albisola Mare, on the Italian coast.

In 1964, he received the Guggenheim International Award, and in 1966–1967, there were multiple retrospectives of Lam's work at the Kunsthalle Basel; the Kestner-Gesellschaft, Hanover; the Stedelijk Museum, Amsterdam; the Moderna Museet, Stockholm; and the Palais des Beaux-Arts, Brussels. His work belongs to the permanent collections of many internationally known museums such as the Museum of Modern Art (MoMA), Tate Modern, Guggenheim, and Metropolitan Museum of Art.

Maroesjka Lavigne's work has been shown internationally at the Foam Talent exhibition, Amsterdam; Robert Mann Gallery, New York; Galerie Hug, Paris; Museum Saint Guislain, Ghent, Belgium; and elsewhere. She was selected for the Talent Call at Fotomuseum Amsterdam (FOAM) (2012) and was the winner of the Emerging Talent competition of Lensculture in 2014 with the series *You Are More Than Beautiful*. In 2015, she won the Harry Penningsprijs in Eindhoven, Netherlands; and in 2016, she won first place in the Landscape Category at the Sony World Photography Awards.

Recent exhibitions include *Floating Japan*, Kasteeltuinen Arcen, the Netherlands (2017); *Brassage Photographique*, Villers-la-ville, Belgium (2017); Paris Photo with Robert Mann Gallery, Grand Palais, Paris (2016); Jeonju International Photography Festival, Seoul, South Korea (2016); Sony World Photography Awards Exhibition, London, Somerset House (2016); AIPAD photo fair with Robert Mann Gallery, New York (2016); and *Land of Nothingness*, Robert Mann Gallery (2016).

Eva Leitolf critically examines the practices of image production and contextualization in her art, exploring contested societal phenomena such as colonialism, racism, and migration.

Her works have been shown at international institutions including the Pinakothek der Moderne, Munich; Kunstverein, Frankfurt; Sprengel Museum, Hanover; Rijksmuseum, Amsterdam; the Netherlands Photo Museum, Rotterdam; KunstHausWien, Vienna; National Gallery of Kosovo, Pristina; and the Wallach Art Gallery, New York. Leitolf's work is also regularly featured in the color supplements of the *Süddeutsche Zeitung* and *Die Zeit*. Her publications include *Postcards from Europe 03/13* (2013); *Deutsche Bilder—eine Spurensuche* (2008); and *Rostock Ritz* (2004). In 2016, she was awarded the City of Munich's Art Prize.

Dana Levy has had solo shows at Rosenfeld Gallery, Tel Aviv (2004); Haifa Museum of Art (2004); Tavi Dresdner Gallery, Tel Aviv (2008); Habres and Partner Gallery, Vienna (2009); Nicelle Beauchene Gallery, New York (2010); Center for Contemporary Art, Tel Aviv (2012); Loop Art Fair, Barcelona (2012);

Ron Mandos Gallery, Amsterdam (2012); the Petach Tikva Museum of Art, Israel (2014); and the Israel Museum, Jerusalem (2015).

Select group exhibitions include *Open Plan Living,* Museum on the Seam, Jerusalem (2008); *Lush Life*, Invisible Exports, New York (2010); *Unnatural*, Bass Museum of Art, Miami (2012); *Magic Lantern: Recent Acquisitions in Contemporary Art*, Israel Museum, Jerusalem (2012); and *The Compromised Land*, Neuberger Museum, New York (2013).

Her works have been screened at various film festivals, including the Tribeca Film Festival; Rotterdam Film Festival; Hamburg Short Film Festival (where she won the 2006 Jury Award); Oberhausen Festival; Impakt Festival; Rencontres Internationales Paris/Berlin/Madrid; Chicago Underground Film Festival, among others.

In 2008, Levy received the Young Israeli Artist Award, and in 2010, she won the Dumbo Arts Festival Best Studio Award. In 2013, she was awarded the Beatrice Kolliner Award from the Israel Museum. Her works are in the Israel Museum Collection, Jerusalem; Petach Tikva Museum Collection, Israel; Donald Rothfeld Museum Collection, American University, Washington, DC; and other private collections.

Yao Lu's concern about the impact of China's rampant path toward urbanization is portrayed in photomontaged manipulations that borrow from the classical Chinese aesthetic style of painting. Lu's environmental message crosses borders and raises pressing questions about the hidden costs of modernization and global sustainability. In 2008 Lu won the Paris Photo BMW Prize for contemporary photography; he was short-listed for the prestigious Prix Pictet the following year. He made his New York debut with a major solo exhibition, *New Landscapes,* at Bruce Silverstein Gallery in 2009.

He has participated in numerous exhibitions and festivals, including the Museum of Photographic Art, San Diego; Royal Academy of Art, London; Fotofest International in Houston; multimedia art exhibition *Space and Transportation*, Graz, Austria; Paris Photo, France; and GETXOPHOTO Festival, Bilbao, Spain.

Lu's work has been viewed in prominent institutions in the East, including the Istanbul Museum of Modern Art, Turkey; National Museum of Fine Arts, Beijing; A9 Art Gallery, Beijing; Beijing Art Gallery; *Brisbane Photography Exhibition*, Australia; Daegu Photo Biennale, South Korea; Lianzhou International Photo Festival, China; Made in China Fotofestival, Lodz, Poland; Pingyao International Photography Festival, China; and the SuoLuo Gallery, Beijing.

Pedro Neves Marques is a writer, visual artist, and filmmaker. He has exhibited in art venues such as the Tate Modern, London; Anthology Film Archives, New York; V-A-C Foundation, Venice; Museu Colecção Berardo, Lisbon; Contour Biennale 8, Mechelen, Belgium; PAV, Turin; Sursock Art Museum, Beirut; Kadist Art Foundation, Paris; e-flux, New York; Casa do Povo, São Paulo, Brazil; 12th Cuenca Biennial, Cuenca, Ecuador; Sculpture Center, New York; Elizabeth Foundation for the Arts, New York; EDP Foundation, Lisbon; Serralves Museum for Contemporary Art, Porto, Portugal; as well as in art galleries such as Galleria Umberto di Marino, Naples; Pedro Cera, Lisbon; and Gallerie Martin Janda, Vienna.

His first short-fiction film, *Semente Exterminadora* (Exterminator Seed), produced by Capivara

Filmes and Curtas Metragens—CRL, premiered at the IndieLisboa Film Festival in 2017. His short-film essay *Where to Sit at the Dinner Table?* premiered at DocLisboa International Film Festival in 2013. Together with fellow artist Mariana Silva he runs www.inhabitants-tv.org, an online channel for exploratory video and documentary reporting.

Noelle Mason is a multidisciplinary artist whose work is about the subtle seductiveness of power facilitated by systems of visual and institutional control. Mason has shown nationally and internationally in a variety of nontraditional spaces, galleries, and institutions, including the National Museum of Mexican Art, Chicago; Orlando Museum of Art, Florida, and Museum of Fine Arts, St. Petersburg, Florida. She is the recipient of a Joan Mitchell Foundation Artist Grant, Jerome Fellowship, Santo Foundation Individual Artist Grant, the Florida Prize for Contemporary Art, and the Southern Prize. In 2004, Mason was a resident at the Skowhegan School of Painting and Sculpture. Mason currently is Associate Professor of Art at the University of South Florida.

Mary Mattingly's work explores issues of sustainability, climate change, and displacement. Her most recent project, *Swale*, is a floating food forest for New York. In 2015, she completed a two-part sculpture, *Pull,* for the International Havana Biennial with the Museo Nacional de Bellas Artes de la Habana and the Bronx Museum of the Arts. Mattingly's work has been exhibited at the International Center of Photography Museum, New York; Seoul Art Center; Brooklyn Museum; New York Public Library; deCordova Museum and Sculpture Park, Lincoln, Massachusetts; and Palais de Tokyo, Paris. In 2009, Mattingly founded the *Waterpod Project*, a barge-based public space and self-sufficient habitat that hosted more than 200,000 visitors in New York. In 2014, an artist residency on the water called *WetLand* launched in Philadelphia. It is being utilized by the University of Pennsylvania's Environmental Humanities program.

Her most recent solo exhibitions include *Objects Unveiled: Boxing, Rolling, Stretching, and Cutting*, Institute for the Humanities, University of Michigan (2017); *Blockades Boulders and Weights*, Light Work, Syracuse, New York (2017); *Pull*, Museo Nacional de Bellas Artes de la Habana, Cuba (2015); and *Mary Mattingly*, Bemis Center for Contemporary Art, Omaha, Nebraska.

Mattingly has been awarded grants and fellowships from the James L. Knight Foundation; Eyebeam Center for Art and Technology; Yale University School of Art; Harpo Foundation; NYFA; Jerome Foundation; and Art Matters Foundation.

Gideon Mendel explores the struggle against apartheid in his work, which has received global attention and was highlighted in Axis Gallery's exhibition *Shooting Resistance* (2002) and Okwui Enwezor's *Rise and Fall of Apartheid* (2012). His work on HIV/AIDS, spanning more than twenty years, includes *A Broken Landscape: HIV & AIDS in Africa* (2001); *The Ward* (2017) on Middlesex Hospital's AIDS wards in 2002; as well as *Through Positive Eyes*, a project that turned over the camera to the subjects themselves.

Mendel's decade-long *Drowning World* project spotlights climate change in a dozen countries, reflected in the shared trauma of the flood victims in Mendel's *Submerged Portraits*, and his video project *The Water Chapters*. *Drowning World* also includes formal images of flooded interiors (the *Waterline* series) and a series on damaged photographs found in flood zones (the *Watermarks* series). *Drowning World* has been exhibited at Les Rencontres de la photographie, Arles, France (2017); Wits Art Museum, Johannesburg (2017); the Eli and Edythe Broad Art Museum, Michigan State University (2016); and in a Prix Pictet exhibition, *Disorder*, at Musée d'Art Moderne, Paris; as well as in many other venues.

Mendel's awards include the Greenpeace Photo Award (2016); the Pollock-Krasner Foundation's Pollock Prize for Creativity (2016); the Eugene Smith Award for Humanistic Photography; and six World Press Photo Awards.

Ana Mendieta was a Cuban-born artist who, in her brief yet prolific career, created groundbreaking work in photography, performance, film, video, drawing, sculpture, and site-specific installations. Mendieta is a pioneer among artists dealing with identity politics and feminism.

Mendieta's work has been the subject of six major museum retrospectives, the most recent of which, *Ana Mendieta: Traces*, was organized by the Hayward Gallery, London (2013) and traveled to the Museum der Moderne Salzburg, Austria, and the Galerie Rudolfinum, Czech Republic. *Ana Mendieta: Earth Body, Sculpture and Performance 1972–1985* was organized by the Hirshhorn Museum and Sculpture Garden, Washington, DC, in 2005 and traveled to the Whitney Museum of American Art, New York; Des Moines Art Center, Iowa; and Miami Art Museum, Florida.

Recent exhibitions including her work have been held at Galerie nationale du Jeu de Paume, Paris (2018); Colby Museum of Art, Waterville, Maine (2017); Sugar Hill Children's Museum of Art & Storytelling, New York (2017); State Museum of Contemporary Art, Thessaloniki, Greece (2017); Alison Jacques Gallery, London (2017); St. Louis Art Museum, Missouri (2016); NSU Art Museum, Fort Lauderdale, Florida (2016); and Berkeley Art Museum, University of California (2016).

Kimiyo Mishima is a contemporary Japanese ceramic artist best known for creating highly realistic versions of "breakable printed matter" such as newspapers, comic books, and boxes out of clay. Mishima began her artistic career as a painter, then started working in ceramics in 1971. At this time, she began to use the silk-screen technique to print newspaper and ad poster images onto clay.

Major solo exhibitions of her work have been held at Art Factory Jonanjima, Tokyo (2015); Gallery Yamaki Fine Art, Hyogo (*Painting Period 1954–1970* [2013]); Gallery Nii, Tokyo (2004); Contemporary Art Museum, Ise, Mie (2004); and Minami Gallery, Tokyo (1974). In 1986, she received a Rockefeller Scholarship ACC and lived and worked in New York for a year. Her works are included in the Permanent Collections of the Everson Museum of Art, New York; First National Bank of Chicago; Museum of Art Olot, Spain; Korean Culture and Arts Foundation, Seoul; Museum of Contemporary Art, Tokyo; National Museum of Art, Osaka; Benesse Art Site Naoshima; and National Museum of Modern Art, Kyoto.

Richard Misrach is one of the most influential photographers of his generation. In the 1970s, he helped launch the renaissance of color photography and large-scale presentation. Misrach has had one-person exhibitions at the National Gallery of Art, Washington, DC; Art Institute of Chicago; Los Angeles County Museum of Art; and Centre Pompidou, Paris; among other venues. His photographs are held in the collections of most major institutions, including the Museum of Modern Art, Whitney Museum of American Art, and Metropolitan Museum of Art, New York; National Gallery of Art, Washington, DC; and San Francisco Museum of Modern Art. In the fall of 2010, on the five-year anniversary of Hurricane Katrina, the exhibition *Untitled [New Orleans and the Gulf Coast, 2005]* made its debut at the New Orleans Museum of Art and was also shown at the Houston Museum of Fine Arts and the San Francisco Museum of Modern Art.

Misrach is the recipient of numerous awards in the arts, including four National Endowment for the Arts Fellowships and a Guggenheim Fellowship. In 2002 he was given the Kulturpreis for Lifetime Achievement in Photography by the German Society for Photography and, in 2008, the Lucie Award for Outstanding Achievement in Fine Art Photography.

Beth Moon has gained international recognition for her large-scale, richly toned platinum prints. Since 1999, Moon's work has appeared in more than sixty solo and group exhibitions in the United States, Italy, England, France, Israel, Brazil, Dubai, Singapore, and Canada. Her work is held in numerous public and private collections, including the Museum of Fine Arts, Houston; Museum of Photographic Arts, San Diego; and Fox Talbot Museum, Wiltshire, England.

Recent exhibitions including her work have been held at Verve Gallery of Photography, Santa Fe, New Mexico (2016); Louisiana Art and Science Museum, Baton Rouge (2016); Ph-Neutro Fotographia, Pietrasanta, Italy (2016); Open Shutter Gallery, Durango, Colorado (2016); and Center for Photographic Arts, Carmel, California (2016).

Richard Mosse's photography captures the beauty and tragedy in war and destruction. Mosse is the winner of the 2014 Deutsche Börse Photography Prize. In 2013, Mosse represented Ireland in the Venice Biennale with the *The Enclave,* an immersive six-channel video installation that utilized 16mm infrared film. Mosse has exhibited work at the Palazzo Strozzi, Florence; Weatherspoon Art Museum, Greensboro, North Carolina; Bass Museum of Art, Miami Beach, Florida; Künstlerhaus Bethanien, Berlin; Centre Culturel Irlandais, Paris; the Dublin Contemporary Biennial; FotoMuseum Antwerp (FoMu); FOAM, Amsterdam; and the Tate Modern, London. Mosse's first monograph, *Infra*, which captures the ongoing war between rebel factions and the Congolese national army in the Democratic Republic of the Congo, was published by Aperture Foundation and Pulitzer Center on Crisis Reporting in 2011. His most recent monograph, *The Enclave*, was also published by Aperture Foundation in 2013 to accompany his presentation at the Venice Biennale.

Recent solo exhibitions include *Richard Mosse: The Enclave,* Hafnarhús, Reykjavík Art Museum, Iceland (2016, 2017); Nasher Museum of Art at Duke University (2015, 2016); Portland Museum of Art (2014, 2015); DHC/ART, Montreal (2014, 2015); Louisiana Museum of Modern Art, Humlebæk, Denmark (2015); and National Gallery of Victoria, Australia (2015, 2016).

Jackie Nickerson makes photographs that examine identity and the physical and psychological condition of working within a specific environment. Her photographs challenge conventional notions of making portraits and landscapes and offer a more engaged view of her subjects.

Major recent solo exhibitions have taken place at National Underground Railroad Freedom Center, Cincinnati (2017); Samsøñ Gallery, Boston (2016);

Jack Shainman Gallery, New York (2014); Brancolini Grimaldi, London (2014); Accademia d'Arte, Bologna (2013); Galerie Satellite, Liège, Belgium (2013); and Light Work, Syracuse, New York (2013).

Nickerson's photographs are held in many collections, including MoMA, New York; Irish Museum of Modern Art, Dublin; Nerman Museum of Contemporary Art, Overland Park, Kansas; Pier 24, San Francisco; Vatican Museums; Rubell Collection, Santa Barbara Museum of Art; Progressive Art Collection, National Gallery of Ireland.

Gabriel Orozco works in media including drawing, installation, photography, sculpture, and video. Orozco began exhibiting his work in 1983. He has had solo exhibitions at the Musée d'art moderne de la Ville de Paris (1995, 1998); Hirshhorn Museum and Sculpture Garden, Washington, DC (2004); Serpentine Gallery, London (2004); Museo Nacional Centre de Arte Reina Sofía, Madrid (2005); and Guggenheim Museum, New York (2012).

Major traveling solo exhibitions have been organized by the Kunsthalle Zürich (1996–1997); Museum of Contemporary Art, Los Angeles (2000–2001); and Museum of Modern Art, New York (2009–2011). His work has been included in the Venice Biennale (1993, 2003, 2005); Whitney Biennial (1995, 1997); Carnegie International, Carnegie Museum of Art, Pittsburgh (1999); and *Documenta 10* and *11*, Kassel, Germany (1997, 2002).

Orozco has received numerous honors, including the Secció Espacios Alternativos prize at the Salón Nacional de Artes Plásticas in Mexico City (1987); a residency with Deutscher Akademischer Austauschdienst, Berlin (1995); and the German blueOrange prize (2006). Orozco lives and works in Mexico City, New York, and Paris.

Trevor Paglen is an artist and writer whose work spans image-making, sculpture, investigative journalism, engineering, and numerous other disciplines. A midcareer survey exhibition, *Sights Unseen,* is on view at the Smithsonian American Art Museum, Washington, DC, from June 21, 2018, to January 6, 2019. Paglen has had additional one-person exhibitions at the Nevada Museum of Art, Reno; Secession, Vienna; Berkeley Art Museum; Kunsthall Oslo, Norway; and Kunsthalle Giessen, Germany. His work has been included in group exhibitions at the Metropolitan Museum of Art, New York; Tate Modern, London; San Francisco Museum of Modern Art; BALTIC Centre for Contemporary Art, Gateshead, United Kingdom; Museo Reina Sofia, Madrid; MIT List Visual Arts Center, Cambridge; Haus der Kunst, Munich; and Walker Art Center, Minneapolis. He participated in the 2009 Istanbul Biennial; 2012 Liverpool Biennial; 2013 ICP Triennial, New York; and the 11th Gwangju Biennale, South Korea.

Paglen has launched an artwork into distant orbit around Earth in collaboration with Creative Time and MIT, contributed research and cinematography to the Academy Award–winning film *Citizenfour,* and created a radioactive public sculpture for the exclusion zone in Fukushima, Japan. He has received numerous awards, including a 2017 MacArthur Fellowship; the 2014 Electronic Frontier Foundation Pioneer Award for his contributions to countersurveillance; and the 2016 Deutsche Börse Photography Foundation Prize.

Abel Rodríguez is a Colombian artist and an elder of the Nonuya people who is known among his people as the "Namer of Plants," a designation of wisdom. He holds special expertise in the plants and ecological systems of the Amazon Basin, a knowledge that is traditionally passed down through generations. After leaving his homeland with his family in the 1990s, Rodríguez began to create intricate drawings and paintings of Amazonian plants and vegetation.

He received the 2014 Principal Prince Claus Award. His work has been exhibited at the National Gallery of Canada, Ottawa; Prince Claus Fund Gallery, Amsterdam; Biblioteca Luis Ángel Arango, Colombia; the Cultural Center of the Universidade Federal de Minas Gerais, Brazil; and Salón Nacional de Artistas (National Artists' Exhibition), Colombia.

Allan Sekula is concerned with the consequences of the economic changes arising from globalization and questions the function of documentary photography in the media, in art, and in society. Allan Sekula's recent solo exhibitions include *OKEANOS,* Thyssen Bornemisza Art Contemporary, Vienna (2017); *Fish Story, to be continued,* NTU Centre for Contemporary Art Singapore, Gillman Barracks (2015); *Dockers' Museum*, Johan Jacobs Museum, Zürich (2014); *Meditations on a Triptych*, Stedelijk Museum, Amsterdam (2013); and *Polonia and Other Fables*, Ludwig Museum, Budapest (2010).

Select group exhibitions include the Museo de Arte Reina Sofia, Madrid (2016); Museum of Modern Art, New York (2015); Leal Rios Foundation, Lisbon (2015); Whitney Biennial, Whitney Museum of American Art, New York (2014); Victoria and Albert Museum, London (2014); MAXXI National Museum of XXI Century Arts, Rome (2014); 55th Venice Biennale, Catalan Pavilion (2013); 29th Bienal de São Paulo (2010); and *Documenta 12* and *11*, Kassel, Germany (2007, 2002).

His work is in the collections of the J. Paul Getty Museum, Los Angeles; Art Institute of Chicago; Museo de Arte Reina Sofia, Madrid; Museum of Modern Art, New York; Tate, London; Thyssen-Bornemisza Art Contemporary, Vienna; Museum of Contemporary Art San Diego, San Diego; and Walker Art Center, Minneapolis; among others.

Taryn Simon is a multidisciplinary artist working in photography, text, sculpture, and performance. Guided by an interest in systems of categorization and classification, her practice involves extensive research into the power and structure of secrecy and the precarious nature of survival. Simon's works have been the subject of exhibitions at the Louisiana Museum of Modern Art, Humlebæk, Denmark (2016–2017); the Albertinum, Dresden (2016); Galerie Rudolfinum, Prague (2016); Garage Museum of Contemporary Art, Moscow (2016); Jeu de Paume, Paris (2015); Ullens Center for Contemporary Art, Beijing (2013); Museum of Modern Art, New York (2012); Tate Modern, London (2011); Neue Nationalgalerie, Berlin (2011); and Whitney Museum of American Art, New York (2007).

Permanent collections include Metropolitan Museum of Art, New York; Tate Modern, London; Guggenheim Museum, New York; Centre Georges Pompidou, Paris; and Los Angeles County Museum of Art. Her work was included in the 56th Venice Biennale (2015). Simon's installation *An Occupation of Loss* (2016), commissioned by the Park Avenue Armory and Artangel, premiered in New York in 2016. Simon is a graduate of Brown University and a Guggenheim Fellow. She lives and works in New York.

Nicole Six and Paul Petritsch are based in Vienna and have been collaborating since 1997 on performative, filmic, photographic, displays and sculptural works. Recent solo exhibitions are *Un-Curating the Archive*, Camera Austria, Graz (2017); *Das Denkmal*, Kunstraum Lakeside, Klagenfurt, Austria (2015); *Das Meer der Stille*, Landesgalerie Linz, Austria (2014) (cat.); *Aussicht kann durch Ladung verstellt sein*, Kunstverein Medienturm, Graz (2012) (cat.); *Raum für 17 Minuten 6'23*, Galerie im Taxispalais, Innsbruck, Austria (2011) (cat.); *Atlas*, Secession, Vienna (2010) (cat.); and *Nicole Six / Paul Petritsch*, Gesellschaft für aktuelle Kunst, Bremen, Germany (2006).

Their investigation of space and the human condition were part of *Yesterday, Today, Today*, Kunstraum Buchberg, Gars am Kamp, Austria (2018); *Stretching the Boundaries*, Fluca, Plovdiv, Bulgaria (2017); *Psst. . . There is still Space in Outer Space!*, Pavelhaus/Pavlova hiša, Radkersburg, Austria (2016); *Fictitious Tales about the History of Earth*, MAK Center, Los Angeles (2015); *Archives, Re-Assemblances and Surveys, On Austrian Contemporary Photography*, Klovicevi dvori Gallery, Zagreb, Croatia (2014) (cat.); *Suicide Narcissus*, Renaissance Society, Chicago (2013); and *Keine Zeit, erschöpftes Selbst*, 21er Haus, Vienna (2012) (cat.), among others.

They are regularly invited for displays and interventions in public space and realized projects like *Klimt Schiele Moser*, Lentos, Linz, Austria (2018); *Mehr als Zero—Hans Bischoffshausen*, Belvedere Museum Wien, Austria (2015) (cat.); *Places of Transition*, Freiraum MuseumsQuartier Wien, Austria (2014); *Das Bauhaus in Kalkutta*, Bauhaus Dessau, Germany (2013); and *Art Is Concrete*, Camera Austria, Graz, Austria (2012).

Laurencia Strauss navigates hope and doom as she investigates vulnerabilities and ingenuities of people and the places they inhabit. Combining socially based art practices with landscape experiments, she creates mixed-media, often participatory experiences that contend with our interdependencies. A culturally mixed queer interdisciplinary artist and landscape architect based in her hometown of Miami, she is currently researching South Florida's relationship with water and responses to sea-level rise. Amid environmental activism and speculative solutions, she attends to anticipatory loss and climate change grief.

Her work has been shared nationally and internationally. Recent solo exhibitions include *Hope and Doom*, Satellite Art Show, Miami Beach (2016, 2017); and *Infiltração*, Galeria Península, Brazil (2016). Group shows include *The Miami River Project*, Miami (2018); *RAW*, Miami (2017); *Opposing Futures*, Fort Lauderdale (2017); *Flooded Sanctuaries*, Miami Beach (2017); *Waterscapes*, Fort Lauderdale (2016); and *Hightide* at Satellite, Miami Beach (2015). Recent residencies include ArtCenter/South Florida; Kansas City Art Institute; Vermont Studio Center; Studios of Key West; Curatoria Forense (Chile); La Paternal Espcacio Projecto (Argentina); Float with Radical Intention and the Luminary (St. Louis).

Thomas Struth has had work featured in comprehensive retrospective exhibitions organized by the Kunsthalle Bern (1987); Institute of Contemporary Art, Boston (1994); Carré d'Art, Musée d'Art Contemporain, Nîmes (1998); Dallas Museum of Art (2002); Museum für Gegenwart, Berlin (2004); and Museo de Art de Lima (2005). Recent solo exhibitions of his work have been held at Moody Center for the Arts, Houston (2016); Museum Folkwang, Essen, Germany (2016); Senior and Shopmaker Gallery, New York (2016); Marian Goodman Gallery, London (2015); Galleria Monica de Cardenas, Milan (2015); and Galerie Rüdiger Schöttle, Munich (2015). Recent group exhibitions of his work have been held at Kunstmuseum Bonn (2016); Brooklyn Museum of Art, New York; Museum Rietberg, Zürich (2016); Philadelphia Museum of Art (2016); and National Gallery of Art, Washington, DC (2016).

He is the recipient of numerous awards in the arts, including the Spectrum International Prize for Photography, Kulturstiftung, Niedersachsen (1997); and the Royal Photographic Society awards Centenary Medal and Honorary Fellowship (2016).

Bethany Taylor works to reveal ecological and sociopolitical narratives embedded in everyday materials and employs textiles as a form of social and political activism. Her work has been exhibited nationally and internationally at venues such as the Seattle Arts Commission; Post, bG Gallery, and Los Angeles Center for Digital Art, Los Angeles; New Mexico State University Art Gallery, Las Cruces; Orange County Center for Contemporary Art, Santa Ana, California; Museum for Arts and Sciences, Macon, Georgia; Florida Museum of Fine Art, Tallahassee; Huntsville Museum of Art and Wiregrass Museum of Art, Alabama; Alexandria Museum of Art, Los Angeles; Bellevue Arts Museum, Washington; Bob Rauschenberg Gallery, Fort Myers, Florida; Musei di Genova Raccolte Frugone, Genova Nervi, Italy; Limerick City Gallery, Ireland; Werkstadt, Berlin; and Nelimarkka Museum, Alajärvi, Finland; among others. Her large-scale installation *River Unraveled*, confronting the complexities of ecological change and drought in the New Mexico Rio Grande region, was recently published in the *Center for Sustainable Practice in the Arts, Quarterly 15: Hyperobjects*.

Taylor is an Associate Professor of Drawing and Co-Coordinator of Workshop for Art Research and Practice (WARP) at the University of Florida.

Frank Thiel is widely renowned for photographing the architectural spaces of Berlin. The architectural spaces in his photographs reflect not only a turbulent social and political history but also the emergence of new patterns of urban existence. Previous bodies of work have focused on such topics as state surveillance and the privatization of public space.

Thiel has exhibited extensively in museums and galleries worldwide; his works are included in the collections of many major international museums including the Centro Galego de Arte Contemporánea, Santiago de Compostela, Spain; Museu National Centro de Arte Reina Sofia, Madrid; National Gallery of Canada, Ottawa; Fotomuseum Winterthur, Switzerland; Moderna Museet, Stockholm; Hirshhorn Museum and Sculpture Garden, Washington, DC; and Phillips Collection, Washington, DC.

Recent solo exhibitions include *Frank Thiel: Nowhere Is a Place*, Sean Kelly Gallery, New York (2014); *Los Arados de Dios*, Galerie Krinzinger, Vienna (2014); *Nowhere Is a Place*, Galeria Leme, São Paulo, Brazil (2014); and *Frank Thiel*, Galeria Leme, São Paulo (2010). Recent group exhibitions include *Viajando Pelo Mundo*, Paço Imperial, Rio de Janeiro (2017); *For a da ordem—obras de Coleção Helga de Alvear*, Pinacoteca, São Paulo (2016); and *Viaje alrededor del mundo*, Instituto Cultural Cabañas, Guadalajara, Mexico (2016).

Sergio Vega has focused his artistic research for the last two decades on *Paradise in the New World,* a book written in 1650 by Antonio de Leon Pinelo. According to this text, the Garden of Eden was located at the center of South America. Vega traveled in search of Pinelo's paradise and found it—or its afterlife—in Mato Grosso, a large central state of Brazil. Employing a range of mediums, Vega has produced artworks that explore contemporary and historical discourses related to Tropicalism.

His work has been featured in *Documenta 13*; 51st Biennale di Venezia; 3rd Moscow Biennale; Sharjah Biennial 8, United Arab Emirates; 5th Biennal de Lyon; 1st Yokohama Triennale, Japan; Sonsbeek 9, Holland; 2nd Kwangju Biennale, South Korea; and Site Santa Fe III International Biennial, New Mexico. Vega has been a faculty member of the School of Art and Art History at the University of Florida since 1999.

Andrew Yang is an artist and scholar whose work interweaves across ecology, history, and the naturalcultural. He works across media integrating sculpture, collage, text, photography, and video. His projects have been exhibited from Oklahoma to Yokohama, including a commission for the 14th Istanbul Biennial (2015) and a solo exhibition at Museum of Contemporary Art, Chicago (2016). Recent group exhibitions took place at the Four Boxes Gallery, Denmark (2017); Peale Museum, Baltimore (2017); PlatteForum, Denver (2017); and Muzeum Sztuki, Poland (2017). His writings appear in *Art Journal*, *Leonardo*, *Antennae*, and *Biological Theory*, among others. He is associate professor at the School of the Art Institute of Chicago and research associate at the Field Museum of Natural History.

Haegue Yang's practice spans a wide range of media, from paper collage to performative sculpture and large-scale multisensorial installation. Her reflections on specific historical or contemporary figures and concrete, domestic phenomena are translated using her meticulous language of formalistic abstraction. In her light sculptures (ongoing since 2006), electric cables, light bulbs, and ready-made and handcrafted forms are assembled on clothing racks, as intimate configurations of objects and anthropomorphic figures. Yang's ongoing research draws on art history, literature, political biographies, and history as well as invisible social structures to reimagine a possible community, through which she reinterprets themes that recur in her works: migration, postcolonial diasporas, and social mobility.

Selected recent solo exhibitions include *Silo of Silence—Clicked Core,* KINDL–Centre for Contemporary Art, Berlin (2017), *Lingering Nous*, Centre Pompidou, Paris (2016); *Haegue Yang: Come Shower or Shine, It Is Equally Blissful*, Ullens Center for Contemporary Art, Beijing (2015); *Accommodating the Epic Dispersion—On Non-cathartic Volume of Dispersion,* Haus der Kunst, Munich (2012); and *Arrivals*, Kunsthaus Bregenz (2011). Her work has been included in the 13th Biennale de Lyon (2015); Sharjah Biennial 12 (2015); *Documenta 13*, Kassel, Germany (2012); and 53rd Venice Biennale (2009).